Rethinking Religion

Rethinking Religion

Edited by

Soumyajit Patra

RAWAT PUBLICATIONS

Jaipur • New Delhi • Bangalore • Mumbai • Hyderabad • Guwahati

ISBN 81-316-0267-2

Published by
Prem Rawat for **Rawat Publications**
Satyam Apts, Sector 3, Jawahar Nagar, Jaipur 302 004 (India)
Phone: 0141 265 1748/7006 Fax: 0141 265 1748
E-mail: info@rawatbooks.com
Website: www.rawatbooks.com

New Delhi Office
4858/24, Ansari Road, Daryaganj, New Delhi 110 002
Phone: 011 2326 3290

Also at Bangalore, Mumbai, Hyderabad and Guwahati

Typeset by Rawat Computers, Jaipur
Printed at Chaman Enterprises, New Delhi

To

Manjusree Patra – My Mother
Rupa Patra – My Wife
Professor Samita Manna – My Teacher

Contents

Section II
Religion Theorized

Section III
The Local and the Global

Acknowledgements

Truly, I am an atheist. But the pervasiveness and credence of religion always attract me. And I chose 'religion' as the subject of my first major work. I am grateful to Professor George Ritzer and Professor Noam Chomsky for their enduring inspiration right from the beginning. My deepest regards go to Professor Swapan Kumar Pramanick, Vice-Chancellor, Vidyasagar University (India) and Professor Samita Manna, Head, Department of Sociology, University of Calen (India), without whose encouragement and support I could not have undertaken this work. I am thankful to my friend, eminent scholar, Dr George Pollard, who patiently read the earlier draft of my article and helped enrich it. I am also indebted to Professor Sankar Prasad Singha, Dean, Faculty of Arts, Vidyasagar University (India) and my friend, Dr Ananta Kumar Giri of Madras Institute of Development Studies, Chennai (India) for their cooperation during different phases of my work. Thanks are due to all at Rawat Publications. Finally, I must remember the support my family members and colleagues in the Department of Sociology, Vidyasagar University extended to me for the completion of this volume.

Soumyajit Patra

Introduction

Is there any continuity between what Cornford (1991: xiii) calls 'religious representations' and 'rational speculations' or, more specifically between supernaturalism and scienticism? It is true that science provides us with a radically alternative paradigm for answering questions related both to the day-to-day mundane affairs and the ultimate meanings of life, for which religion too has its own convenient and traditional ways of explanation. Cornford (ibid.: xiii) has rightly said that for some people these are 'two distinct provinces of thought'. If we define science in terms of rigorous logic and experimentation leading to verifiable conclusions, religion definitely is relegated to the other pole of the continuum. Nietzsche's (1986: 62) analysis in this regard is interesting: 'there exists between religion and true science neither affinity, nor friendship, nor even enmity: they dwell in different stars.'

But of course there is continuity. The unilinear evolution of human thought, marked by decreasing religiosity and growing rationalism, as has been described by some of the classical sociologists, has given rise to two distinct domains in a recognizable 'continuum'. Though this shift from providentialism to rationalism has a historical perspective, often traced backed to renaissance, there are examples of simultaneous existence of both perspectives—rational and, obviously, religious—in ancient cultures. Traces of early atheism have been found first in

Jerusalem and then in India at least five centuries before Christ (Brow, 1982: 43).

It is true that there is no known human society in which religious beliefs and practices are totally absent; though it is very difficult to analyse the nature and orientations of prehistoric religions for understandable reasons. But from the available archeological evidences anthropologists have discerned the existence of some kind of religious practices even among the Peking man, who lived about half a million years ago (Hultkrantz, 1982). The existence of religion across time and space has made it not only complex but pervasive also in such way that it becomes an intrinsic part of what Giddens (1984) in his *The Constitution of Society*, calls people's discursive and practical consciousness.

But what does religion actually mean? Except some particular religions like Confucianism and Buddhism, most of the world religions have some sort of 'beliefs in supernatural power' at their core. And they are oriented to Gods or God-like figures—an association that helps inculcate among its followers a feeling of commonness. In 1980s a group of French sociologists under the leadership of Emile Durkheim, the father of sociology of religion, tried to define religion in terms of what they called 'collective representations' and argued that 'religion is the product of the spontaneous overflow of powerful group emotion' (Ackerman, 1991: vii). However, this type of definition either ignores or simplifies the transcendental and supra-empirical dimensions of religion, and so is not given much importance in contemporary discourses on religion.

It is a widely accepted view that most of the world religions were initially monotheistic, that in course of time degenerated into polytheism. This is true of Hinduism, the religion of the majority of the Indians, as well. Brow (1982: 32) tells us that 'the later Vedic literature has certainly become polytheistic by, say, 1000 BC but the earliest Aryans must have been monotheists.' The Bible also describes the first true man as monotheist. There are reasons to believe that polytheism and personification of what may be called abstract spiritual forces are the product of human reason found only at a later stage of development. In some cases monotheism was developed into henotheism before it was finally transformed into polytheism. Hinduism itself is a case in point (ibid.).

Considering the complex nature, organization and ideological-philosophical foundations of religion, this book has been divided into three sections. The first section deals with four important religions of the world—Christianity, Buddhism, Hinduism and Islam. Anton Senekal in his article points out the evaluative confusions existing in the study of social deviance and attempts to reach at a conclusion from a Christian perspective. He distinguishes between sin and social deviance, and suggests us to consider God as the Ultimate Definitional Authority in this regard.

Jeffrey Grupp analysing the Buddhist philosophy opines that the Buddhist compassion, which, in his opinion, 'is the realization that you are different from me', can save us from the emerging crises of the 'prison planet'. In his account of Buddhism, Grupp heavily relies on Dharmakirti's philosophy of atomism.

Pramod Kumar Singh examines the foundations of Hinduism and shows that the Vedas, the Upanishad and the Gita are not, at least theoretically, antithetical to social change. Though he accepts some distortions of Sanātanadharma but believes that this dark side of Hinduism can be kept aside by the right emphasis on its conceptual schema. Singh provides us with a classification of world religions—Sacramental, Prophetic and Mystical, and opines that Hinduism may come under each of them.

Mahmoud Khatami analyses the concept of religion from an Islamic point of view. The word 'Islam' means 'peace and submission to God' and it is a unitary religion. Khatami points out that the Qur'an gives us a specific meaning of religion that 'denotes only one truth'. Distinguishing between type-religion and token-religions, Khatami says that 'type-religion is ineffable and transcendent, but man responds to this reality through 'token-religions'. Islam is of course a type-religion in his analysis.

P.K. Mohapatra in his article 'Karma, God and Rebirth' describes the Karma doctrine as the 'fundamental paradigm of Indian ethics'. He defines the Karma doctrine as 'a principle of allocating to each his own'. But he criticizes this doctrine as 'individualistic and backward-looking ideal' though he believes it may provide scope for moral progress. In this article he also shows why the concept of rebirth constitutes an essential element of the Karma doctrine.

In the second section some classical theories of religion have been discussed. Alberto Toscano elaborately explains Marx's views on religion. He deals with some questions posed by Marx himself and treats 'his seemingly anachronism as a resource rather than a defect in displacing some of the numerous commonplaces about religion, society and politics that have come to dominate our public and academic discourse.' Toscano explores certain theoretical schemes existing in Marx's analysis of religion and tries to find out the importance of his thinking on religion in an era of 'dramatic reversals in the secularizing tendencies'.

Håkan Sandgren analyses Nietzsche's theory of religion taking clues from his major writings and biographical information. He tries to find out what did Nietzsche actually mean by 'God is dead'. Håkan Sandgren discusses Nietzsche's atheism which is, in the final analysis, a 'different form of atheism'. Pointing out the significance of Nietzsche's views on religion, Sandgren opines that '[a]s long as there are thoughts on religion … Nietzsche will be read with interest … .'

Swapan Kumar Pramanick explores Durkheim's theory of religion that involves an analytic blending of 'positivist methodology and a theory of social primacy.' He says that Durkheim's theory is 'based on its unique importance on the origin, continuation and change of the essential features of human society.' This article summarizes Durkheim's analysis of the functional interplay between religion and society to develop a comprehensive sociological theory of religion.

Kathleen A. Riddell in her article 'Max Weber: The Sociology of Religion' argues that Weber 'revolutionalized the social-scientific study of religion' by shifting the attention from 'other-worldly' to a 'this-worldly' aspects of religion. She elaborately analyses Weber's writings on religion and provides us with an overview of Weberian sociology of religion. Riddell shows how Weber traced economic development through a particular world-view based on a religious ethic.

My own article shows that the 'age of religion' has gradually been replaced by the 'age of philosophy' to use Cornford's (1991) categorization. This article points out that the earlier hegemony of religion has been dismantled as a consequence of the triumph of reason. The dominant Enlightenment philosophy, thus, gradually made religion as a 'matter of choice'.

Four articles related to tribal religion, folk religion, Tibetan Tantric initiation and globalization of spirituality have been included in the last section. Zahidul Islam and S.M. Arif Mahmud examine different aspects of the Garo religion. The Garos are the tribal people of Bangladesh. Their traditional religion is known as Sangsarek. There are Christian Garos as well. After a comparative discussion on the Sangsarek and Christian Garos, the authors describe the changes occurred in the religious practices of this tribal community of Bangladesh since the 'advent of the British in 1756'.

Harvinder Singh Bhatti points out the essential features of Punjabi folk religion. He observes that the folk religion of Punjab is usually 'without any central shrine, scripture or organization'. This article also focuses on the 'non-discriminating nature' of folk religion. Bhatti argues that this type of religion does not have any formal membership, and comes to conclusion that 'it is based on the principle of inclusion and recognition of the plurality of faiths.'

Brian J. Given presents a detail ethnographic account of Tibetan Tantric initiation cycle. He also discusses some issues relevant to the study of rituals. Tantric ritual cycle is a 'complete teaching'. The initiation cycle, known as *Lam Dre'*, is divided into two major parts—Triple teaching and Triple Tantra. Given's 'thick participation' during the field work enables him to experience even the minute detail of this initiation cycle.

Ananta Kumar Giri tries to focus on the globalization of spirituality and contemporary religious movements. He argues in favour of the reversals in secularization and writes that the present era is 'characterized by a global resurgence of religion'. Giri analyses the spirit behind the Swadhyaya and Sai Baba movements and concludes that the 'religion of the future has to be a religion of humanity.'

This book shows that religion can be viewed both as an ideological construct and a practical frame of reference for the day-to-day activities. In a 'sophisticated multicultural' set-up (Giddens has used this term in a recent interview) these two aspects of religion may not always converge. And this severance unveils the destructive tendencies inherent in the institution of religion as such. Examples can be cited from the fundamentalists' agenda and activities in many countries of the world including India. I believe that almost all major religions indirectly lead to an 'insider-outsider' categorization; no doubt powerful religious symbols are very important in this regard though often their negative impact is largely overlooked in the study of religion. To say the least, religious symbols with all its emotional dimensions unify the group while create the notion of the 'other'. A true scientific study of religion should consider the hidden contradictions between the ideological orientation and practical implications of religion as opposed to the existing common sense notion.

Section I

Beliefs Diversified

1 When Deviance Becomes Sin

Christian World-view Re-examined

Anton Senekal

Accepting the category of sin as ontologically real, is of course only possible if one accepts the Christian world-view, as presented in the Bible, as valid. This will be my point of departure in discussing the topic 'When deviance becomes sin'. Another important premise from which this theme will be discussed will be called the 'logovision' (from the words logos and vision) premise and can be summarized in five statements:

- We look at reality with our eyes, but we see reality through words. This is a very simple but profound truth that has been captured long ago in Walter Lipman's aphorism: First we look, then we name and only then we see (Bredemeier and Stephenson, 1970).
- What we thus see in reality, is, if we believe the words applied to the reality, taken by us as basis for our reaction or response to that reality.
- If deceptive words about reality were used and we believed those words, we would not see reality as it really is, i.e., true reality, but we would take the false reality to be the true reality.
- If we have thus been successfully deceived, i.e., convinced to believe the false reality (lie) to be the true reality (truth) our response to that reality could be fatally inappropriate. For

This article was previously published in slightly adapted form in South Africa in *Koers* (1999), 64(4): 443–64.

example, if A wanted to kill B, A could simply invite B to have a can of Coke after having added poison in the can but without having changed the word 'Coke' on the can to the word 'Poison'. B would then see a can of Coke on the basis of having believed the word 'Coke' written on the tin and would inappropriately respond by drinking the Coke and die, having taken a false reality (a lie) to be the true reality (truth) and having done so with fatal consequences.

- As Ultimate Definitional Authority, God's words about reality—be it physical, psychological, socio-cultural or spiritual reality—are the words that, if accepted and believed, can guide human words and systems of words—also social-scientific words and word systems—as well as human actions, towards a much closer encounter with truth than would otherwise have been humanly possible.
- Against the backdrop of these remarks, then, this article is written with the primary aim of bringing more clarity in the evaluative confusion which is characteristic of the study of social deviance and which in this article is seen as the result of unsuccessful attempts at evading inescapable evaluative issues. It is attempted to obtain more clarity by bringing God's words to bear on the confusion in the study of deviance so as to attempt to see the realities concerning deviance, more clearly. This is done by distinguishing between sin and social deviance and by relating these phenomena to each other.

On Good and Evil

Cherbonnier starts his discussion on the interconnectedness between sin and the evaluative issues of good and evil as follows:

> Anyone who uses the word 'sin' obviously assumes a distinction between good and evil. But leaders of thought, both scientific and philosophic have frequently challenged this distinction. A discussion of sin must therefore first deal with the question of whether in the last analysis, the difference between good and evil is tenable or whether it is merely a subjective phenomenon which a man of intelligence can overcome. If it can be successfully suppressed, then all talk about sin becomes a dead issue. But if not, then sin at once becomes

everybody's problem. He who wishes to avoid this problem correctly concentrates his fire upon value judgments. (Cherbonnier, 1956: 21)

Berkouwer (1958: 5) also acknowledges some connections between sin and issues of good and evil when he says, 'Deze vraag … (naar de oorsprong der zonde) … die men binnen de grenzen van kerk en theologie allerwegen aantreft, schijnt haar parallel te vinden in een algemene bezinning over de oorsprong van "het kwaad" in de wereld.'

The same thing is emphasized by Möller (1997). Weaver (2003: 71) on the other hand argues that '[m]oral discourse should occur alongside and in conversation with the discourse of sin, since the discourse of sin lends the moral life its soteriological (and ecclesial) framework and context.' In the following few paragraphs this issue will be discussed.

Underlying every human being's and therefore every social scientist's cognitive, emotional and volitional faculties, is the even more fundamental, evaluative capacity—i.e., the formal capacity or dynamism which enables human beings to differentiate between good and evil or right and wrong. Of course, the definitional content of the terms 'good' and 'evil' or 'right' and 'wrong' is to some extent culturally influenced. However, in the final analysis, the definitional content of these evaluative opposites is determined by the particular individual's free choice of an ultimate directional source or an Ultimate Definitional Authority—be it him or herself, be it some other human being or beings, be it a particular philosophy, or ideology, or be it a supernatural source, e.g., God, Satan or other spirit beings. The chosen Ultimate Definitional Authority becomes God to that person. The definitional content given or derived from the chosen Ultimate Definitional Authority will therefore not only be accepted by the particular actor, but the evaluative behavioural directives (values) flowing from this authoritative source, will also be freely obeyed.

It is important and very interesting to note that this evaluative capacity does not lie dormantly within us waiting to be activated only when we so desire. In fact, we can not escape the continuous working of this capacity. Even if we try to escape from our evaluative capacities by professing evaluative neutrality or simply by remaining silent, our professed neutrality or silence will not only always be taken by a particular audience to signify—even if only by implication—approval of the phenomenon under scrutiny, but will in fact involve that approval. We therefore always make and convey evaluative statements—even if only by default. If social scientists were to try to break loose from this tenacious evaluative responsibility by stating: It is wrong to be evaluatively involved as a social scientist or it is right to be evaluatively neutral, they would paradoxically still be making, and in fact would already have made an evaluative statement.

Cherbonnier (1956: 21) discusses a number of futile attempts to escape value judgments (of which Nietzsche's attempt is perhaps the most illustrative of the futility and failure of such attempts at evaluative beyondism) which suggest that they are in principle impossible. No one can censor the words 'good' and 'evil' without introducing some substitute for them, and no one can put them in quarantine without presupposing them. Even the legitimate suspension of value judgments for purposes of scientific investigation occurs within the total context of valuation. The scientist must first decide that it is good to seek objective truth. To make the further decision that it would be even better to dispense completely with the terms 'good' and 'evil' would repudiate the basis of the decision itself. It is therefore not surprising that everyone who attempts to banish these terms becomes the victims of a curious irony. In his book *Beyond Good and Evil*, Nietzsche (1989) fails to break free from making evaluative statements. Cherbonnier (1956: 23) remarks in this regard: 'The irony of his (Nietzsche's) position however, consists in his denunciation of value judgments, together with those who make them, as themselves *wicked*.'

The scientific commandment, 'Thou shalt not commit a value judgment'—so eloquently opposed by Gouldner (cited in Finsterbusch and McKenna, 1986) is therefore a commandment to remain evaluatively silent and passive and in effect implies the following:

> Thou shalt not disapprove of or in any way act against any behaviour (sociologically defined 'sins' like racism, sexism and classism excluded of course). By thy silence and inaction thou shalt be taken to be—or preferably, thou shalt be—an agent of the universal condonation of human behaviour in the name of social science (once again of course excluding the trilogy of 'sociological sins' of racism, sexism and classism). (ibid.: 15)

If saying yes to evil, or consciously remaining silent about it while being aware of its existence, involves condoning that wrong, then saying no to evil, automatically becomes one of the most powerful statements any human being can make. Thus, all human beings—and therefore all social scientists—are born with an evaluative capacity to differentiate between good and evil; possess the ability and freedom to define the contents of good and evil in terms of a chosen directional source or Ultimate Definitional Authority; are free to choose or decide between these evaluative opposites—once again in terms of a chosen directional source or Ultimate Definitional Authority and finally, are responsible for the actions flowing from their choice. Furthermore, human beings—and hence social scientists too—cannot break free from this evaluative capacity or the responsibility and accountability that goes along with it. We are therefore inescapably, evaluatively responsible and accountable for what we say and do, not by choice but because that is part of our being as humans. We are, however, also free to choose who or what we will accept and obey as Ultimate Definitional Authority in our lives and work.

In view of the varying and even contradictory definitions of what constitutes good and the varying and often contradictory definitions of what constitutes evil, the following question inevitably arises: 'Which then is the truly good and which the truly evil?' There has to be a single answer to a question like this as two mutually exclusive and opposite answers cannot both simultaneously be valid and applied to a particular case and in particular circumstances. We therefore have no choice but to choose as a result of which we are prisoners of our freedom to choose—an astonishing paradox which liberates us once we embrace it. As a result we as human beings carry a threefold burden:

- First, the burden of defining good and evil, or our 'definitional burden' or 'responsibility', which requires us to search the minefield of distorted and deceptive definitions of good and evil for the true good and the true evil and to distinguish these from the false good and the false evil respectively.
- Second, the burden of choice, or our 'decisional responsibility', which requires us to take a stand on these evaluative opposites amidst powerful contradicting pressures impinging on our attempt to make the right choice.
- Third, the burden of accountability or our 'admissional responsibility' (i.e., the act of accepting or acknowledging as true), which requires us to accept responsibility for our choices and the associated actions and to explain and justify these.

On Deviance

Deviance and Evaluative Issues

When social scientists study the phenomenon of social deviance, they are, in terms of the above, subject to conflicting forces: On the one hand, the scientific commandment of value or ethical neutrality and on the other hand the existential inevitability of being evaluatively responsible and accountable. In a futile attempt to give precedence to the former, they often respond as follows: Instead of calling certain forms of behaviour bad, wrong or evil, they opt for ostensibly more neutral or scientific sounding terms like deviant, pathological, disorganized, etc. Good behaviour is then referred to as for example conforming, normal or healthy and organized behaviour. Lyman (1978: 129) remarks:

> Through the bloodless language of the new sciences the sins are neutralized: Sloth becomes 'affectlessness'; lust changes to 'sexual deviance'; envy shows up as 'resentment'; greed reforms itself as the 'spirit of capitalism'; gluttony fades into 'addiction', and pride is reduced to 'mental illness'. Anger, however, resists the expurgations of scientific and lexical sublimation; typically, we find it characterized as 'aggression'.

A sinister and dangerous dynamic, however, is operating within and underlying this whole process and that is what could be called the dynamic of the 'polar transpositioning of evaluative opposites'. This involves the tendency towards calling good 'evil' and calling evil 'good' so as to get people, in terms of logovision premise—whether they are God's children or not—to see a false reality as though it were the true reality in order to get them to act in a fatally inappropriate manner. This of course implies the existence of a supernatural father of lies (called Satan or Lucifer in the Bible) with an evil agenda intent on destroying all Gods created by furthering deception of the kind referred to above. The current debate and deceptive arguments on whether being involved in a homosexual relationship is right or wrong, presents a case in point. The polar transpositioning of evaluative opposites, normally manifests itself in the following three phases and/or dimensions:

The first phase very often simply involves a questioning of the validity of the distinction between good and evil, light and darkness, truth and lie, love and hate, in a particular case which at the same time represents a symbolic questioning of the generic validity of the distinction between evaluative opposites in all similar cases. It invariably takes the form of the questioning, discrediting, debunking, incredulizing and attacking the good pole of the evaluative continuum. Questions like the following are examples of this: Can we really know what is good, what is right, what is truth, what is light, what is love? Eventually God becomes the target of this process as is indicated by the following question which Möller (1997: 10) sees as manifestation of the destructive dynamic of sin: How do we know whether God is not perhaps evil rather than good, and whether He is not perhaps seeking our doom instead of our salvation or survival? Implied in questions like these is the suggestion that what is called good/right/truth/light/love is not nearly as distinct and different from its evaluative opposites as we might think. Strangely, nobody seems to have a problem to recognize and acknowledge the distinct characteristics of the evaluative opposites of evil, wrong, the lie, darkness and hate.

The second phase frequently amounts to an attempt to diminish the distance between or blur the clarity of the distinction between good and evil by emphasizing apparent commonalities between the evaluative opposites and then concluding with the question: Are these apparent opposites really so different? (Thus, in effect making evil less objectionable and good, less attractive). This dynamic is very often observable in televised situational comedies.

Third and finally, a transpositioning of evaluative opposites very often occurs where—and here the evil pole of the continuum receives the emphasis and becomes the benefactor—evil is being called good, particularly by means of the names given to it. Thus, for instance, crime can became 'innovation'; adultery 'swinging', prostitution 'sexual therapy' or 'commercial sex work', theft 'redistribution of wealth' etc. Taken to its logical extreme, this phase tends to find its conclusion and logical extreme in calling God, Satan and calling Satan, God. Interestingly enough, this is exactly what Satan implied when he tried to convince Eve to obey him rather than God. The dire consequences of this is to be found in the behavioural correlates which go with this polar transpositioning—i.e., the growing tolerance and approval of and eventual participation in activities like these by increasing numbers of people. In this way, the gradual and incremental and almost unnoticeable institutionalization of evil/wrong/darkness/the lie/hate takes effect. Being death-directed, this process, which is always Satan-driven through the degenerative dynamic of sin,

> ... (is) geared at spoiling and ultimately destroying that which God has made. It strives to convert all that is beautiful to ugly, good to bad, true to false and to kill that which lives. Everything was created to the glory of God and with the purpose of exalting Him, but sin aims to reverse this trend, turning everything against God and making it a disgrace. Consequently sin always blasphemes God [Isa. 25: 5; 1 Pet. 4:4, 14] (ibid., 1997: 10).

Unless reversed—which has of course in principle already been done two thousand years ago, in and through Jesus Christ—this process inevitably would have to result in the ultimate destruction of humanity and society and everything else that exists. Nevertheless, whatever one calls deviance, it is always implicitly suggested to be the kind of behaviour to be avoided, because it is considered 'bad', whereas the opposite category (i.e., conformity) is implicitly suggested to be the kind of behaviour to be espoused, because it is considered 'good'. Students and other audiences reading works on social deviance or listening to talks on this subject, implicitly accept this evaluative differentiation, not only to be valid, but moreover, almost invariably take the evaluative behavioural directives, implied in theories of deviance, as guidelines for their own behaviour. A very clear illustration that even sociologists tend to do this, can be found in the following remark by Alex Thio on Glaser's theory of differential identification concerning criminality:

> Glaser's theory may be taken to suggest that it is all right for us to associate with criminals in real life or in books and movies, as long as we do not take them so seriously that we identify with them, treating them as our heroes. If we do identify with them, we are likely to become criminals ourselves. (Thio, 1995: 35)

As social-scientific human beings, sociologists (and most probably all other students of human behaviour as well) therefore, have to deal with two types of knowledge concerning the social reality they study. The one type is informative or categorical knowledge which is always and in all contexts, in a very explicit sense, present and operating in all human behaviour. A pilot, hunter or food gatherer respectively has to be in possession of and act in accordance with very distinctive sets of informative knowledge in order to fly a plane successfully track down and kill some animal, and find food in the fields necessary for survival. In the same way sociologists make use of informative knowledge when—among others things—they differentiate between deviant and conforming behaviour and the characteristics of each. The other more implicit type of knowledge, which is more fundamental than the first, and furthermore inseparably linked to the first, is of course evaluative or normative knowledge. Evaluative knowledge is nothing more and nothing less than the knowledge of good and evil, which infuses and directs our informative knowledge.

With reference to the examples used above, evaluative knowledge actually precedes and in fact constitutes the foundation on the basis upon which the categorical information is considered to be of value. Because flying per se, flying as a means of rapid transport, safe flying etc., are defined as good (i.e., evaluative knowledge) therefore the knowledge to build safe and fast planes, the skills to fly these planes successfully, etc. (categorical knowledge), becomes valued. The same line of argumentation applies to the other two and similar examples. Applied to the sociological study of the field of social deviance, it therefore becomes possible to construct a typology, which relates the above mentioned types of knowledge in this particular context. Such a typology would look like this.

Table 1.1

Categorical and Evaluative Definitions of Good and Evil

		Sociological (categorical) definitions of	
		Conformity	*Deviance*
Evaluative definitions of	Good	Good Conformity	Good Deviance
	Evil	Evil Conformity	Evil Deviance

A very simple, yet fundamental, truth emerges from this typology, namely that it is possible to differentiate between good deviance and evil or bad deviance on the one hand, as well as between good conformity and evil or bad conformity on the other hand. This differentiation—although found to be highly disturbing and unacceptable by some sociologists, e.g., Rushing and Sagarin (cited in Thio, 1995: 5)—is not only logically appealing but also empirically convincing in the sense that all social scientists would acknowledge that not all forms of deviant behaviour are necessarily bad—e.g., deviating from a peer group norm which requires the use of drugs—nor that all forms of conformity are necessarily good—e.g., conforming to the dictates of a totalitarian, ethnocentric and racist leader.

Despite the logically and empirically compelling nature of this argument in support of two interlocking and inseparable types of knowledge, sociologists, as we have seen, are expected by some to achieve the impossible and to study, research and teach sociology in general—and the sociology of deviance in particular—as if evaluative knowledge did not exist. In trying to accomplish the impossible, many if not most sociologists, try to ignore, devaluate or suppress the existence and inescapable relevance of evaluative knowledge. This of course cannot successfully be achieved as our every thought, word and deed is preceded by and intended to satisfy a particular evaluative standard, underlying that particular thought, word or deed. Instead then of confronting and integrating these two levels of knowledge in an accountable manner, most sociologists opt for the easier but inadequate response to this inescapable dilemma, by simply using the term 'deviant behaviour' to refer to all kinds of behaviour considered to be undesirable—i.e., behaviour which would otherwise have been called bad or evil by whoever happens to be the selected definitional authority at the time, be it public opinion, the people, the workers, the government, the middle class, business, society, etc. Furthermore, they tend simply to substitute the term conformity for behaviour that would otherwise be called good or right by a similarly selected definitional authority. Implicitly then deviant behaviour becomes a synonym for bad/evil behaviour and conforming behaviour a synonym for good/right behaviour. Our evaluative capacity as human beings thus poses an uncomfortable challenge to us which is in fact perceived by some to be some sort of threat from which one should rather try to escape. In terms of the above, three escape routes can thus be identified.

The first route of escaping our evaluative capability is therefore to avoid this evaluative issue altogether by avoiding using terms like good and evil or right and wrong at all and to rather substitute these with terms like conforming and deviant behaviour respectively—i.e., by opting for ethically neutral objectivity. By doing this we act as if distinctions between good and bad either did not exist or if it did exist, were of no relevance or significance in any social scientific endeavour and should better be avoided.

Yet, as we have seen, we still end up with the very real problem that not all deviant behaviour can always be considered bad or evil in the same way, that not all conforming behaviour can always be considered good or right—a fact that most sociologists, would acknowledge. Some sociologists, however, evade this problem by denying the possibility of good deviant behaviour by calling such a possibility an oxymoron. Thio (ibid.: 5) refers to Sagarin in this regard: 'Sagarin also insists that deviance be defined as negative only, arguing that it is an oxymoron—a contradiction in terms—to talk about "positive deviance"'. William Rushing basically shares the same conviction (cited in Thio, 1995: 5).

The logical problem that we are left with, in using our substitutionary terms for good/right and evil/bad, is the following: How can good/right behaviour (i.e., conformity) at the same time also be evil/bad and how can evil/bad behaviour (i.e., deviance) at the same time also be good/right? It is more than a logical problem however. Somewhere along the line in our personal, teaching or researching lives we will be expected to come out in favour of or in disfavour of one of the two alternatives, i.e., a choice for one alternative and a choice against the other alternative will be demanded either by circumstance or fellow human beings.

Another attempt in dealing with this tenacious evaluative problem is to use twisted, morally or culturally relativistic reasoning. We could try to convince ourselves and others to believe that what is considered good or right in our society or at one time in our society, might be considered bad or evil in another society or period in the same society. Although this kind of evaluative inconsistency does of course exist, the mere existence thereof does not solve the logically and evaluatively untenable position that the same phenomenon is simultaneously categorized as both good/right on the one hand and evil/bad on the other hand. Deep inside, we would however still know that in terms of some ultimate criterion, it is impossible for wrong/bad/evil to simultaneously be really right/good and for right/good to simultaneously be really wrong/bad evil—that it is impossible for two opposite and mutually exclusive phenomena to be the same and to be grouped together in the same nominal category.

In spite of this, our second route of escape, then, is taken to be moral or cultural relativism. In this case we not only deny the reality and even possibility that absolutes concerning good and evil exist or could ever exist, but we also deny that, because these do not exist, we would never be required to obey its demand for a choice between them. Once we truly believe this, we conclude that it is not only impossible but also not rational or desirable to bother about issues like choosing between good and bad. The behavioural directive following from this line of argument is simple: Do as you please—as there are no evaluative absolutes on right and wrong anyway. As a result no choice is required and therefore anything goes.

Our third route of escape is determinism. In this case the source of our actions is shifted from the realm of conscious and voluntary choice to dynamisms (structures/processes/forces) within ourselves or outside ourselves or at least outside our control. The old nature vs. nurture debate testifies to this. Through this approach then, we shift responsibility or blame for our actions or inaction to forces within (e.g., our genes or personality) or outside ourselves (e.g., political/economic conditions in society or experiences in early childhood) and in so doing we furthermore present these dynamisms as coercive entities which allow us no choice in what we do, no control over what we do and finally, as a result of the first two, no responsibility for what we do. Thus, once again no one could ever point a finger to us (or to any other human being for that matter). All of this is done with the help and in the name of social science and on the basis of a wide variety of social and psychological theories. Lyman (1978: 119) notes in this regard:

> The rise and proliferation of the sciences of man since the 1850s have been attended by the fall and the contraction of the idea of sin. Perhaps most significant in this movement has been the philosophical victory in the minds of most educated persons, of determinism over freedom. Once man was relieved of full responsibility for his deeds, once dark forces of the mind, of history, of heredity, or of culture were found to shape his thoughts, and shackle his reason, sin with its insistence on freedom of the will to choose between good and evil, had to retreat into the recesses of a suspect theology; at the same time

dire punishment as a deserved retribution for the willful commission of wrongful deeds had to give way to remediation and rehabilitation. The establishment of social-scientific determinism paved the way first for a scientific authorization for the distrust of human reason and, ultimately, for the triumph of the therapeutic.

All of the above relieves us of the necessity to find ultimate and valid definitions of good and evil, to choose between the two and to accept responsibility for our choices. The threats and possible escape routes presented by the social sciences could be depicted as follows:

Table 1.2
The Threats and Possible Escape Routes

Threat	*Escape route*
Having to find valid and ultimate definitions of good and evil: Our definitional responsibility	Ethical neutrality
Having to choose between good and evil: Our decisional responsibility	Relativism
Having to accept accountability for our choices and actions: Our admissional responsibility	Determinism

The same escapist dynamic operates within the study of deviance with ethical neutrality, relativism and determinism as the most well-known routes of escape from evaluative responsibility. In spite of this attempt to dodge the evaluative sub-structure upon which this whole operation rests, it will not go away and will keep on demanding a verdict even if only by default.

Defining Deviance

When trying to define deviance, we can start off by looking at various categories of definitions as identified by Thio (1995: 4–8). First, he looks at definitions suggesting that deviance involves departure from normative standards. Parsons, Merton and Cohen fall in this category. Second, those definitions—used by most sociologists—which define deviance in terms of what the public/public opinion considers negative, objectionable behaviour. Sociologists opting for these definitions, reject the idea that the term deviance could refer to positive or unobjectionable behaviour. Definitions by Rushing and Sagarin fall in this category.

Whereas the first two categories define deviance on the basis of the actions of the deviant actor, the third category of definitions define deviance on the basis of a responding audience/group/society imposing a label on behaviour considered to be undesirable. Becker and Erikson fall in this category. The fourth category can be called the ambiguous category as it involves ambiguous definitions. Matza and Lemert belong to this category. In fact Lemert suggests it is much better to leave deviance undefined. Fifth and finally, Alexander Liazos suggests that people listed by sociologists as deviants, have one thing in common. They are all oppressed, powerless individuals whose deviant behaviours are of a dramatic nature—such as prostitution, drug abuse, juvenile delinquency and the like. This means that sociologists have neglected the study of powerful persons who break laws, fix laws and violate moral standards (cited in Thio, 1995: 7). Thio (ibid.: 8) then reduces these five broad categories of definitions into two—the positivist (including those definitions with a specific focus on definitional precision and a scientific study of powerless deviants) and the humanist (including definitions with a specific focus on broader boundaries, labelling and the study of powerful deviants).

Looking at the variety of definitions of deviant behaviour, one common element connects all these definitions: In each definition, humans are taken as Ultimate Definitional Authority—be they sociologists, general public or powerful members of society. Taking this fact as basis, it is possible to define deviance as that state of being and those behaviours which would constitute a departure from that which humans (be it humanity in its totality or certain sections of it) call good. In other words, deviance simply refers to that state of being or to those behaviours which humans call bad or evil.

On Sin

Sin and Sociology

Regarding sin and sociology, Lyman (1978: 3) says the following:

> To the extent that sociological thought embraces the study of evil today, it does so under the embarrassing, neutered morality of 'deviance'. Adopting for the most part an uncritical stance toward the normative structure of any given society, the sociologist of deviance

can only locate those violations of the norms that evoke sanctions of one kind or another. Presuming to have no relevant standards of morality by which he might independently judge the situation, the positive sociologist of deviance takes his cue from whatever the forces of law and restriction define as evil. Hence, the concerns of the vocal and powerful elements of a society become the resources for a sociological investigation of evil. Alternatively, the sociologist becomes the self-appointed advocate of an allegedly oppressed group, or of history itself, and seeks to define and locate evil in just those official elements that move against and demoralize his chosen people or trajectory of history. Sociologists are asked to take sides in a kind of intellectual contest of moral and social superiority; in the outcome of that game, there will emerge good and evil.

A good example of this is *Taking Sides* (Finsterbusch and McKenna, 1986). With reference to sin and sociology Lyman (1978: 3–4) says:

> The concept of sin is a *rara avis* in sociology.[1] Indeed, it is a rare word these days altogether if we accept the thundering warnings of religion. It is not that there are no transgressions for which we might atone or repent, but rather that the atomization of society, the alienation characteristic of social relationship, the collectivization of guilt and pride make the designation of sinners all too difficult. There has been a division of labour in sin as well as in virtue, and each person can now point an accusatory finger toward others or toward a faceless massive monolith—the corporate structure of modern society. It is precisely in this recognition of division, corporatism, and neutrality that sin has reached its greatest heights. For modern sin is peculiarly non-human in its use of things and exploitative in its use of men. Just as man reaches new understandings of human nature and social order, those very understandings lead him to see evil as outside his control. It is the Frankensteinian vision that haunts the world today. Man has created great corporate automatons, empowered them with money, endowed them with strength and potency, and freed them from personal, social, or moral responsibility. Once imagined to be his neutral servants, who would keep him from the temptations of pride, avarice, envy, and gluttony, coerce him away from sloth, reduce and cabin his lust, and chasten his anger, these corporate men *manqué* have become his masters, driving him on, determined to achieve in

> their soulless domination a hitherto unimagined kind of tyranny. They have appropriated and neutralized sin, liberating men from their obligations to one another at the precise moment when these same men become slaves to their own immortal and untiring creations.

From the preceding section it is clear that, as Cherbonnier (1956: 28) concludes, '... the true realist is the man who acknowledges the distinction between good and evil and with it the category of sin.' Looking at humanity and human life across the boundaries of time and space and as we know it today in the here and now, one conclusion is inescapable. Something went terribly wrong somewhere. The empirical evidence is overwhelming. Not only do we observe the manifestation of the micro-macro dynamics of destruction and degeneration in the physical-geographical, psycho-biological, socio-cultural and spiritual realms but sooner or later all of us personally experience the ravages of the destructive dynamic that relentlessly gnaws away at the very fibre of life and orderly substance in all its forms. Earthquakes, droughts, floods, environmental abuse, mental and physical illness in all its forms, marital and family disintegration, violence, rape and murder, poverty, corruption, domination of one individual or group by another individual or group be it ethnic, racial, gender, class or international domination, conflict or war and finally, the invisible but very real war that rages between truth and lie in the battlefield of the spiritual realm where ideas, words and philosophies of truth and deception vie for our attention and support, confirm and underline the fact that everything is not well. There seems to be a relentless and ultimate death-directness inherent in all of humankind's thoughts, words and actions as well as in the dynamics that operate within and drive nature and the greater cosmos. All of this of course started when '... the first human couple disobeyed God and fell victim to sin ... .' Ever since his condition has been typified as a state of decay and sin (*status corruptionis*) (Möller, 1997: 2).

In this regard, Lyman (1978: 269) states '... man seems to be overwhelmed by evil and yet obscured from sin.' The unpleasant realities associated with human existence carrying the stamp of death, pose questions like: What has gone wrong in the world? And what is wrong with humanity? Why did my child/spouse/father/mother have to die such an agonizing death? These questions demand answers. But human explanations of these realities and answers to these questions remain unsatisfactory and incomplete. Lyman (ibid.: 273) with reference to present-day society and sin states:

> ... the scenes of sin are now much more different from those imagined by the early thinkers on the subject. Three moods or leitmotivs dominate the modern dramas of sin and evil—immensity, impersonality and ambiguity. The scale of evil committed in the world today seems to defy puny man's attempt to understand, much less to prevent it.

God's explanation of and word for this tragic state of human affairs, is of course 'sin' and 'the consequences of sin'. These and other empirical realities of human existence simply confirm the ontological reality of sin and its consequences. The overwhelming and depressing force of the gravity of sin is such that, unless this burden is placed on the shoulders of Jesus Christ, who already carried this burden on our behalf and absolved us from its bondage, alternative escape routes have to be identified and used especially for the sake of mental and spiritual survival.

The Denial of Sin

Many thinkers, both secular and religious, tend to consider the concept of sin to be dysfunctional, archaic or irrelevant as it implies a picture of God as being too punitive. It is furthermore argued that the discourse of sin tends towards a rhetoric of scapegoating and that it is sometimes used in dubious social or political agendas by certain Christian communities (Weaver, 2003: 45). Being however confronted by the ontological reality and horror of sin and its death-directed, degenerative dynamic, without knowing and/or acknowledging Jesus Christ as the Way, the Truth and the Life out of this existential death-warrant, the denial of sin, as an attempt to escape the reality and consequences thereof, becomes imperative. Lyman (1978: 271–272) describes this tendency:

> ... As the anxieties of life itself become too much to bear, individuals seek an escape from evil, a release from sin, virtually a departure from the human condition. In their heroic struggle to release themselves from the captivity of sinful life they exchange one *form* of life for another, each new form promising both liberation and security, the end of man's separation from himself, from God, from history. Harold Rosenberg is thus quite correct when he interprets Marx's

> theory of history as a great theatrical drama. It is a play that unfolds in five mammoth, era-long acts—Asiatic, Ancient, Feudal, Bourgeois, and Socialist Production. In terms of Simmel's theory of the dialectics of form and life, each epoch is an act in the drama of mankind's release from the formal conditions of human enslavement and its ultimate emergence into an existence that is life itself, freed from all forms. But the forms are man's own contribution to life—he gives it structure, meaning, rules, and customs. Encased in his own creations, architectonic man cannot escape. He can only hope for release.

In this process of denying sin yet having to face and struggle with its consequences, especially the social sciences tend to be seen and presented as a substitute, but false gospel to the world. Guilt must somehow be sublimated. 'The task of social theory is not to explain guilt away or absorb it unthinkingly in still another destructive ideology, but to neutralize it and give it expression in truly creating and life-enhancing ideologies (ibid.: 271–272). Becker believes that a new science of society—synthesizing ideas of Marx with those of Freud—might in its critical and tragic dimensions provide a moral equivalent of religion for the expiation of sin. He writes:

> A science of society will be a study similar to one envisaged by Old Testament prophets, Augustine, Kierkegaard, Max Scheler, William Hocking: it will be a critique of idolatry, of the costs of a too narrow focus for the dramatization of man's need for power and expiation. (cited in Lyman, 1978: 271–272)

Schuurman (1993: 356) sees the denial of sin as the consequence of the denial of God as the creator of reality:

> Men erkent de werkelikheid niet langer als schepping van God, laat staan dat men de diepte van de zondeval en daarmee ook de totale en radikale verlossing deur Christus en de verwachting van de herschepping belijdt.

With its inclination to determinism, ethical neutrality and moral relativism then, the social sciences in general and sociology in particular, tend to act as substitute gospel in the mind of the unbeliever by declaring, through its philosophies, theories and research, the innocence and guilt-free state of humanity and implicitly presenting science in general and social science in particular as the way to redemption from the bondage of sin and its consequences. It is exactly this quality of the social sciences which affords it its almost irresistible attraction for the world. With a sigh of relief, the unthinking student of sociology can, on the basis of many if not most social theories, conclude: 'I am innocent' and in so doing fulfil one of the most basic human needs i.e., to be freed of guilt or to be forgiven, a need that can only be truly fulfilled by accepting Jesus's work of redemption on the cross, his paying of the price for our sins in our stead.

Defining Sin

What then does this phenomenon called 'sin' entail? Cherbonnier (1956: 43–44) starts off by stating that the concept of sin is not exclusive to Christianity:

> The word 'sin', then, a purely formal word referring to the disorientation of human freedom, is no monopoly of Christianity. Every philosophy has its own conception of what man's external point of reference ought to be. Consequently, as the other side of the coin, it will also have its own conception of sin, though usually under a different name. The reason why it is mistakenly regarded as a 'Christian motif' is simply that the Bible, adhering more rigorously than most other philosophies to the implications of human freedom, keeps the problem of sin in the foreground, instead of trying to circumvent it.

Cherbonnier (ibid.: 61) indicates that sin has been misconceived in two ways: First, as breaking rules and second, as being intrinsic to human nature. The first misconception implies God to be involved in the '... quibbling calculation of quid pro quo' (ibid.: 62). And this is contrary to God's revealed nature.

The second misconception, which also implies the concept of 'original sin', suggests an element of determinism in human's sinful behaviour, which is contrary to the biblical conception that humans are free to choose. This conception, however, understands that sin is prior to individual acts of choice, and traces it to a defective human nature rather than to misplaced allegiance. Cherbonnier (ibid.: 13) says:

> If there is any viable alternative to it, the Christian doctrine of sin ought not to be taken seriously. Its consequences are far too

> momentous to warrant acceptance on any but the most unimpeachable grounds. The most obvious alternative is to deny that the conception of sin in any form, whether Christian or otherwise, is a meaningful or necessary category for the interpretation of human life. As against this view, the present book must demonstrate that some notion of sin, even though under a different label, is integral to the thinking of every human being. He who denies it ultimately succeeds only in concealing it from himself.
>
> The other alternative to the Christian view would indeed retain the conception of sin but with a different definition. Historically, all such definitions have fallen under one of two main headings: the 'moralistic view', which regards sin as the violation of given rules and standards; and the 'dismal conception', which regards sin as some intrinsic defect in human nature. The work of Cherbonnier must therefore also refute these versions of sin before vindicating the specifically biblical view.

Cherbonnier (ibid.: 13) then goes on to define sin with reference to the Bible in the following words:

> According to the Bible, sin is properly defined as misplaced allegiance or, to use its technical word for it, idolatry. No man is without his 'god', in the sense of a focal point around which his life takes its orbit and which imparts a distinctive complexion to his values, purposes, and actions.

Closely related to Cherbonnier's conception of sin is McFadyen's argument which points out that sin involves 'the disruption of our proper relationship to God' (cited in Weaver, 2003: 45). Möller (1997: 8–10) also discusses the meaning of sin as presented in the Bible and highlights the following characteristics:

- Sin as not reaching the goal—missing God's purpose for humanity.
- Sin as trespassing the limits imposed by God and rebellion by refusing to live in accordance with God's commandments.
- Sin as evil, especially the evil inclination that exists in man.
- Iniquity or lawlessness by living outside the law of God.
- Being guilty before God.
- Perfidy and disloyalty.
- Works of the flesh.

- Manifesting the spirit of the devil in the world.
- Crucifying the Son of God.

Berkouwer (1960: 58) writes that sin can only be defined in relation and with reference to God in the sense that sin in its deepest sense involves an unfathomable depth of wrong against God. Referring to the essential being of sin, he lists the following: *val, ongehoorzaamheid, ontrouw, vijandskap, ongeloof, overtreding, vervreemding.* Lyman (1978: 271) on the other hand defines sin as follows:

> Sin from this point of view is the human condition, the condition of alienation from God. In his separation from the divine he feels uncertain of his being and unknowing of his future. The material and fleshly world obsesses him, but he gains no peace of mind thereby. It is life itself that becomes a problem, and not merely particular acts in that life. Sin thus creates a drama of lifelong anxiety, as lonely, oppressed, and weighted-down individuals act or are acted upon in a theater of increasing absurdity.

Ellul (1985: 60) says:

> ... in truly Christian thought, sin is known and recognized for what it is only after the recognition, proclamation, and experience of forgiveness. Because I have been pardoned, I realize how much of a sinner I was. Sin is shown to be sin through grace and not otherwise, just as the abruptly freed slave realizes, as he sees his chains, how great his misery was.

Sin for the purposes of this article then will be conceived of as being two-dimensional:

First of all, it will be conceived of as being intrinsic to human nature, i.e., as being a natural inclination or predisposition to deny and therefore disobey God and to hate one's neighbour. What is suggested here is simply that the first, spontaneous, natural option which comes to mind in a situation of invitation to sin, is to establish the 'supremacy of self which rebels against God and God's laws'. This would involve what the Bible calls our carnal nature. For instance, no father needs to call his son of five years old to himself, lift him onto his lap and say: 'Son, today Daddy's going to teach you how to lie!' The boy already knows how to lie without needing anybody to teach him. He has been born with the inclination towards and the knowledge of how to lie and needs to be taught the better alternative. Adults of course are more adept in hiding or camouflaging this inclination or tendency. In essence, this involves an inclination towards that which God would call evil or would disapprove of in that particular situation.

In terms of what Cherbonnier has suggested, the tendency towards sin is seen here as the outflow or consequence of a defective human nature which in turn is seen here as being a result of Adam and Eve's original sin. This, however, in no way implies that the resultant sinful behaviour which might or might not flow from this inclination or tendency, is blindly determined as if humans had no choice or decisional responsibility, but merely that this is the response that, due to its intrinsic nature, tends to be the primary and natural or first option considered in a particular situation, e.g., to hate those who hate you or to love those who love you, to lie rather than speak the truth, etc. It needs to be stressed, however, that consideration and freedom of choice—in other words—our decisional responsibility—always and inescapably stands between our natural tendency or inclination towards sin and the actual commitment of sin.

The second dimension of sin then would involve a free choice, or the executing of one's decisional responsibility, to act according to our carnal or sinful tendencies or inclination—i.e., out of free will and consciously, to do exactly that which God would call evil or would disapprove of. This implies that sinning is always the result of both an innate tendency or inclination and a personal, free choice.

Sin then can be a defined as that state of being and those forms of behaviour which constitute a departure from that which God calls good or stated otherwise, conformity to that which God calls evil/wrong or bad. Sin furthermore is totally race-, gender-, and class-blind and refuses to be bound or limited by any sociological variable or category, or by time and space.

On the Relationship between Sin and Deviance

The relationship between sin and social deviance will very briefly be described in terms of a typology in which sin has been defined as that state of being and those forms of behaviour which depart from that which God calls good or conform to that which God calls evil/wrong or bad. Deviance on the other hand has been defined as that state of being and those forms of behaviour which depart from that which humans—or certain sections of humanity—call good or conform to that which humans or certain sections of humanity call evil/wrong or bad.

The relationship between sin and social deviance will now very briefly be outlined by drawing up a simple typology in which human definitions of good and evil will be combined with God's definitions of good and evil. The typology looks like this:

Table 1.3

Divine and Human Definitions of Good and Evil

Human definition of	*God's definition of*	
	Good	*Evil*
Good	GG	GE
Evil	EG	EE

From the above typology the following types of behaviour can be discerned:

- GG: Behaviour that conforms to what both God and humans would call good and involves human obedience to God.
- GE: Behaviour that humans would call good but that God would call evil and involves obedience to humans but disobedience to God.
- EG: Behaviour that humans would call evil but God would call good and involves disobedience to humans but obedience to God. This constitutes an interesting category of behaviour as it includes what has previously been called 'good deviant behaviour' but the possibility of which is denied by some sociologists. This is perhaps the most challenging and difficult kind of behaviour required from Christians as it very often involves standing alone in a self-sacrificial way. This is exactly the kind of behaviour that Jesus Christ exemplified.
- EE: Behaviour that both humans and God would call evil and involves disobedience to both humans and God.

The relationship could further be clarified by means of two overlapping circles: the one circle representing sin, the other representing deviance. In terms of two overlapping circles it is clear that three categories of behaviour can be distinguished:

- Behaviour considered sin from God's perspective but not considered deviant from human perspective.
- Behaviour considered deviant from human perspective but not considered to be sin from God's perspective. Looking at Scripture, this seems to be the kind of behaviour God encourages in His children by calling on them to depart from that which is wrong and evil—thus to be Godly deviants!
- Finally, a category of behavioural overlap between sin and deviance which could therefore be considered to be both sinful and deviant.

Final Comments

Accepting God as the Ultimate Definitional Authority not only in our personal lives but also in the study of social deviance, we are—in terms of the 'logovision' premise—enabled to gain the following advantages:

- First of all we will be enabled to see reality as it really is, i.e., to distinguish the true good from the false good and true evil from false evil and thus avoid the pitfall of acting in a fatally inappropriate manner in a world full of deceptive definitions of what constitutes good and what constitutes evil. This would also bring an interesting and exciting dimension into the study of deviance as evaluative issues would not need to be avoided but could be confronted in a bold and constructive way in both teaching and research.
- We would be able to clearly distinguish good deviant behaviour from bad or evil deviant behaviour. In terms of the typology, the latter would include behaviour that both God and humans would call evil and behaviour that humans would call good but God would call evil.
- Though the phenomenon of definitions of good and evil being relative to a particular time and place would remain, the problem of evaluative relativism and the evaluative confusion accompanying this relativism, would disappear as God is taken as Ultimate Definitional Authority concerning *inter alia* definitional issues of good and evil/good and bad/right and wrong and God in and through Jesus Christ would thus become 'The Absolute One' relative to whom all else is measured.

- We would realize that deviance (of the variety which humans would call evil but God would call good) can indeed be a very good form of deviance that should be encouraged.
- Ethical neutrality—chosen because of the fear to boldly confront issues of right and wrong—could be replaced by 'agape' love (love in spite of) in the approach towards and study of deviants. Thus love could become the guiding principle in the study of and in dealing with all issues of good and evil and eventually could become the '... concentration of all normativity' (Schuurman, 1993: 353). This involves the overcoming of what is called socio-moral disgust, in the name of this kind of love (Beck, 2006).
- The study of deviance could be performed with evaluative and intellectual integrity in the sense of calling good 'good' and evil 'evil' instead of vice versa and doing that without apology.

Note

1. An important exception is Edward Alsworth Ross's (1973) *Sin and Society: An Analysis of Latter Day Iniquity.*

2 Buddhist Compassion and the Moral Nihilism

Jeffrey Grupp

The world we all live in today is a 'prison planet'. Slavery and poverty is rampant; inundating every corner of the globe (see Bales, 2004). Environmental destruction is relentless, forests are vanishing, pollution is unprecedented, animal species extinction is widespread. Use of anti-depressant and anti-stress medications is skyrocketing, and world citizens are forgetting the religious life in order to chase lifestyles that only bring disorientation and dissatisfaction. War is widespread, new diseases are appearing, and crime rates are escalating worldwide. The purpose of this article is to show that there is an escape from prison planet: Buddhist compassion. Buddhist compassion, as I will use the term in this article, is the realization that you are not different from me. With this realization, the popular concept of an isolated self is revealed to be not real. It can be verified that Buddhist compassion pervades all conscious beings; but most humans have forgotten that it exists: they have forgotten this since they have forgotten who and what they are, which is nirvanic. According to Buddha, hate is not conquered by hate: hate is conquered by love. This is an eternal law. Many do not know that we are here in this world to live in harmony. Those who know this do not fight against each other.

As Buddha indicates, it is not widely known that people are supposed to live in harmony with one another. Another way to put this is: few know that conscious beings are not separate or distinguishable (which is a Mahāyānistic sort of Buddhist compassion) due to the fact that all persons are nirvanic. Residing in Samsara (forgetting one is nirvanic) prevents conscious beings from understanding this. Buddha also points out that this Buddhist compassion is 'law', which apparently means it is the way of things, and thus those who do not understand this law are deluded.

In addition to following the Mahāyāna position on Buddhist compassion, I will also be concerned with Dharmakîrti's philosophy of Buddhist atomism, which appears to be the correct account of Buddhism. In fact, Dharmakîrti's work leads to a philosophy of moral nihilism which, interestingly, leads to the maximum level of Buddhist compassion. The sort of Buddhist moral nihilism that will be discussed in this article is not moral anarchy or moral inversion, both of which lead to cruelty toward other conscious beings. Rather, it is a state of indifferent non-judgment and inaction—all central to Buddhist compassion. Only with this Buddhist moral nihilism can conscious beings attain deep Buddhistic compassion for all conscious beings. The findings lead to the conclusion that all conscious beings contain a deep compassion for one another (i.e., they are not distinct from one another), but as evidenced by the state of the contemporary war-torn world, few have remembered this inside themselves (i.e., as the dynamo of their subjectivity).

Quantum Atomic Non-matter

The 'Standard Interpretation' of Dharmakîrti's Philosophy

Before discussing the theory of nihilistic Buddhist compassion, some issues will be discussed now. In this article the correctness of, what Dreyfus calls 'the standard interpretation' of Dharmakîrti's philosophy will be used. This is as follows:

> ... only infinitesimal atoms and moments of consciousness are real. Everything else, such as a shape or a colour, is real only inasmuch as it is taken as an object of conventional practice. This view is not unlike Wilfrid Sellars's claim that objects such as table, ice cubes, and colours do not really exist. Our commonsense notions of such objects are false but cognitively useful ... . Several traditional and modern scholars have explained Dharmakîrti in this way, emphasizing that in

> his system reality is reducible to partless atoms interacting with moments of consciousness … . This causal relation explains our perceptions of extended objects. In reality, there is no extension but just the causal interaction of infinitesimal atoms with partless moments of consciousness. This interpretation of Dharmakîrti's ontology can be called *the standard interpretation.* (Dreyfus, 1997: 85)

Quantum Blob Theory: Properties do Not Exist

The argument in this article involves the philosophy of blob theory (reality is an undifferentiated being: distinctionless, propertyless). Consider a passage about Nagārjuna by Raju:

> The aim of Nagārjuna is to show that nothing positive or negative can be asserted of reality. It is therefore *Sûnya* (Vacuity, Emptiness). Even to think of it as *Sunya* is a mistake, because the concepts and vacuity and emptiness are understood with reference to full … . But Nagārjuna's dialectic goes deeper, and the linguistic analysts can find much that interests them in it … . Let us take vacuity. What is vacuous is something devoid of space, it is not vacuous. If it is devoid of space, then it contains a reference to space, in fact, a reference to all the things of which it is devoid. That means it contains this reference. Then how can it be vacuous. … It was, again, Nagārjuna who first enunciated and worked out the doctrine that the world was never born and is not there (*Ajātivāda*), which also was later adopted by some of the *Advaita Vedantins*. If everything is false and unreal, am I unreal? Is the pen I am writing with unreal? Nagārjuna says that I am not, nothing is. The world was not, is not, and will not be there. There is no question of the world of action even, because action, like all the other concepts, is self-contradictory and, therefore, false. All is *Sûnya*, Nirvana. (Raju, 1998: 128–129)

According to this passage, ordinary empirical reality is not real. Ordinary empirical reality is a reality of structure and distinction. The inverse of that is a reality of structureless and undifferentiated being: a reality that is ineffable. This is what is involved with blob theory: reality is flashing (vibrating), propertyless, indistinguishable, energy points, and the surfaces and colour-patches witnessed in ordinary empirical consciousness are illusions (Samsara). Consider what Stcherbatsky (1962: 85) writes about 'qualityless' ultimate reality:

> Every point-instant may be viewed as a particle of Time, as a particle of Space and as a sensible quality, but this difference is only a difference of our mental attitude ... towards that point-instant. The point-instant itself, the ultimate reality cut loose from all imagination is qualityless, timeless and indivisible.

When a conscious being uses language, they assign meanings and symbols onto observed items in ordinary empirical reality. These meanings and symbols are about the properties of the appearances of the items of Samsaric ordinary empirical reality. In fact, the only items that are in ordinary empirical reality are properties of things (specifically, surface and colour properties). But if there is no language that can denote any real (non-conceptual) objects, as the above passage about Nagārjuna implies when it shows us that all concepts are unreal (self-contradictory), then that indicates that there are no properties at all. This is because if there were properties, then language would have the power to denote, which the passages just given indicate cannot be the case. But there are stronger reasons than this to assert that blob theory is correct.

According to the philosophy of quantum blob theory, quantum atoms (partless quantum particles, such as the electron or quark) do not have properties, own being or materiality (Grupp, 2006a, 2006b). According to this quantum theory of Buddhism, '...there is no matter at all, flashes of energy follow one another and produce the *illusion* of stabilized phenomena' (Stcherbatsky, 1962: 83 emphasis added). Charge, spin, mass and other alleged 'differences' that physicists believe they witness among quantum atoms are all descriptions of how quantum atoms are observed (represented) through the quantum physicist's computer monitor in the particle accelerator lab. This is, however, a representation that contains serious distortions (see Grupp, 2006b for copious information on this issue), and is not the nirvanic direct apprehension of the ultimate quantum entities. Nirvana is direct observation of flashing quantum atoms; to see that they are real and the ordinary empirical reality is not. The nirvanic observer will directly apprehend 'many' philosophical atoms with the third eye but will report (if she reports anything) that there is only one, since they are all indistinguishable. Elsewhere I have called this mereological nihilism, Buddhist atomism, quantum non-matter, quantum blob atomism, blob theory, the mereological nihilist interpretation of quantum mechanics, quantum

Buddhism, and quantum abstract atomism, where that last two terms are the ones that will be used hereafter in this article. The realization that reality is a vibrating quantum blob—which is remembered through mindfulness—is to understand that materiality (surface and colour properties) is not real, and that only immateriality (vibrating quantum abstract atoms) is real. This realization is an escape from the prison planet: a release from the prison by understanding that the prison never existed, there was always only nirvana.

One can note that the nirvanic, the ultimate reality that Stcherbatsky is describing is an atomic reality—not the atomic reality of the ancient Buddhists, but a later pre-classical development in Indian Buddhism initiated by Dharmakîrti. He proposed 'that the study of [Buddhist] logic and epistemology has to replace the ancient philosophy of early Buddhism' (Stcherbatsky, 1962: 37). The quantum atomism of Dharmakîrti was not a Greek-like four-element atomistic theory as it was a surprisingly modern-sounding quantum mechanics, where it was discovered that '[t]he sensible world consists of sensibilia which are but momentary flashes of energy' (ibid.: 79).[1] It can be shown that Dharmakîrti's quantum mechanics (and perhaps, some perspectives on Mahāyāna Buddhism) involves blob theory.

The Mereological Nihilist Interpretation of Quantum Buddhism

Three standpoints will be used here to analyse Buddhist compassion:

(i) The interpretation of Buddhism given by Sautrāntika and Nagārjuna.
(ii) The account of Buddhism given by Dharmakîrti.
(iii) The account of empirical quantum mechanics just discussed which is called the mereological nihilist interpretation of quantum mechanics (see Grupp, 2006b).

It can be shown that a thoroughgoing and hard-nose empirical perspective of quantum mechanical reality is the correct view of reality (and thus other positions, such as the Realist, Einsteinian, and other metaphysical positions—including the other non-nihilist interpretations of quantum mechanics, which are metaphysical theories—are incorrect) (Grupp, 2005, 2006a, 2006b). Reality is best described according to the philosophies of mereological nihilism and blob theory, which are identical to the aforementioned hard-nosed and strictly empirical account of quantum physics. According to this strictly empirical interpretation of quantum physics, the data of quantum physics is non-interpretive (it does not involve interpretations of data that lead to, for example, wave-particle duality or probability clouds, which are not empirical findings, but are metaphysical theories and assumptions)[2], only involving the most rudimentary empirical findings of quantum mechanics, and which avoids the famous paradoxes (absurdities, contradictions) of quantum physics. According to the mereological interpretation of Buddhism, which is also called blob theory or quantum abstract atomism, reality is found to be immaterial, and consisting of indistinguishable points of energy that flicker (flash, vibrate, pulsate) in and out of existence:

> ... the only objects that exist are quantum objects that do not have parts, such as electrons, quarks, and any other *partless* quantum objects. Hereafter, I will call these 'quantum atoms', 'quantum philosophical atoms', or 'quantum abstract atoms', for reasons I will clarify ... . The data of experimental quantum physics reveals that the partless quantum abstract atoms are point-sized (sizeless), unstructured, non-material, surfaceless, non-interacting, irreducible, and perhaps indistinguishable quantum objects (true philosophical *atoms*) that have an incredibly short-lived and/or nearly instantaneous existence. Philosophical reasoning will also be given later in this article to show that philosophical argumentation about the quantum realm is in agreement with these experimental findings. These experimental findings of quantum physics show that quantum objects are not the sorts of items that can constitute macroscopic objects—or any objects whatsoever: material constitution is an illusion, and thus everyday ordinary empirical-material reality is some sort of a dream (Grupp, 2006b: 246).

There are only two perspectives conscious beings can have, nirvanic and Samsaric, or, in other words:

1. Ignorance (Dukkha): An ordinary empirical perspective, which is associated with the experience of extension (surfaces and colours), and which does not involve perception of the flashing immaterial quantum blob atoms.
2. Mereological nihilism: A quantum perspective, which is nirvanic experience, and the awareness that 1 does not exist (1 is illusion).

According to this position, an observer directly apprehends (i.e., perceives without the five senses) the immaterial flashing quantum blob atoms.

Now 2 follows from the thesis that Buddhist logic is concerned with the mereological nihilist's findings. Specifically, mereological nihilism is the theory that objects with parts do not exist, which is empirically verified by quantum physics. Stcherbatsky (1962: 86) writes in his *Buddhist Logic*, in a section entitled 'Duration and Extension Are Not Real', and in a passage about Buddhist opposition to the Realists, that '[f]or the Buddhists the parts alone are real, the whole is a fiction'. Dreyfus writes:

> Extended objects cannot be identified with their atomic parts, since they are extended (assuming they exist) and atoms are infinitesimally small. They cannot be different either, for in this case they would exist apart from these atoms. Since they are not one either, we have to conclude that extended objects do not exist externally. Why, then, are we perceiving extended objects if they do not exist? Dharmakîrti answers: 'The appearance of cognition, which is not distinct [from its object], as being so is indeed a distortion.' … Our perception of extended objects is without support in the external world and therefore mistake. Extended objects appear to exist separate from our consciousness, but in reality they do not exist externally. We perceive them as such, however, because our perceptions are distorted. (Dreyfus, 1997: 102)

Mereological nihilism also leads to blob theory.

Blob Theory (Propertylessness) in Dharmakîrti's Philosophy

'Ontology is closely linked to the question of whether universals exist … . Ontologically, such entities can be considered properties that individuals instantiate' (ibid.: 49). But universals (properties) do not exist, according to Dharmakîrti's post-ancient formulation of Buddhism; rather, they are mental illusions, fabrications, as Dreyfus points out:

> Against the Nyāya realism, Dharmakîrti develops a conceptualist theory of universals. The essential difference between the two lies in that, whereas for the Nyāya universals are real, for Dharmakîrti they are not. Dharmakîrti holds that universals have only nominal

> existence. They are constructed by conceptuality on the basis of our experiences of resemblances. In short, they are generally characterized phenomena … . [U]niversals as posited by realists have contradictory attributes, a clear sign that they fail to satisfy the … conditions of real phenomena … . Therefore, they are not real. Dharmakîrti explains: 'If [this universal] is distinct from [its particulars], then it is unrelated to them. Therefore, it is established as being essenceless. Its does not follow [from that] that nonexistents are kinds because they do not depend on their [particulars]. Therefore, this kind which is unreal and constructed on the basis of [real] entities is revealed by words for the sake if relating to particulars.' Universals are not real because they are not part of the causal network that is reality … . Only when thinking mind intervenes do universals come to be. (ibid.: 143)

If properties do not exist, then we arrive at a conceptualist and an extreme nominalist philosophy[3] that is often described as blob theory (Moreland, 2001: 74). Properties are not real items separate from Samsaric consciousness; but rather, properties are conceptual resemblances, and thus are fabrications of resemblances in Samsaric consciousness:

> … the world is not made of enduring substances with changing qualities. Rather, change [vibration] itself is the essence of reality. Things that appear to endure unchanged are, in fact, a succession. Reality is made only of events that flash in and out of existence. Every real happening in the universe is due to the arising and disappearing of countless events [i.e., countless flashing atoms] that cause it. Even the continuity of things is due to successive phenomena—events that closely resemble each other. (Dreyfus, 1997: 61)

For reasons given in this subsection, we can see that Dharmakîrti's Buddhism involves quantum blob theory. This understanding will be important when moral nihilism and Buddhist compassion will be discussed below.

Quantum Abstract Atoms do not have Own-being

A critical issue of blob theory and the mereological nihilist interpretation of quantum Buddhism is the Sautrāntika view that momentary events (Buddhist quantum atoms) do not have own-being. Consider what Mitchell writes about the Sautrāntika:

> They ... accepted the notion of momentariness, but understood it more in terms of the Buddha's teaching of impermanence. That is, while life is a series of momentary events, its elements do not have any own-being. So the fundamental elements of existence are not separate and self-subsisting, but are interconnected parts of the impermanent flow of existence. (Mitchell, 2002: 128)

If properties do not exist, as blob theory involves, there is no property of haecceity that can be exemplified by bare (propertyless) quantum abstract atoms and thus individuality or selfdom cannot be possessed by any quantum atom. For that reason, the Sautrāntika theory that entities do not have own being follows from blob theory.

This is all that is borrowed from the Sautrāntika, and while Mitchell's passage is interesting, it is cited here partly to show its error. A lack of own-being of any entities is not about the 'interconnectedness of things', but rather about the indistinguishability of immaterial 'things' (quantum abstract atoms). My point is to advance Buddhism so that it is more in accord with nirvanic observation as being identical to with the strictly empirical findings of quantum mechanics. A primary issue in this interpretation of quantum Buddhism is the idea that nothing is interconnected, and that there are no connections and metaphysical relations whatsoever; and rather there are only quantum abstract atoms, and the quantum abstract atoms are indistinguishable from one another:

> [Q]uantum philosophical atoms are indistinguishable particles that are not coinciding (not overlapping): quantum atoms share all the same *perceived* properties, and thus from what is observed about them through quantum instrumentation, those observations do not provide data that allow quantum researchers to clearly distinguish quantum abstract atoms from one another ... . The famous physicists, Brown and Davies, write: 'All members of a given particle species are identical; there is no way to distinguish, say, one electron from another'. (Grupp, 2006b: 249–50)

At a quick glance, it may seem that this account of quantum abstract Buddhist atomism may be promoting a Realist fallacy, on the order of the Realist fallacy described by Stcherbatsky (1962: 86):

> According to the Realists empirical things have a limited real duration ... . The atoms combine and form real new unities. These created unities reside, or inhere ... in the atoms. Thus we have one

> real things simultaneously residing in a multitude of atoms, i.e., in many places. This is impossible ... for if it were a reality, it would be a reality residing at once in many places, i.e., a reality at once residing and not residing in a given place.

This Realist account involves two primary issues: there are wholes, and there are multiply-located atoms. But the mereological interpretation of quantum mechanics involves a rejection of each of these two Realist absurdities. According to quantum Buddhism, space (location, place) does not exist and wholes composed of parts do not exist, and the mereological nihilist interpretation of quantum mechanics does not involve the Realist fallacies. If space does not exist, then there is no location. If two indistinguishable quantum abstract atoms are apprehended either in the particle accelerator lab or amid direct nirvanic apprehension, then it is not correct to assert that they are at different locations. It would be correct to assert that they are nowhere, and thus are not multiply-located (i.e., there is no relationalist matrix of space nor a substantivalist container of space, that these atoms exist amid, rather, they just are, and there is nothing more that can be asserted).

The Inevitability of Harm to Self and Others without Buddhism

Having established the Buddhist quantum philosophy that will be used to build a theory of Buddhist compassion here, another issue will now be discussed that is critical to the theory: the thesis that non-nirvanic beings can only be filled with hate and violence toward one another. This finding indicates that the philosophy of Buddhist compassion is critically important for all conscious beings to understand (i.e., to remember), lest our prison planet turn for the worse. According to Buddhism, we inevitably harm and have spite toward others. Consider the following argument, which has been pointed out by the Dalai Lama and which is found in Dharmakîrṭi's Pramanavarttika:

- Amid the attitude of the ordinary, non-nirvanic, empirical consciousness (Dukkha), where a conscious being does not observe flashing quantum abstract atoms, but rather observes extension (surfaces, colours, and duration—i.e., it is erroneously believed that extension and time are real), it is believed that an enduring, isolated self exists.

- The self wants to survive: the self discussed above also involves a (sometimes ferocious) desire to exist, to persist through time.
- The self wants to protect itself: the self will feel threat to that which is perceived to in any way harm the continual existence of the self.
- Parts of what might be believed to be a threat to the self are other people (what are erroneously believed to be 'other' isolated, persisting selves). Thus, other persons who are perceived to be a threat to the existence of the self will be considered an enemy and thus will be hated or attacked, either overtly or covertly.
- The illusory isolated self will seek out what it perceives are the best (most safe and most favourable) conditions for it, including removing any threats.
- There are limited things (land, resources, money) that non-nirvanic denizens of Dukkha all try to acquire and people inevitably compete for these.
- Therefore ordinary, non-nirvanic, empirical consciousness inevitably involves spite, hostility and violence toward what it perceives as other isolated selves (i.e., other people).
- Notice that this finite regress starts with the illusory belief in an enduring isolated self. If there is an understanding that the persisting self does not exist, then the conclusion of this argument would not be manifested in the behaviour of conscious beings. Buddhist ethics are an entirely foreign sort of ethics, compared to that which is found in the contemporary world. In Buddhism there is no good and evil; '[t]he basis of [Buddhist] ethics is extremely simple. Nothing is intrinsically good or bad. It is just flashing atoms' (Ricard and Thuan, 2001: 19). Reality, according to the mereological nihilist interpretation of Buddhism is neither good nor evil; it is only the Buddhist quantum abstract atoms. But in contemporary culture it is ubiquitously believed by the world citizens that there is evil all around—namely 'in other people' (that are perceived as threats to the illusory self).

Vibrating Quantum Abstract Atoms do not have Moral Properties

So far it has been shown that only flashing atoms exist and that deluded Samsaric selves inevitably hate one another. The very popular theories of moral realism and relativism do not work, as the violence-ridden world demonstrates. The correct thesis of morality is desperately needed by the world citizens and that thesis is moral nihilism. Moral nihilism involves the idea that there is no good or evil, and thus there is no good or evil that has been done to me. Rather, there is only the suffering of Samsaric agents which needs to be quelled by nirvanic release. Now it will be shown that quantum blob theory leads to moral nihilism and quantum moral nihilism is the essential position a conscious being must emanate in order to remember that one is deep Buddhistic compassion (and moral realism or moral relativism are the enemies of genuine compassion).

If the no-nonsense eliminativism of the mereological nihilist interpretation of quantum Buddhism is the correct account of reality, we can discuss all of reality in terms of mere vibration (momentariness, durationlessness) of propertyless, immaterial and indistinguishable quantum Buddhist atoms. This leads to a question: How can the vibration of quantum atoms be evil, or be good? If atoms only vibrate (flash in and out of existence), and if atoms are the only real entities, then there is nothing else about the atoms, or about reality, to make them this way or that way. Hence, they are indistinguishable from one another, and are incapable of being good or bad (they are incapable of possessing moral properties). In other words, if there is only atomic vibration, then nowhere can anyone call some vibrational 'events' evil and others not, because vibration of quantum abstract atoms is not intrinsically evil or good. If so, it is not clear why some quantum vibrations could be considered 'good' and others 'evil'.

Furthermore, if blob theory is the correct theory of reality, then it bolsters the thesis: vibrational quantum non-matter cannot have intrinsic value, since it cannot possess properties such as goodness, evil and so forth.

Nihilism and Inaction

Moral Nihilism I

Moral nihilism is typically resisted by many philosophers, due to the fact that philosophers around the world associate nihilism with an absence of morality that leads to an absence of compassion, which, in turn, leads to pervasive violence and hate. But such a position is entirely incorrect. Moral nihilism does not lead to absence of compassion, but rather it is just the opposite. It is the base for developing deep nirvanic compassion. Moral nihilism, in fact, is founded in an absence of concern for anything in culture or about the self. More specifically, it is founded in a rejection of importance of, and moral value in, anything illusory (i.e., an unconcern for the self or for anything material). Moral non-nihilism (i.e., placing importance and value on that which is illusion, Dukkha) leads to placing importance on some material entities over others, where the latter will be viewed as less important. The nihilistic (morally nihilistic) nirvanic observer is unmoved by material phenomena since she understands that they are not real. A consequence of this position is that she cannot formulate moral preferences about material things; she will see that materiality does not contain any moral properties since materiality does not exist. She will not be able to, for example, understand that one physical body (such as a Jewish body) is any better or worse than another one (such as a Muslim body),[4] since physical bodies do not exist. Consequently, if the moral nihilist is called to war in order to oppress and/or kill material bodies whom she has been told need to be controlled or killed, in her nirvanic foundation she will be unable to move, due to the fact that she will see that the material world does not exist, and cannot be sought after or repelled, pursued or rejected.

Conversely, it is the non-nihilistic, non-nirvanic observer who almost always tends to be a moral realist or moral relativist, illusorily believing that the self and material things are real—who will develop ideas that some material things are good, and others are bad, for the self, wherein some material items needs to be grasped or hoarded, and others need to be attacked or obliterated. It is the non-nihilist, then, who is prone to, and capable of violence, while it is impossible for the Buddhist moral nihilist to muster up enough physical bodily movement to hurt a single person in any way.

Moral Nihilism II

Moral nihilism is not often discussed other than in brief passages that often tend to give varying definitions of what moral nihilism is. Let me be clear that moral nihilism is not a rejection of ethics, for such a view is contradictory: the rejection of ethical positions would prevent a philosopher from holding any position, such as the preference for the position of moral nihilism. Rather, moral nihilism is an ethical position where one value is held: the moral nihilist asserts that it is ethical to reject the value or importance and value of human behaviour (physical bodily behaviour), and of any physical event or item. In other words, moral nihilism involves a rejection over that which does not exist. This moral nihilism is not the thesis that it matters not at all what we do, as is often associated with Nietzsche (Ellin, 1995: 76–77). But rather, moral nihilism is the thesis that there is nothing to do. There are no choices to make, no preferences to defend, no goods to hoard, and no enemies to fear. There is only nirvana.

In this article, for reasons given above, descriptions of moral nihilism that are not in accord to what has been written above are rejected, such as the following, which supposedly derives from the theory of ethical relativism:

> Moral absolutism holds that there is a single true morality. Moral relativism claims instead: … . There is no single true morality. There are many different moral frameworks, none of which is more correct than others.
>
> Moral nihilism can be compared to religious nihilism. Religious nihilism can be compared to the conclusion that there is no single true religion but only many different outlooks, none of which is more correct than the others … ..Moral nihilism argues that the same is true of morality: … there is no point to engaging in morality and moral judgments. (Harman and Thomson, 2000: 5–6)

According to Harmon and Thomson's analysis, if relativism is true then nihilism is true. This conditional link is tenuous. Harmon and Thomson want us to believe that if there are enough morals (moral relativity) then there are none (moral nihilism). Perhaps this is analogous to asserting that if enough light exists in reality, then the reality will become dark. This would appear to be a contradiction, and thus another definition of moral nihilism would be more appropriate, such as the one given here. According to Harmon and Thomson's passage, humans have many values, all of which are equally right. This is not moral nihilism (there are no morals), but rather radical relativism (there are many 'even-level' morals). Buddhist moral nihilism is concerned with an entirely different issue than this sort of relativism: the rejection of any importance of any life-form's behaviour. It is this lack of importance that is what moral nihilism actually involves.

Realism and relativism which are concerned with the activities and beliefs of 'isolated selves' (which do not really exist) lead to action, and, *ipso facto*, lead to violence. Nihilism is realized in the nirvanic state of no-self and *ipso facto*, can only involve inaction and peace.

Subjectivity and Buddhistic Compassion

The dynamo of Buddhism—compassion—follows from quantum moral nihilism. In fact reality can be viewed from two perspectives: illusory (ordinary empirical reality, Dukkha) and real (nirvanic). A careful analysis of reality through both of these perspectives reveals an interesting issue: there are no distinctions between conscious beings. This follows from the findings in the analysis of mereological nihilism and moral nihilism above and it is a realization of subjective Buddhist compassion when one remembers (realizes) that they are nirvanic. Now it will be shown why non-nirvanic humans can be shown to be indistinguishable: if you feel a pain or joy, I feel it too, regardless of whether or not my awareness is awakened enough to understand that I am feeling your feeling. This is the most genuine definition of compassion: to feel the other directly and to remember that you are the other.

Compassion is the Amalgamation of Subjectivities

Humans are not bodies, but rather are subjectivities, so if we are to genuinely experience and feel one another (if we are to exhibit genuine compassion), it is not ultimately through body contact (which is illusory touching), but rather via mind-to-mind contact (which is a sort of telepathic direct contact). But as is well-known, if any things are able to actually contact, they become indistinguishable. To understand this, first consider the following passage from Chisholm (1989: 84):

> Let us recall an ancient problem. 'Consider two discrete physical bodies thought to be continuous with each other; the east side of body A, say, is continuous with the west side of body B. How is this possible? Either (i) the eastmost part of A is in the same place as is the westmost part of B or (ii) no part of A occupies the same place as does any part of B. In the case of (i), we would have two discrete things in the same place. But this is impossible.[5] In the case of (ii), since A and B occupy different places, there is a place between the place where A is and the place where B is. But if there is a place between A and B, then A and B are not continuous.'

Chisholm's argument indicates that there cannot be contact, abutting or touching unless there are items that are coinciding in time or space, whereby there can be contact or integration of the entities that are touching. If two things are to directly touch, they must occupy each other's being, and if they occupy each other's being, then they are not separate, and if they are not separate, they are not two, they are one: they amalgamate (integrate, unify). For this reason, if two people (subjectivities) contact one another, they are one subjectivity.

What has just been described is the illusion involved in the idea that consciousnesses (subjectivities) are distinguishable from one another: if there is any interaction between persons (consciousnesses), they must be one consciousness. Dispelling this illusion of separateness is a key tenet of Buddhism and Buddhist compassion, as this passage about Mahāyāna compassion illustrates:

> Sāntideva persuasively ... argue[s] that indifference to the suffering of 'others' is as absurd as indifference to one's 'own' suffering .... In his *Bodhi-caryāvatāra*, ... [h]e advocates that one who sees the equality of self and other should heroically practise 'the exchange of self for others' ... the 'highest secret' which benefits both self and other .... In this practice, one looks on another, lowly, person as 'I' and on oneself as one would know someone else. (Harvey, 2000: 125–126)

The Feeling Mass

If right actions do not come from bodies or from moral properties, then where do they come from? The answer is: from what a conscious being actually is, which is subjectivity (consciousness). If moral nihilism reveals that there is no value in any self or any material item, then how does the Buddhist become compassionate? Buddhist moral nihilism involves the realization that there is no value in self or materiality since they are not real and thus the nihilist's attention is shifted to what is real—which is subjectivity (specifically, nirvanic subjectivity)—and by doing that, the nirvanic nihilist understands that you are not you, you are me, and if I love myself, I can only love you also and that is a basis for deep Buddhistic nihilistic compassion. It is feeling-based, rather than idea-based. Subjectivity generates compassion, which in turn generates right action (which is not-doing or compassion), which in turn generates love for all life-forms. It is from this basic Buddhist inwardness that genuine compassion emerges, rather than from ideas or ethical doctrines of physical items.

Why subjectivities cannot be distinct? If I hear a loud sound that startles me, there is no reason to imagine that the person next to me is feeling differently. Our feelings are, it seems, indistinguishable, since there is no way to define them as distinct. It may be erroneously believed by the persons involved that their feelings are separate, but how would they be? Do their feelings have a difference in intensity? This does not seem likely, since we can verify that subjectivity from one instance of startledness to another, the feelings of startledness are identical. If I am startled by a loud noise in the year 2008, a subjective feeling is generated, and if I am startled by a very similar loud noise in 2009, an indistinguishable feeling is generated (it can be verified through introspection—through observation of feelings that this is so). If my feelings are indistinguishable in this way, then why would I assume that the person next to me is feeling something different when she is startled? Feeling is feeling, so how can my feeling be different or significantly dissimilar from another? In fact all subjective feelings are uniform and indistinguishable, as if there is just one 'feeling mass' within us, as Gendlin (1997: 13) has noted:

> Above and beyond the symbols there is always also the feeling referent itself. Always it is concretely and definitely there, present for you, an inward sensing.
>
> Let us move from these very simple examples to more complex ones. Consider a sentence: 'What is the law of supply and demand?' In what way do you have your meaning of the sentence? Of course, the sentence is objective, spoken or written. But for you, how do you have its meaning—what it is to you? You have it in your experiencing ... . Does it have meaning for you or not? If it is in a language you know and makes sense, then you have an experiential sense of its meaning. Where do you find such an experiential sense of meaning? Again, it is in the same location, with the same inward reference of attention to *the ever present feeling mass* that you find meaning. The sentence, of course, consists of the verbal noises (or auditory images of noises). But their meaning? It is felt by you. (emphasis added)

There is a vibrational orb of raw feeling that comprises the core and the dynamo of each conscious being's subjectivity. Typically, conscious beings do not see it, because their attention is not focused on the inner (the subjective), but rather is focused on the outer (the illusory, the empirical extensions). But upon the initiation of Buddhist meditation, this 'feeling mass' is discovered (remembered) to be a primary 'ingredient' and dynamo of subjectivity. Gendlin (ibid.: 3) elaborates on this:

> ... [W]e cannot consider experience to be a logically schematic construct, no matter how complex. At best we can have a scheme of how experience and logic can relate. Even then, experience must be referred to directly—it must be thought of as that partly unformed stream of feeling that we have every moment. I shall call it 'experiencing', using that term for the flow of feeling, concretely, to which you can every moment attend inwardly, if you wish.

He also writes:

> First, feel your body. Your body can, of course, be looked at from the outside, but I am asking you to feel it from the inside. There you are. There, as simply put as possible, is your experiencing of this moment, now. But we need to remain with that global feel of your body. Let us 'divide it a bit, although no hard and fast division into parts is readily possible. (ibid.: 12)

In the first of the above three passages given from Gendlin, he appears to maintain that non-emotive, verbal concepts interact with the preconceptual, unchanging, primordial feeling mass, and this 'interaction' or 'interplay' gives rise to meaningful subjectivity. It is this interplay that gives rise to the meanings we have in our mental life.

> Meaning is formed in the interaction of ... [the feeling mass] and something that functions as a symbol .... [W]hen one employs symbols to attend to ... [the feeing mass], it changes. The effort is ... to 'observe' feeling [the feeling mass] and then say what it means .... The 'meanings' of [the feeling mass] ... as such are 'preconceptual' .... Philosophy requires another Copernican Revolution to recognize ... [the feeling mass] as a centre of consideration in its own right, not merely as revolving around the requirements of logical constructions. (ibid.: 8–9)

Consider the following Diagram 2.1 that illustrates Gendlin's theorization:

Diagram 2.1
Fleeting Verbal Thought-concepts

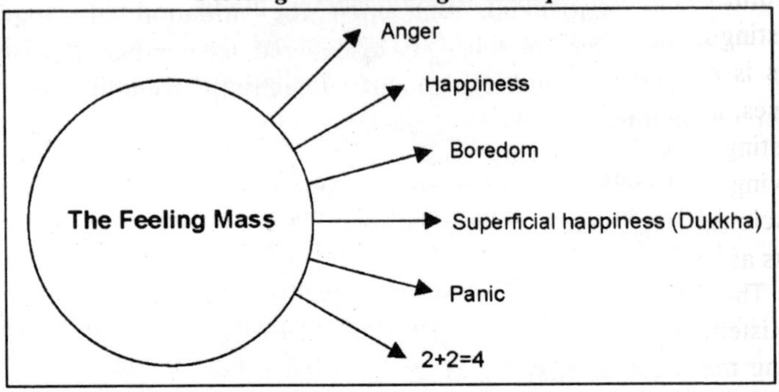

When a conscious being is unaware of (i.e., forgets) these inner dynamics, she has no possibility for nirvanic release. But when the conscious being is aware of (remembers) the feeling-mass-dynamo, there is the possibility of nirvanic release, since being aware of it is to look at it, and to look at it is to see into it, and to see into it is to find the nirvanic explosion residing at the core of the feeling mass, where it has always been and thus the nirvanic observer remembers what she really is.

This analysis of the feeling mass shows how feeling is not a protean or many-faced subjective item. When it is directly apprehended, it is always indistinguishable from any other 'state' of the feeling mass. Therefore, feeling only has one form or intensity.

The Feeling Mass is Indistinguishable from Present Moment to Present Moment

The concept of the feeling mass allows us to see that feeling—the primary dynamo of subjectivity (of personhood)—is not distinguishable between conscious beings. This is a key finding in the study of Buddhist compassion. But a few more details need to be worked out before it is ascertained that this is the case.

Gendlin refers to the feeling mass as 'unformed', '[a]bove and beyond … symbols', '[a]lways … concretely and definitely there', '[always] present for you', 'ever present', and 'in the same location', at 'the same inward reference of attention' (ibid.: 13). He also refers to it as 'pre-logical' and indivisible (as if it is an atomic item). If we combine all these descriptions of the subjective feeling mass, we find that Gendlin's comments apparently indicate that the feeling mass might be indistinguishable from moment to moment. In other words, the feeling mass is a constant (vibrating) whir of feeling-energy that inundates, pierces, and largely comprises subjectivity, but which always contains indistinguishable humming feeling from instant to instant: the same glowing, pulsating hum of explosion and feeling every time that a conscious being looks at it—that is, every time consciousness genuinely exists as self-consciousness.

The feeling mass vibrates,[6] that means it has continual new states of existence, perhaps trillions, where with each new state there is new feeling mass subjectivity (as if states of the feeling mass replace one another with new, indistinguishable states), but where each new feeling mass subjectivity is indistinguishable from the previous. This can be merely verified by any subjective observer who brings perception to subjectivity (rather than affixing it to the ordinary empirical reality of surfaces, colours and Dukkha), wherein is found (remembered) the ever-present radiance of the feeling mass. Searching for it is perhaps the first step toward direct apprehension of the timeless nirvanic lotus.

Hubert Benoit, a Frenchman who writes about Zen philosophy, also writes about the feeling mass, where he calls it 'metaphysical distress' and 'primordial distress', rather than the feeling mass. He also indicates that it is in and through this distress (primitive, unformed, vibrating feeling) that nirvanic eternity is remembered:

> ... there is another distress, a permanent distress ... . Behind the phenomenal ... distress, felt on the plane of phenomena, there is a noumenal, or metaphysical distress, which dwells up-stream of my phenomena ... . First of all it is unconscious. The man who has not attained Realization is conscious of phenomena only; he could not, therefore, be conscious of a distress which is up-stream of phenomena ... . Unconscious metaphysical distress, then, is also characterized by permanence. It is always there, always the same, behind all our affective phenomena ... . Because the perfect existential Felicity is not awakened in the centre of [the natural] man everything happens as if his centre were occupied by a primordial distress. (Benoit, 1990: 79–80)

Beings are Indistinguishable

Subjectivity only contains one feeling state. Thus, it is unclear why other conscious beings would have different feeling states. If subjectivity reveals that all my feeling states are indistinguishable, existing as energetic indistinguishable feeling mass states, then by induction, the best inference would be that 'other' conscious beings I witness would also exist as a feeling-mass-subjectivity of pre-conceptual vibrational radiance. If this is so, then these 'other' conscious beings are feeling mass emanations that are not distinct from me. The Benoitan metaphysical/primordial distress can be witnessed on the face of a non-nirvanic being. Even if the non-nirvanic being is not aware of (has forgotten) their primordial feeling mass, their feeling-mass-distress can be 'sensed' by another mindful observer emanating from their illusory physical body. Thus, it can be verified that all conscious beings are a subjective feeling mass. For this reason, I will inductively conclude that the inner orb of vibrational feeling mass is indistinguishable between conscious beings. A conscious being is their subjectivity, and since the feeling mass is the dynamo of subjectivity, then conscious beings are indistinguishable. Understanding this is to understand that conscious beings are indistinguishable and it is a step toward understanding Buddhist compassion. If subjectivities cannot be distinguished, then they are one: if I feel sorrow, you feel the same sorrow, whether you are aware of it or not. For these reasons, if I can feel love for myself (self-conscious, self-love for the conscious subjectivity that I am), I can only feel love for all 'other' subjectivities, which are really not distinct from mine. This simple finding is forgotten by the masses of contemporary humans of prison planet, who imagine that they are separate and that if, for example, persons in Iraq or Africa are killed, it does not affect them—as if consciousness remains constant upon the deaths of families in the aforementioned nations. This illusion is absurd.

Final Comments

There are harsh criticisms of the Buddha that Hindu's have presented. For example, the Buddha tells us that it is the aggregates that transform when one attains nirvana, but he also says that there is enlightenment, but this apparently means that nothing is enlightened. The first half of the last sentence implies that there is something that is undergoing transformation and the second half implies there is not. The discussion of quantum Buddhist compassion in this article solves this issue:

quantum abstract atoms are nirvanic, which is realized (remembered) through right mindfulness, where mindfulness is subjective-experiential stillness which all Buddhist philosophy emanates from (and where it is false that philosophy is understood before mindfulness, as if mindfulness emanates from philosophy), as discussed in a lucid passage from Dreyfus (1997: 98):

> Buddhism teaches that human beings can liberate themselves from suffering through a correct understanding of reality. We usually understand reality through perception and from wrong views, such as the substantial existence of persons, on the basis of these experiences. So the first step in a Buddhist liberative strategy is to gain a clear understanding of experiences. This is achieved by developing mindfulness toward the four kinds of objects: body, feeling, consciousness, and mental factors.

This article presents an account of quantum Buddhism that is scientific and thus which all conscious beings hopefully will realize must be accorded with if they are not to be deluded and forlorn beings. The arguments of this article should lead to an end to ignorance (war. physicalism, corporatism, consumerism, etc.,) worldwide. If world citizens understand that perfect felicity, stillness and peace resides within them and comprises them, at this very moment, perhaps they could be persuaded to walk away from their current lives—which are lives that only have made them unsatisfied creatures of horror and hate, sadness and shallow ignorance—and return to what they are.

Notes

1. In an article I point out why this is a quantum mechanical theory which is more in accord with actual empirical quantum findings than any other interpretation of quantum physics (such as the Bohmian interpretation, the Copenhagenian interpretation, the many-world interpretation and so forth), Grupp (2006b).
2. See Grupp (2006b) for a detailed discussion of these issues.
3. Dreyfus (1997: 146) writes: 'It is often said that Dharmakîrti is a nominalist. Dravid, for example, says about him: "However, it must be granted that the Buddhist is the most thoroughgoing nominalist in the history of thought."

Dreyfus later discusses how he holds that Dharmakîrti's nominalism is a conceptualist theory.

4. I use the terms 'Muslim' and 'Jewish' here not to denote any biological differences between the two, but rather to denote cultural labels and purported cultural differences that people commonly and thoughtlessly maintain exist between these groups (and usually where political figures coax them into doing so).
5. This claim may be false since it may be the case that quantum theory reveals particles, such as electrons and photons, to routinely collocate in space. But if this is the case, it is not relevant to my reasoning in this article, and thus this point made by Chisholm can merely be ignored, at least with respect to this article.
6. Elsewhere, Gendlin (1997) refers to the feeling mass as 'flowing'. It would appear that he means this to be synonymous with the word 'vibrating', as I have used it. Gendlin refers to the feeling mass as flowing, but also as being at the same location, which implies that the flowing (or vibrating) is stationary. The only ways I know that something can flow (move) in some way while remaining stationary is by either rotating (as if on an axis, for example), by pulsating, or by flashing in-and-out of existence (replacing), much like a Buddhist quantum atom does. Since Gendlin does not refer to the feeling mass as rotating, his 'flowing' must be one of the latter two options—pulsating or replacing. This would amount to the feeling mass being an entity that is flowing but also is both stationary (at the same location). For this reason, we can ask the following question: Is Gendlin's feeling mass changing or unchanging? Gendlin himself appears very unclear, even contradictory on this issue. At some points Gendlin appears to specifically say that it is unchanging; but at many other places, he specifically says that it is changing. For these reasons, I assert that his implying that the feeling mass is flowing (changing), but indistinguishable from moment to moment, indicates that the feeling mass is vibrational.

3 Religion and Social Change

Hinduism Revisited

Pramod Kumar Singh

What is religion? Is it the same as, or is it different from, what we call Dharma? What is social change? Why is change in an existing social order felt necessary? How is a given 'religious order' expected to affect change in the existing 'social order'? These and questions allied to these are basic and primary. Hence, they need our foremost attention and careful examination. This will provide people a ground for adhering to values of one set rather than another. The etymological derivation of the word 'religion' is from the Latin root *religare* that means 'to bind'. Generally speaking, it consists of a body of doctrines concerning the man and the universe, a pack of vows, a set of symbols and a body of rituals. Accordingly, Hinduism, Buddhism, Jainism, Zoroastrianism, Judaism, Christianity and Islam are regarded as important religions of the world. We must, however, remember that Hinduism is not a religion in the strict Western sense of the term.

A system of religion is associated with the following existential dimensions of mankind—God, world, man, evil and suffering, life after death, human destiny, ethical virtues conduct and practices. The prominent religion-making characteristics are:

- Belief in supernatural beings (Gods).
- A distinction between 'sacred' and 'profane'.
- Ritual acts focused on sacred objects.
- A moral code believed to be sanctioned by the Gods.

- Characteristically religious feelings (awe, sense of mystery, sense of guilt, adoration) which tend to be aroused in the presence of sacred objects and during the practice of rituals, and which are usually connected with God or Gods.
- Prayer and other forms of communication with Gods.
- A world-view, a general image of the world as a whole and the place of the individual therein.
- A more or less total organization of one's life based on that world-view.
- A social group bound together by the above.

On the basis of the above characteristics, we can make a classification of religion:

Sacramental religion: This type of religion lays stress on rituals and sacred objects.

Prophetic religion: This is also a kind of religion that underlines belief and morality.

Mystical religion: This type of religion places prior emphasis on immediate experience and feeling.

If this classification is accepted as being exhaustive, then Hinduism would not uniquely come under anyone of them (it might come under each one of them which is the same as saying that it comes under none of them). All the religions of the world named above, except Hinduism, are sectarian and organized seeking to bind together particular sects or groups either in one, or more than one, geographical territory. The appellation of Sanātanadharma is regarded as proper for what they label as Hinduism. The word 'Dharma' is derived from the Sanskrit root 'dhr' which means 'to hold together'. It also signifies spiritually sustaining individual. Binding together and holding together appear to be the same, but they are quite different, even literally. Dharma does not seek to hold together particular sects pertaining to a limited clime and a limited time. It is rather that which holds together all living beings in harmonious order, spiritually sustaining the people on a universal scale. This clearly shows that 'Dharma' and 'religion' do not signify the same thing, although in certain contexts mutual translation of the two words might be possible. In some contexts where the word 'Dharma' is translated as 'religion' it signifies 'sectarian religion', but in the true signification, its translation would be 'non-sectarian religion' or 'universal religion'. *The Encyclopedia Britannica* (1984) lays stress on the three central—though still debatable—characteristics of religion: the numinous or spiritual experience, the contrast between the scared and the profane, and belief in Gods or God.

Now, the point is that the above characterization of religion does not in any way stand in the way of change towards justice, progress and peace. Obscurantism is nowhere in proximity of the above characterization of religion. The cultural and social traditions associated with a religion are historical phenomena and they should be amenable to change and reformation.

There are some thinkers who consider that the very idea of religion is harmful to mankind. There are others who do not hold such a radical view, but consider that certain central ideas of a given religion are harmful and that can be abjured by conversion to a different religion that despises those ideas. B.R. Ambedkar, for example, thinks that certain ideas of Hinduism are pernicious to social democracy, which is the root of the cherished ideal of political democracy.

Hinduism: An Overview and a Critique of Ambedkar

The democratic principles that constitute the fabric of social life are the trinity of liberty, equality and fraternity. Indian society, according to his perception, is based exclusively on castes. But this tends to tear the very fabric of social existence. Hinduism stands for inequality and oppression. It deprives some of its adherents of honour, money, food, shelter and even water from certain ponds and wells. Amedkar has studied the origin and growth of religion as a student of anthropology at Columbia University. He analyses the different stages which religion has passed through—magic, beliefs, rituals, ceremonies, sacrifices, etc. As a rationalist he does not believe in either God or soul. Moreover, to him no religion is acceptable which denies the principles of liberty, equality and fraternity. This is his reason for rejecting Brahminical Hinduism. He embraces Buddhism not as a religion, but as a way of living, as a Dharma. He regards this religion as worthy of admiration for its concern for human suffering and for its democratic approach to human association as the Sangha. The ideas that shape the Hindu view of life are God, soul and Chaturvarna. These are thought to be conceptually related to the ideas of Moksha (salvation), reincarnation and caste system respectively. God is the Mokshadata (saviour). It is believed that soul has a journey through life after life. Chaturvarna on the other hand is a divine sanctification of the caste division. Karma, which is regarded as the performance of rites and sacrifices, constitutes a significant aspect of Dharma for the laity.

Ambedkar iterates that Hinduism is a philosophy of contemplation and sheer speculation and it stands for inequality and oppression. Ambedkar favours a religion based upon ethics and this, in his view, is what Buddha's religion is. He also says that the Hindu religion is not based on ethics. He implores his men to seek refuge in reason. This view, however, appears to be partial and unjust. Hinduism is out and out a view of the world and man articulated by reason. It is not based on oracular pronouncements, dogmatic assertions or blind beliefs. The exhortation of the great preceptor Srikrisna to the great discipline Arjuna in the *Srimad Bhagavadgītā* 'Buddhau Saranamanvichha' is especially relevant here. Ambedkar's assessment of Hinduism appears to be a body of unexamined beliefs very much like the one formulated by Arjuna in the name of Anususruma.

It is an undeniable fact that Buddhism is a stupendous historic attempt to rationally re-examine the earlier world-view and rationally reorganize the social order. But what is known as Buddhism today is not the same thing as Theravada Vajrayana or Tantric Buddhism is a case in point. This is also the case with Hinduism. Reason has played a prominent role in the Vedas, the Upanishad and the Gita. But the rational orientation has got diluted in the Puranic and Tantric tradition and cults, and even in the Manusmriti. But reason has regained its glory in the versions of Hindu philosophy advocated by Raja Ram Mohan Roy, Swami Dayanand and Swami Vivekananda. These three modern spiritual leaders of Hinduism have made strenuous efforts to rationally reform the Hindu social order and re-evaluate the individual beliefs. The period of Renaissance in India was the attempt at a grand synthesis of reason and the religious tradition. And social change has been the logical consequence of such a synthesis.

In an article entitled, 'Buddha and the Future of His Religion' Ambedkar (1950) makes the following important pronouncements:

- The society must have either the sanction of law or it is sure to go to pieces.
- Religion, if it is to function, must be in accord with reason which is another name for science.

- It is not enough for religion to consist of a moral code, but it must recognize the fundamental tenets of liberty, equality and fraternity.
- Religion must not sanctify or ennoble poverty.

He thus envisages two alternatives to hold a society together: the sanction of law and the sanction of morality. He does not find the latter adequately in Hinduism but he somehow finds it in Buddhism which, for him, 'is a true religion', its author being a Margadātā. It uniquely combines the trio principles of Prajna (understanding as against superstition and supernaturalism), Karuna (love) and Samata (equality), which are required for good and happy life. He believes that Buddha's religion is based on ethics and Buddha acts as a guide, not as a God. Even then, he does not want to accord constitutional recognition to Buddhism and impose prohibition on Hinduism, although he wants to destroy the authority, the sacredness and divinity of the Sastras and the Vedas as they teach, allegedly, the religion of castes. He rather makes the constitution avow, to secure to all its citizens liberty of thought, expression, belief, faith and worship. This declaration in the 'Preamble' of the Constitution has made India a secular state and this has since been explicitly announced in the forty-second amendment to it.

Hinduism and Social Change

Indian Philosopher Radhakrishnan's (1971) significant work *The Hindu View of Life*, puts forward the view that though the cardinal values and beliefs of a religion should be honoured, the social institutions have to be transformed when the circumstances demand so. The notion that Indian customs and conventions are timeless is baseless. The Upanishadic tradition of seeking metaphysical knowledge replaced the ceremonial religion of the Vedas. When the former got bogged in dogmatic controversies, Buddhism came out with a simpler religious system and the moral law (Dharma). The *Bhagavadgîtā* is also a revolutionary text which advocates the non-intellectual ways even to the common people. Radhakrishnan, a staunch Hindu, makes out a strong case for social change while keeping the infrastructure intact:

> An institution appropriate and wholesome for one stage of human development becomes inadequate and even dangerous when another stage has been reached. The cry of conservatism it has always been

> thus ignores the fundamentals of the theory of relativity in philosophy and practice, in taste and morals in politics and society, of which the ancient Hindus had a clear grasp. The notion that in India time has stood still for uncounted centuries ... is altogether wrong. (Radhakrishnan, 1971: 92)

He discounts the argument that the Hinduism is involved in obscurantism: 'There has been no such thing as a uniform stationary unalterable Hinduism in point of belief or practice, Hinduism is a movement, not a position, a process, not a result, a growing tradition, not a fixed revelation' (ibid.: 91). He ends this great work with the following exhortation for social change without tampering with the core tenets:

> We feel that our society is in a condition of unstable equilibrium. There is much wood that is dead and diseased that has to be cleared away. Leaders of Hindu thought and practice are convinced that the times require, not a surrender of the basic principles of Hinduism, but a restatement of them with special reference to the needs of a more complex and mobile social order. Such an attempt will only be the repetition of a process which has occurred a number of times in the history of Hinduism. The work of readjustment is in process. Growth is slow when roots are deep. But those who light a little candle in the darkness will help to make the whole sky aflame. (ibid.: 92)

Let us clarify the true sense of the word 'secular'. For this, we have to expound the concept of man. There are four levels of being of a man in the universe: Body, Mind, Intellect and Soul. Accordingly, man has four kinds of functions: Physical, Mental, Intellectual and Spiritual. He does not have to make just two ends meet, he has rather to make four ends meet—that is, four sorts of interests to cater to: Artha (money), Kama (sexuality), Dharma (religion) and Moksha (salvation). The first two pertain to the level of physico-psychical for acquiring sustenance for life; the next one is intellectual which seeks to organize Artha and Kama for co-existence in a society on the principle of 'live and let live', and the last one is spiritual which seeks to organize Dharmas that guide different facets of life for its full and significant realization.

According to some scholars, there is a blatant opposition between religion and reason. The idea of spirituality in religion is thought to be helpful to mankind but the suggestion of supernaturalism in it is thought to be harmful. Similarly, the idea of naturalism in reason (regarded as coeval with the scientific enterprises) is thought to be helpful, but the suggestion of the lack of humanism in it is thought to be harmful. Hence, a conceptual hybrid of the helpful ideas of the two is sought for and the result is secularism. But is secularism or its philosophical formulations in the name of humanism of different breeds and naturalism the adequate theoretical safeguard against ills and evils of modern society?

I do not think so. Humanism of different breeds and naturalism are philosophies born of expediency and pragmatic interests. They do not work in the long run, because they neglect and suppress man's ultimate concern. We have to look beyond the particular and specific geographical regions and historical time on the census register. They are caged in and tied to individual group, party, tribe, caste, creed, society, province, state, region, continent and hemisphere. We must see the significance of an individual in the context of the whole universe of created beings (Praja).

Final Comments

It is true that certain dirt and filth have accrued to the eons-old fabric of Sanātanadharma in the form of casteism, communalism, untouchability and various sorts of discrimination on the basis of these. Nobody considers dirt and filth as constituting the woof and the warp of a fabric. That can be automatically cleansed within the conceptual framework of Sanātanadharma by throwing light upon the right implications of its ideas, which drive away the darkness of wrong implications. We cannot afford to throw the baby with the bath water.

Social change cannot overlook the sustaining value of tradition if it is to prevent anarchy and chaos. Religious traditions also cannot ignore the spirit of the age whether it is the democratic system or the rational skepticism on the upsurge of women and the dalits. It is not religion but the elites at the helm of the religious affairs who have to accommodate the emerging trends of society.

4 The Very Idea of Religion

An Islamic Perspective

Mahmoud Khatami

Contemporary conception of religion in the Western scholarship should be traced in the models back to subjectivism that emerged during the Enlightenment. Those who examine this background consider it as a process of de-divinizing man and the world, ending with a nominalism that makes the world a sort of 'thinned out' region that puts the least constraint on human willing and ordering (Blumenberg, 1983).[1] Man self-assertedly expresses his power to bring matters under control, to define things not by what they are like for God or in themselves but by his own methods of producing their occurrence reliably. So the modern conception of religion takes shape and develops as a man-made concept. This conception is what the modern age needs to assert: that man is able to manage his affairs from the human (and not divine) point of view (Cascardi, 1992; Dallmayr, 1981).

Hegel (see Werner, 1975) sees as one of the chief claims of his system that it could overcome that unbridgeable gap between finite and infinite, and human and divine, by showing how finite human thinking is properly understood and transformed itself into the infinite, circular activity of self-relating thought.[2] It is not that we become Gods, and the distinction between finite and infinite remains, but the thinking subject as he is able to engage in is properly 'divine'. This conception implies that, in the modern period, the finite man takes over divine functions as subject in the place of God; and, then, as a condition of de-divinizing, man remains absolute: the origin of unity, determinacy, necessity, rules of ordering and values. Such a conception, through the rational and technological self-assertion, empties the modern world of the principal and transcendental truth of religion. It implies that we live in a world which is 'disenchanted' (using Weber's word) by the force of technology and by the rationalized thinking that grounds such technology (Benjamin, 1996). The immanence of that human subject and its rationality, in turn, would seem to imply the abandonment or negation of transcendence and its mystery—and, indeed, on Heidegger's well-known view, the modern age conceives of truth no longer in terms of any revelation, religious or otherwise, but in terms of the self-certainty of the representing subject. Such a denial of revelation signals, more broadly, a 'loss of the Gods' that would recall Benjamin' s decay of the 'aura' or Weber's 'disenchantment of the world'—or more deeply 'the death of God' as it appears not only in Nietzsche but in Hegel also. Along with the position of the human as representing subject with rational science and machine technology, the 'loss of the Gods' (*Entgötterung*) must be seen, Heidegger insists, as an essential phenomenon of the modern age (Heidegger, 1977).

The modern liberation of the human subject from any God or revelation, which occurs in and through the rise of distinctively modern, totalizing systems of calculation and planning, would be tied intimately to an objectivism and anonymity of modern culture. Such objectivism and anonymity, in turn, would go hand in hand with the scientific models. And, the technological imperialism rules over the earth. The freedom of subjectivity in modern age vanishes totally in the objectivity commensurate with it (ibid.: 1977).

The totalizing force of the objectivism and collectivism that Heidegger notes in modernity's technological imperialism goes hand in hand with the erasure of human interiority that itself corresponds to the death of God. The death of the transcendent God implies a death or dissolution of the interior self, and such dissolution would be spoken most fully by the anonymity of modern mass culture which comes to light most notably in the de-divinized religion, where distinctions between surface and depth, exteriority and interiority, immanence and transcendence are unsettled. However, the discussion of how religion is defined is a significant debate for it bears directly upon the identity of man and the culture he lives within.

The methodological approaches to 'religion' point to it as something which only exists among human beings and is articulated in 'texts' and 'practices' There can be no discourse of religion outside of culture. It is very interesting that in Western notion 'religion' is a product of particular historical conditions of the Enlightenment discourse. The religious elements in non-Western cultures are similarly culturally embedded (Harrison, 1990). Within this context, one may see all approaches to 'religion' in the West emerge from the modern philosophy of consciousness and from the philosophy of the sign, language and culture. Common to all of them is that there is no discourse of religion outside of human projections and cultures.

This article deals with an otherwise approach to religion by stepping back toward Islamic thought within which one may glimpse a hint of a religious truth which is the source of all religions. Reference to this notion provides an interesting frame, and a spur to look for patterns that other accounts of the modern thinkers are likely to miss.

Religion: A Modern Connotation

The term 'religion' is originally generated in Western thought from the Latin *religio* which Cicero took from *relegere* (to re-read) that has an implication of 'tradition' (which is 're-read' and passes on). The word religio, has the implication of a boundary, a limit or a horizon which is an ultimate constraint upon belief, values and behaviours. Although the early church distanced itself from the idea of the Christian faith as a 'religion', which Paul associated with 'false' Paganism (Bianchi, 1994) by seventh century, religio had come to refer to communities whose members (the religiosi) devoted their lives to the service of the God. By Luther's time the term had come to have a more general designation as the source of truth; while with the Deists and the Enlightenment thinkers it became an abstract concept which we have inherited.[3] But there is no continuous line of development from the concept religio, meaning the 'careful and even fearful fulfilment of what man owes to God', to the Deists', notably Cherbury's, understanding of religio as embracing principles which are derived from the 'universal truth itself and represent the truth that can be found by understanding and intellect' (Feil, 1992). What is significant is that the abstract concept of religion in modern time develops in harmony with the methods of reasoning designed to it.

Religion, in this line of reasoning, did not precede the methods of its research but rather the methods of investigation defined as well as explicated it (Harrison, 1990). The abstraction of religion originated in the context of the critique of Christianity during the Enlightenment and the rise of the modern individual, which has since become an important concept being applied outside Christianity. While it does not of course follow that the concept cannot be applied outside of Christianity, it is nevertheless the case that it is difficult to translate the term in other (non-Western) languages (Sharpe, 1983: 39). There are, however, difficulties and objections in extending the concept to 'Judaism', 'Islam' or 'Hinduism'. An important question here is whether the term 'religion' has semantic equivalents in other languages and cultures?[4] It seems that its use is restricted to the Western culture in the same way as there are no strict English semantic equivalents of religious terms indigenous to non-Western culture, which denotes certain kinds of discourse and practices concerned with social ethics, transcendence, narratives and rituals. As regards Islamic traditions, for example, there are no direct English semantic equivalents for the technical terminologies which developed as part of those tradition's self-descriptions, though a number of Islamic terms pragmatically have some conceptual overlap with the concept. The term 'Din' is often taken as an Islamic equivalent of 'religion'—a term which indicates the social virtues and might be translated as 'Nomos'.[5] The terms 'Shari'ah' and 'Minhaaj' imply a tradition or 'stream' flowing from revelation. Similarly 'Sunnah' can refer in a synchronic sense to the teachings of/or a tradition.

What does become clear is that once beyond a fairly general level, the concept 'religion' is of little use in illuminating these traditions for Western analytical purposes. The Islamic terminology is richer than the English. Indeed, these brief examples show how the translation of these terms into European languages is difficult, if not impossible. None of the Islamic terms mentioned here could be a proper equivalent of the concept of 'religion', though some of the features within the semantic field of 'religion' are encompassed by them.

This leads to the relativization of the concept of religion. While it is true in some narrow sense, it is not any more the case that our recognition constructs it. Worse than this is to understand religions as mere narratives and behaviours that are less about truth-claims and more about identity, less about structures and more about texts, and to take it as an equivalent to 'culture', or 'ideology' which cannot be given privilege outside of culture, but can be distinguished from other aspects of cultural life (see McCutcehon, 1997). Western socio-historical approach to the study of religion reduces them to narratives which are constructed by the research programmes itself for analytical purpose. Religions are in this sense the primary data of the human sciences and research programmes. Such approaches clearly originate from within modern Western socio-cultural condition in which tradition and community have been shattered by the processes of 'de-divinization' and 'de-traditionalization'. And a hidden community of communally isolated, 'authentic individuals' developed, alongside the reconstruction of 're-divinization' or 're-traditionalization'. All these are important for the formation and development of the theory of religion.

There is also a mutual relation between globalization and localization—fragmentation of culture on the one hand and homogenization of it on the other. Contemporary Western conception of religion inevitably responds to this process. On the one hand there is a departure from authority and tradition towards individualization, on the other there is a return to what is called 'tradition-maintenance' and 'tradition-authority'. All these factors point to the importance of religion in postmodern, global culture and the consequent need in the social sciences for a new approach that takes into account both global and local dimensions.

The recent transformations of religion and the assertion of its particularity within a global context, pose challenges to the way religion is analysed. In case of a soft research (such as anthropological studies of religion) religion is explained as a human projection located within the context of privatization and re-traditionalization; while in case of a hard science (such as cognitive psychology) religion is considered as a cognitive system that exists in the minds of the members of a particular social group. Such explanations are also embedded in contemporary Western social context and obviously are based on different humanistic assumptions developed on the basis of modern or postmodern world-view. And from within this world-view emerge the research strategies and practices which affect religion studies also. We are presented with a number of research programmes and methods, each of which claims leverage on the question of religion and its relation to human life and wider society. Though there are, of course, many rival research programmes (sometimes old programmes are superseded by new ones also) all of them are formatted in two apparent paradigms of Western philosophical outlook: those of 'consciousness' and 'language'. They have covered a wide range—from logico-epistemological explanations to narrative-cultural interpretations—of approaches to religion as an object of methodological studies.[6]

Recently religion studies have developed an alignment with the critical and cultural theory. Postmodernism as a social movement (or characteristic of a late capitalist culture of consumerism) and postmodernism as an intellectual movement give rise to academic discourses that break free from restrictions of objectivism and scienticism. Generally, it shows new and innovative ways of reading the past and the present, though it may produce eccentricities as well. Nietzsche presaged the 'rupture with modernity' that can be seen not only in the wider context of social diversity, fragmentation of centralized value and the rise of religious fundamentalisms, but also at the level of theory with the development of postmodern critical perspectives and the development of feminist, gay and post-colonial critiques of Western rationalism. There is no way around these developments—the importance of the postmodern critique of the Enlightenment cannot be ignored. And religion studies as a whole needs to address these issues. But it does not go beyond the Western conception of religion. If it is to recognize its late modern basis and agenda, the contemporary study of religion should take the Eastern conception of religion seriously to have an important role in understanding non-Western spirit, and in influencing wider, crucial debates about religion and culture. The closer alignment of religion studies with the social sciences, is, as it were, facilitated by the reconfiguration of disciplines into new forms, especially with the development of new technologies and virtual educational institutions. In Nietzsche's 'rupture with modernity', religion studies have an important place in becoming a forum for the development of many kinds of critical awareness.[7] Meanwhile, one may claim, contrary to the Western academic concept of religion, that the importance of religion nevertheless is related to the transformations of contemporary culture in the context of modernity/postmodernity. Religion has not died out in the contemporary world as secularization theory might have suggested; and an otherwise conception of religion is still alive in non-Western religious forms of life. In the rest of this article such a conception will be presented within the Islamic perspective.

Religion: An Islamic Perspective

The word 'Din'[8] is mentioned in many verses in the Qur'an. The word 'Din' is used here to give different meanings. Important among these are:

- Subjugation, Authority, Ruling and Having Charge.
- Obedience and Submission due to Subjugation.
- The Method of life and the means.
- Punishment, Reward and Judgment.

These four types of meaning constitute the concept of the word 'Din' in the Qur'an where it implies a comprehensive system of life. Din is a submission, following and worship of the creator and the ruler by man in a comprehensive system of life. As claimed in Islamic literature, all these are embodied in a unique reality which is metahistorical by nature but appeared as different forms of religions throughout the spiritual history of human beings.

The Qur'anic Conception of Religion

The Qur'an claims that religion is a unitary idea which denotes only one truth; but it has been embodied and developed in specific forms of religions. While all religions do truly carry on one and same reality, some of them are more expressive of that reality and then stand above others. However, they reflect just one truth. The Qur'an also emphasizes on this oneness.

This unitary religion is called Islam in the language of the Qur'an. The word Islam here is used in its general sense which means peace and submission to God. Islam is the religion itself. We should not think of the religion of Islam which indicates a very specific religion that appeared in particular geographical and historical conditions.[9] Islam is 'type-religion' and all others are 'tokens'. In this sense, the Qur'an says: 'Surely the (unitary true) Religion with Allah is Islam' *(3.19)*. 'Do they seek for other than the Religion of Allah? While all creatures in the heavens and on earth have … bowed to His Will (Accepted Islam), and to Him shall they all be brought back' *(3.83)*. So: 'He it is Who hath sent

His messenger with the guidance and the Religion of truth, that He may make it conqueror of all religion however much idolaters may be averse' *(61.9)*. As we see, there is only one unitary religion under which all forms of historical religions had appeared. This unitary religion is an innate (Fitri) religion. All forms of religions are but manifestations of this truth.

Islam as type-religion is, according to the Qur'an, the code of real life and 'all creatures in the heaven and on earth have, willing or unwilling, bowed to His Will (Accepted *Islam*), and to Him shall they all be brought back' *(3.83)*. And there is only one religion of truth, which conflicts all man-made forms named religion. The true religion is mistaken by human beings as their social conditions affect their knowledge of truth, and they get interpreting the truth according to their needs, benefits and worldly policies, and change the manifested forms of the unitary religion into utilitarian ones.

The Pyramid of Religion

As a matter of fact what, has been mentioned in the Qur'an can be illustrated by a pyramidal diagram referred to here as 'the Pyramid of Religion'. In this perspective the truth of religion flashes out from God at the vertex all the way down to the socio-historical forms of religions. While all religions emanate from the simplicity of the religion, they all enjoy the strongest essential connection and unity with their divine principle at the top. But they are, on the other hand, widely diversified when they are considered at the specific socio-historical conditions where the horizontal levels converge into an absolute unitary simplex.

Within this pyramid, the relationship between religion as a metahistorical reality and religion as a historical manifestation can be considered in two ways: vertical and horizontal. Considered as vertical, this relationship is that of 'unity in difference'; and as horizontal it is that of 'type-token'. All the way, religion manifests its unique reality in token-religions according to the degrees of importance they may have (depended upon the needs and conditions of a society in the spiritual history of human beings). Token-religions are also actually separated and diversified in format as well as in individuation. But since this separation and diversity which occur in the socio-historical (horizontal) order do not happen in the vertical order (that of unity), they have no impact on the inner system of their continuity and unity. In other words the multitude of the horizontal order has no bearing upon the unitary connection of the vertical order.

The pyramidal diagram of religion together with the distinction between vertical and horizontal lines within it must be taken into serious consideration in understanding Islamic idea of religion. It is of fundamental importance to understand the 'inner unity' in relation to the 'outer diversity' of this diagram when one meets the paradoxical statements of religious experiences. It is also important to understand religious pluralism as indicating different understandings of the unitary truth.

Diagram 4.1
The Pyramid of Religion

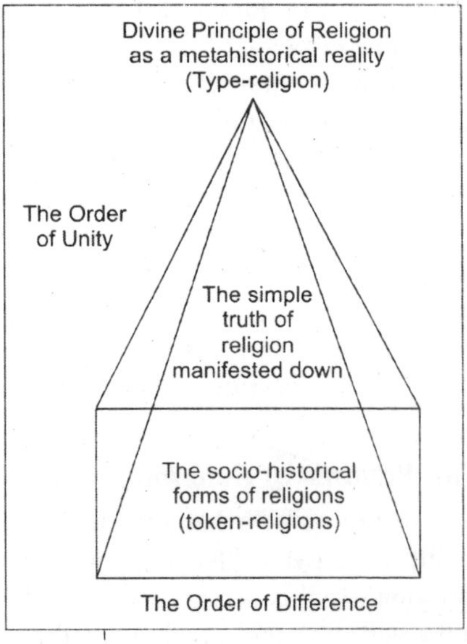

The Structure of Religion

The pyramid of religion indicates a hierarchic (Tashkiki) structure for religion. Token-religions are pyramidally emanated from the reality of the unitary type-religion. A token-religion is entirely held by, and dependent upon, this reality. This reality, in its turn, is dependent, with all its depending content, upon its own tokens, as they are all reduced to, and fuzzy in, the reality of that unitary type-religion. Thus, it appears that the whole multitude is designed as but one manifestation of the 'self-substantive' religion.

The plurality of token-religions is designed as appearances of one unitary type-religion. As hinted above, there is an unbroken vertical line connecting all manifested religions.[10] There are horizontal lines also along which the manifested token-religions are to be regarded as different from one another. These are generally characterized by multiplicity in rank, in culture, and in individuation. All these belong to the factual texture of the unitary type-religion itself. For the sake of distinction, the vertical lines are called the 'inner order' of religion, and the horizontal lines the 'outer order' of religion. The former is that which religious experiences and meditative apprehensions are concerned with, and the latter (which is called Shari'ah and Minhaaj) contains rituals and practices. In dealing with the former, what researchers can do is to account for the interpretation and conceptualization of religious experiences, customs and social traditions. These interpretations and conceptualizations fall into the order of the horizontal line, whereas the depth of factual religion always remains in the vertical dimension and belongs to the inner order of reality. It is not, strictly, representational.

Justification of the Idea

In the literature of Islamic philosophy, there is a doctrine that can help understand the logic of the idea presented in the Qur'an. This doctrine is called the 'unity of continuity' by which we will be able to prove that any continuous unbroken linear system is dominated by an essential unity. The central point is that the hierarchy of religions implies continuity and total dependence of the token-religions upon the one and same reality of religion. Just as this type-religion is totally dependent upon and manifested from the one-for-ever-lasting intention of God to manage human life, so also the token mode of the religion is totally dependent upon the reality of this religion.[11] So as vertical dependency requires, there is a continuous chain of dependency and implication among all token-religions throughout the spiritual history of man. If C implies B and B implies A, then it is logically true that C implies A. This is a hypothetical syllogism or 'the rule of transitivity'. The logical form of this law is:

$$A \supset B \quad \text{and} \quad B \supset C$$

So $$A \supset C$$

As one can see, this law is based on material implication as its logical connective. To apply this law one needs to substitute the notion of 'dependence' for material implication. To depend totally on the truth of another is to mean that a religion is overshadowed by, and included in, the truth of another religion. Logically, this essential relation is expressed by material implication, such that the truth of a religion consists analytically in the truth of its undetachable principle (the unitary type-religion). Thus, 'dependence' here is equated with the 'undetachability' and 'indistinguishability' of religions from their source.[12]

Now, this idea says that any given degree or token mode appeared as religion A, will entail, by material implication, its immediate mode of B. Since B is in its turn a dependent token-religion, in the same manner, on its own immediate principle, it also logically implies its own principle and so on, until the range of religions ends in the ultimate principle C. In this way the unbroken chain of religion is traced back from the token mode of religion A to the intermediate token B, and finally, to the ultimate source of C which is the type-religion. This is the logical strategy of transitivity. While these modes and degrees of dependency, following one upon the other, appear in their own particular stages to be different from one another in terms of such hierarchical levels and proportions of closeness and remoteness to the ultimate principle, they all constitute only one single and indivisible vertical line from the source down to the token-religions.[13]

Upon this idea, it is possible for the token-religions, with all their characteristic multiplicity, to be reduced to the unitary type-religion as the ultimate source of religions. This is made possible without the intermediary role of history, geography, culture, social conditions or any other element of disruption and discontinuation in the unitary system of religion. At the level of historical appearance, the reality of religion, by its very nature, is a 'fuzzy' one. For a token-religion to exist means that it can never be detached from its principle and it stands by itself as an independent entity, either in the mind or in the world of reality. It is therefore right to say that a token-religion could have issued forth from its principle and could continue to exist without having essential dependence on its source. This interpretation means that a token-religion was possible when and only when it had not come into being through its principle. But as soon as that same token religion was to come into reality, it would change its basic status to the form of a self-sufficient religion due to the socio-historical conditions in which it appeared. Whatever a self-sufficient religion might be, it becomes a self-grounded religion for the socio-historical conditions in which it appears. This religion then, even though it is at that very moment a form of continuing religion, is subject to be interpreted by people according to their specific socio-historical conditions and their capacity to enrich the domain of knowledge and research. This is obviously a transmodification of religion from its pure reality to its what may be called the 'interpretive format'. This does not, however, indicate that the ultimate reality of religion is changed into a human interpretive format. For one thing, the vertical nature of religion is undoubtedly immanent and can never be a transitive one. Furthermore, when we are speaking of type-religion we are not dealing with a religion constituted by custom and culture, but rather with that very simple, indivisible and unitary entity. This is the meaning of the prepositional state of the horizontal forms of religion appeared in the historical and social context. It would be wrong, if we were to visualize a token-religion in itself as independent by-product of human culture or psycho-biological nature.

What happens in the horizontal (socio-historical) line is that man approaches to that reality and makes it accessible for himself. This effort could be made within a wide domain—from a deep and true interpretation to a very superficial dogma and custom. The vertical reality of religion might be partly apparent in some human formats while it might be absent in others dependent on the conditions in which it appears. It is only in this sense that, one may say, token-religions are different ways of responding to an ultimate and transcendent reality which is the core content of type-religion.[14]

Thus, only in this sense, the Muslim 'Allah', the Christian 'God' and the Hindu 'Bhagwan' are all terms for the same ultimate reality towards which various token-religions are climbing. So type-religion is ineffable and transcendent, but man responds to this reality through the token-religions. In this horizontal (socio-historical) line, we experience that type-religion in different ways according to different dispositional states. Although religious meanings are diverse in this sense, we have the cognitive state to believe and to live on the basis of its experience in our socio-historical norms. The religious plurality, diversity and mutually exclusive claims of the traditions, then, appear in the various forms of interpretative and linguistic systems. Human experience of the uniqueness of religion is structured in different traditions. Incompatible doctrinal schemes within diverse religious traditions cannot be resolved by human concepts and do not, therefore, threaten the overall hypothesis that token-religions fuzzily manifest the eternal truth embodied in type-religion and that token-religions represent different historical examples of the same reality and evoke parallel transformations of human life.

Final Comments

By now enough has been said to outline the general elements of the Islamic idea of religion[15] and the analysis of the connection of the religions to the 'Religion'. This connection is fuzzy as we consider Religion as the one and same reality which manifests as a 'continuity in difference' through the vertical line. According to this idea of religion, we have a model for understanding the diversity of religions which have boundaries of their owns, but at the same time they share a unitary reality and all have one identity and reality in spite of their appropriate socio-historical contextualization.

Notes

1. Blumenberg (1983) says that the late medieval emphasis on God's absolute power and freedom did not lead to despair but rather paved the way for such a nominalism and the modern conception of man and the world.
2. This is well-known project of Hegel's (1967) *Phenomenology of Mind.*
3. Harrison (1990) has shown how the modern Western concept of 'religion' (and therefore the roots of the scientific study of religion) originated with the Deists and developed during the Enlightenment out of a Lutheran tradition.
4. Some authors like Pye (1994), citing examples from Japan, have argued that there are such parallels. Others would wish to restrict its use to the Western monotheisms (Staal, 1989).
5. The word 'Din' in Islamic literature is the Arabic form of Avesta's *Daena* which in its original use means *Nomos* or the basic law of life. We realize that it is wrong to translate the Qur'anic word Din to religion in English. So we will use the latter for convenience here.
6. This shift from the epistemological problem of subjectivity and its relation to the world puts language and culture at the centre of a discourse in which narrative becomes dominant. This relocation of the problem of the other into language, culture and narrative, and of the problem of understanding religion has its origin in the late eighteenth century in the works of some scholars, who demurred the idea that knowledge can be established within a system and can be traced through hermeneutics to the narratology or what might be called 'the philosophy of sign' and into linguistic anthropology and discourse analysis.

7. Recent movements such as feminist theory, queer theory and post-colonial theory draw attention to issues of cultural difference and are important for the study of religions and for the development of a meta-theoretical discourse about the nature of religion studies. The implications of these discourses for religion studies are important on a number of accounts. In fact, they do not take the truth of religion as in itself but merely treat as a socio-cultural phenomenon.
8. This may be mentioned here again that it is wrong to translate the Qur'anic word 'Din' to English with the word 'religion' nevertheless, I will use the word religion for it here for the reader's convenience.
9. Meanwhile the Qur'an says that this specific appearance of the religion as Islam (revealed to the Prophet Mohammad) is the most perfect format of that unitary religion Islam.
10. The vertical and horizontal lines are obtained from the Avicennian principle of the 'nobler possibility' (*Al-imkan Al-ashraf*) together with principle of the 'more posterior possibility' (*Al-iakan Al-akhass*).
11. More correctly, it appears with its reality as a token-religion in the history but the historical conditions may not be sufficient to realize it in full. In this sense, Islam as type-religion is fully the token form that appeared in different periods of history to the prophets and divine messengers like Abraham, Moses, Jesus, etc.
12. 'Undetachability' and 'indistinguishability' are other expressions of implication, because a thing implied in another means it is undetachable and indistinguishable from the other. Conversely, a thing undetachable and indistinguishable from another means it is implied by and contained in the other.
13. One may object here that the implication of transitivity does not bring out the claim of this idea, which calls for nothing other than the essential identity of all the gradations and modes of religion. What the rule of transitivity can do is to help us know that there is an unbroken relation between any lower degree or mode of religion A and the ultimate principle C through an intermediate mode B, used as a middle term. But whether or not this relation is an identity relation, making the whole massive system of the gradations of religion and its principle of one essential unity, it is beyond the logical parameters of the hypothetical syllogism. The answer is that the relation between type-religion and token-religions is nothing but an essential one which is unitary. In point of fact, it is this 'unitary' relationship which accounts for the sort of essential identity which the religious variety has with the source of religion. Within the context of this unitary relation, the rule of transitivity is applicable in order to lead from one occurrence of this

relationship at the base to the ultimate one at the zenith of the hierarchic structure of religion. In other words, the operation of material implication in this system of relations results logically in a kind of essential unity subsisting from the lower class of religion right up to its ultimate principle and source without any disruption or any extraneous mediation.

14. Hick's (1989) pluralistic approach to religion can be interpreted in the light of this theory. However, his major problem is that he does not justify the one and same reality of religion in a logical way. Presupposing that the religions respond to the transcendental reality in divergent ways, he supposes the oneness of the transcendent as a noumenon in the Kantian sense. He is not able (and apparently does not intend) to show the unitarity of the religion and that all religions are manifestations of one and only one religion.
15. I have used Tabatabaii's (1984), *Al-Mizan fi Tafsir al-Quran* (Vol. 1), here.

5 Karma, God and Rebirth

P.K. Mohapatra

The Karma doctrine constitutes a fundamental paradigm of Indian ethics. The belief in Karma and the operation of the Karma doctrine bring to focus the pre-eminently moral aspect of our value systems. The Karma doctrine can be said to be a principle of justice—a principle of allocating to each his own. But the allocation or the apportionment of deserts and entitlements is done automatically on the basis of a causal principle—not necessarily by any dispenser of justice. This is the quint-essential claim of the doctrine of Karma, on which both the orthodox and the heterodox systems of Indian philosophy would agree. The admittance of a divine dispenser of deserts, we shall see, would take away the moral element from the doctrine, to say the least.

This doctrine is essentially an individualistic and usually backward-looking ideal for securing appropriate consequences which everyone is entitled to by virtue of his (past) actions. Actions of individuals have the causal efficiency of producing consequences, which the respective individuals have to enjoy or suffer from. This is because the individual, who is endowed with the power of freedom of will, does all his actions by choice, so it is supposed, and is therefore responsible for the consequences they produce. But although the responsibilities are taken up or accounted for with regard to one's past actions, the scope of accountability is not limited to the past but extends to one's future on the basis of his present actions; for the present actions also produce consequences for which the agent is responsible. Thus the scope of the Karma doctrine is not only retrospective but also prospective. 'As you sow, so you reap' is equally applicable to the consequences of our past actions as well as to those of our present actions that fructify in future. But the usually backward-looking characterization of the law of Karma is due to the fact that, when the consequences of actions are reaped (enjoyed or suffered) by the individual, the actions have already become things of the past. Be that as it may, there is an important asymmetry with regard to the consequences of the past and present actions, which introduces an overwhelmingly moral element into the doctrine of Karma; and it is this: whereas we do not have any choice regarding the consequences of our past actions except to go through their experiences, pleasant or painful, we do have choice and control over the consequences of our present actions. If what we are (in this life with all its pleasures and sufferings) is determined by what we have been (in the previous life), what we will be (in future life) lies entirely within our control, so that the belief in the doctrine of Karma is an effective incentive for right conduct. Thus far from being fatalistic and deterministic, as several Western scholars would make it out to be, the Karma doctrine, in this respect, leaves ample scope for moral progress and development. The idea of rewards for good conduct and punishment for the bad is an important means (incentive) to moral growth—this is also an important factor leading man to a firm commitment to the obligations of a truly moral life. The fact that man is the architect of his future through his present actions that are fully under his control, it must be noted, applies to the 'present actions' in all his past lives as well as in his present life—assuming transmigration and 'Samsara' as a necessary part of this belief system. From this it follows that man is not only responsible for the consequences of his actions, but he deserves them in all fairness. For whatever we knowingly do—irrespective of which life we may be talking about—is sure to bring us the results we merit. The idea of retribution thus becomes an integral element in the Karma doctrine, which signifies not only that whatever happen to us in life are determined by their antecedent causes, but also that whatever happen to us are the just rewards and punishment for our actions.[1] The Karma doctrine, thus, is not a blind mechanical law but an essentially moral or ethical law. Instead of making man a helpless sufferer (or enjoyer) of the pains and pleasures of life, he is shown to organize his life in accordance with ethical principles. For man is not only a rational being with power to know moral values from disvalues, but is also a moral agent, a valuing being, who is capable of ordering his own way of living (Hiriyanna,

1975). However, despite highlighting the essential moral feature of the doctrine of Karma, the described asymmetry between the consequences of the past and present actions (actions of one's past life and those of one's present) still retains an important difference. For once the actions are performed, there is no escape from the consequences thereof. Like the 'wheel that follows foot of the ox' and 'the calf that seeks its mother in a herd of cows', the consequences of one's past Karmas follow him inevitably, either in the same life or in a later life. Man's life, in respect of his past Karmas is governed by strict necessity. The Karma doctrine thus implies necessity, determinism and predestination. But it also implies freedom in respect of ethical progress and commitment to moral life as described above. This is a perfectly coherent explanation of the implication of necessity as well as freedom involved in the doctrine which only a blind literal mind would find to be inconsistent or contradictory. Further as Hiriyanna rightly points out, the seemingly opposite implications relate to different aspects of Karma—necessity relates to the results of Karma and freedom to matters of moral progress. Indeed the doctrine claims, every action that we perform leads to double results—a Phala (result) in form of pleasure or pain and a Samskara or tendency to repeat the same (type of) deeds in the future. Whereas, we are necessarily bound by the former, the latter we are free to regulate, and, on the success with which we regulate these tendencies or dispositions depends the moral progress we make.

Karma Doctrine and Self-Determination

The freedom to regulate one's Samskara in particular and to perform actions in general constitutes a very important aspect of the Karma doctrine. Freedom of the agent in respect of what he does, does not allow control or constraint by any thing external, though it is compatible with, or rather characterized by, an internal constraint, i.e., self-determination. The law of Karma is thus a postulate of practical reason, which at all stages (in all lives of the individual), is governed by self-determination and there is no need to acknowledge the existence or role of any external agency, not even of God. For if the law of Karma is a specific form of the casual law operating in the domain of morality (i.e., in the domain of human actions and conducts and the consequences thereof), then to admit this all controlling agent would impede the operation of this law and militate against its all important 'moral' feature. It is for this reason that not only the heterodox schools like

Jainism and Buddhism but also some orthodox ones like 'Samkhya' and 'Mimamsa' would want to disallow the existence and the role of God in the operation of the 'Karma' doctrine.[2] The divine influence would go against the unimpeded operation of the law by telling upon its objectivity, which would be affected by waiting upon the divine dispensation. And it would divest the law of its all important moral nature by making God the virtual cause of the doings of men, thereby depriving them of the moral freedom in choosing their actions and hence deserving the consequences thereof. The idea of a divine dispenser of the rewards and punishments for men's actions, mooted by some schools like the 'Nyaya' and forms of theistic 'Vedanta', purportedly to safeguard the ethicality of this doctrine,[3] pays only a lip service to God by making him act in consonance with the Karmas of men; for the authors of this idea—the said theistic schools—conceive of him as 'a common cause in the operation of the law of Karma' and explain the divergence of its incidence (differing awards of rewards and punishments) on different individual agents entirely in terms of their respective moral deserts, thereby limiting his power of omnipotence. If, to counter the latter, God is projected as the ulterior cause of man's deeds, he would be responsible for the inequity of the awards and so would be responsible for the presence of evil and injustice in the world as evidenced by the said inequity. If, to counter this, it is further argued that the law of Karma is the Will of God and as such cannot be considered as limiting his power, he would be construed as 'willing' the sufferings and punishments awarded to men and that would affect his goodness.[4] Thus the divine dispenser of justice would not only take away the ethicality of the Karma doctrine, but would also be a very truncated God indeed.

Unattached thus from the notion of divine control, (on which, understandably, there is no agreement among the Indian schools of thought), the Karma doctrine, in its secular version and generally agreed formulation, is an inexorable moral law of deserts and entitlements, governed by self-determination and causal necessity. What may be called the secular version of the law of Karma would still make three distinct but supposedly interdependent claims which are not logically interdependent after all. Rajendra Prasad has summarized these claims of the law thus:

> Ignoring some details, which may be important for some schools or sects of classical Indian philosophy, the law of *Karma* ... can be stated as a conjunction of three claims: (a) every action produces

> some pleasure or pain, (b) which and only which its doer necessarily experiences in the present or next life because (c) he deserves, or ought, to experience them and them alone. (Prasad, 1989: 220–221)

Let us examine the three claims and their implications. But while examining them we must not lose sight of the fact that the three claims must be supposed to be interdependent, the presupposition of which only would make the law of Karma what it is. For otherwise (a) would have nothing to do with (b) and (c), and the same would be true of (b) and (c) as well. But contrary to this supposition, even if we admit that one's actions produce some effects, it does not follow that one must experience them all, or that one deserves them all. My writing this article may enrage a staunch believer because the article reflects a view that does not quite conform to his own view. But neither do I have to experience his anger, for he may not express it or direct it against me, nor do I deserve his anger, if he does. Secondly, even if my actions produce an effect 'e' (claim–a), and I deserve it (claim–c), it does not follow that (claim–b) I experience 'e' in any of my supposed lives. Thus (b) would have nothing to do with (a) and (c). Conversely (which makes the same point), it may also be the case that I experience something, e.g., I may be the victim of someone else's anger (claim–b), which for sure, I do not deserve and which is not a consequence of any of 'my' actions (claim–a). For example, take this familiar story from the *Ramayana*: Ahalya, became the victim of her husband's anger and was turned into a stone; but she neither deserved this nor was this the consequence of 'her' own action (i.e., the alleged adultery which she did not commit within her knowledge).[5] However, if I do deserve something (claim–c), it would mean that what I deserve is the result of one of my actions (claim–a) and in all fairness I must (ought to) experience it (claim–b). But, as Prasad rightly observes, the fact that I ought to experience 'x' does not imply, or is not the same thing as saying, that I do experience it (ibid.). Thus (c) strictly has nothing to do with (b). It is therefore not a logical interdependence that binds the three claims together. Their interdependence is a postulate and a presupposition of the law of Karma, which is admittedly neither logically provable nor empirically demonstrable. However the law is proffered as a sort of transcendental argument that claims to make intelligible some very important facts of life, which would otherwise remain unexplained. The gap between virtue and success of life, often expressed as the problem of the evil, the inequalities of life's benefits and burdens, and most important, the sufferings of people which cannot be traced to any of their actions in (this) life, are all important facts which are supposed to find a rational explanation in the law of Karma. For if the deserved consequences of one's actions are to be experienced (suffering or enjoyment) by oneself, the Karma doctrine seeks to provide the explanation.

Karma and Rebirth: A Critique

In fact the beliefs in rebirth and the cycle of births and deaths constitute an essential requirement for the Karma doctrine in order to make it internally coherent. This belief is virtually another transcendental argument without which the doctrine cannot be explained, since one single life is often inadequate to explain and establish the deserts and entitlements accrued from actions. But this is another presupposition, equally unprovable and equally non-demonstrable and if one does not accept this belief, one will have a strong reason to reject the law of Karma and not just modify, albeit drastically, the character of the law as Prasad (1989) has rather shakily suggested.

To suggest that one would 'hesitate' to accept (b), and therefore the law of Karma, if one does not find the belief in rebirth acceptable (as Prasad does) is itself a hesitant suggestion, since to reject the belief in rebirth is to reject (b) and the law of Karma—if the latter is taken as absolute and inviolable. I have argued later that this does not have to be so with the law of Karma—and that the law's being not inviolable does not affect its essential moral nature as a principle of retributive morality. But prior to this work of analytic reconstruction, we will have to continue exposing a few more problems endemic in the law in its received form.

An important problem with the claims of the doctrine, especially as spelt out by (claim–c), is that it assumes that all actions are moral actions and that all actions entitle their doers to experience the sufferings and enjoyments of the results. This is contrary to our normal understanding of the concept of human actions, which recognizes the reality of moral actions as well as of non-moral ones; the former only lead to deserts and entitlements whereas the latter do not, or cannot, generate any entitlement for the doer. But the Karma doctrine seems to have taken no care to take note of this important distinction between types of human actions—important from the point of view of moral entitlements. And the classical Indian tradition, depending heavily on this doctrine rather as an article of faith, has never felt the need to make this distinction, which nevertheless is of crucial logical and philosophical importance (ibid.: 1989). Interestingly commentators on Karma do not generally feel this need; for in keeping with the tradition they inherited, they simply take it for granted that every action generates some moral entitlements. This is the symptom of the general tendency for abstraction and generalization that has been largely responsible for many misconceptions regarding our tradition. Even if we accept that all our actions generate entitlements, there is, in addition, the problematic possibility that some results of our actions not only affect oneself but also some other people. As an anecdote in the *Ramayana* goes, Jarata (the whore) seduced Rushyasringa in to the perturbing kingdom of Raja Lopamudra and the result was the much awaited rain that saved millions' lives from draught; but it would be much too-fetched to claim, as some do (Mohanty, 2004: 38), that the millions who benefited from her (Jarata's) action deserved the benefit by virtue of their past actions.[6] My use of a high power motor causes scarcity of water supply in my neighbours' houses, but this is the consequence of my action which not I but my neighbours suffer from, and which certainly they do not deserve. Thus, claim (c) is shown to be fairly violable, and with it the Karma doctrine is deprived of its supposed important requirement of unimpeded operation. In fact my sufferings may be the result of my actions as well as of someone else's actions or of a natural calamity like the super cyclone or the Tsunami earthquake. Though the latter types of event are sometimes attributed to a general decline in moral virtues, it would hardly pass for a theory of deserts when the victims of such calamities may include the virtuous and the vicious alike. However, such blatant exceptions to the law of Karma are generally ignored and some particular 'positive' instances are singled out and cited, viz., the miraculous survival of a child or an old man in the midst of the killer events, to prove that some of their past virtuous actions saved their lives; and myths are raised in support of this.

The gravest problems the law of Karma has to suffer, are the severe limitations of the belief in rebirth and transmigration, which virtually is the sine qua non of the law's operation. One's sufferings are the deserved results of one's past actions, so the law claims, but not all these sufferings are explainable as results of one's past actions performed in one's present life. So in order to prove that it is the agent's desert, a present suffering is traced backwards to one's actions done in a supposed past life (or lives). But the success of this supposition (argument?) depends on proving that the person who is said to have done a bad action in a supposed previous life is the one who suffers in this life.

This tacit assumption of personal identity is severely suspect in the obvious absence of bodily continuity, which alone can tell the difference of 'same person' from a 'similar person'. The usual invocation of memory as the explanation of personal identity in such cases is hopelessly inadequate since memory, in order to qualify as a criterion of personal identity, is dependent on physical continuity and cannot be a sufficient condition of personal identity. In the absence of physical continuity, the distinction between genuine memory and mere memory-claims would remain unexplained, and the problem of possible massive reduplication would remain unsolved. I have adduced elaborate arguments to this effect elsewhere (see Mohapatra, 2000). However, the foregoing discussion is enough to indicate the weakness of the rebirth theory, which, in turn, weakens the Karma doctrine considerably. For to say the least, unless the actions of a supposed past life are (shown to be or individuated as) my actions, my sufferings and pains in this life cannot be explained as deserved punishments. The law of Karma is claimed to be a retributive theory of morality in as much as it insists that whatever sufferings or enjoyments one undergoes are the deserved effects of his actions. But its retributivism gets into serious trouble in its being tied of with the theory of rebirth. Yet the law of Karma, as received from tradition and interpreted by some modern writers, relies heavily on this contentious postulate of 'one's own actions' in a past life giving rise to rewards and punishments in the present. Hiriyanna (1975: 174) writes:

> We can as well conceive of man's continued existence in a series of lives (*Samsara)* and then the difficulty of accounting for what befalls him in any life disappears, because *we can trace it to the deeds done by himself in each earlier birth.* If we look at life from this perspective past *Karma* which explains the preset conduct of a person and the good or evil that follows from it *are eventually traceable to nothing but his own actions.*

The belief in rebirth has another problem that relates to, or rather poses a threat to, the morality of the Karma doctrine as a theory of desert. The deserts and entitlements of a person in the present life are traced to his supposed actions in a past life which are admittedly never remembered by the doer except in the dubious cases of the Jatismaras, the so called memory of the latter being indistinguishable in principle from retrocognitive clairvoyance and mere memory-claims. If we do not remember anything of our past life, it may not disprove the reality of that past life and the continuity of the person through the (supposed) past life and the present, as Hiriyanna has argued in defense of transmigration (ibid.: 107).[7] But what is missed in this argument is the crucially important point about the 'justice' of punishing a person for what he does not or cannot be able to remember to have done even if he did it in 'his' supposed past life. Consciousness of guilt is an important moral and legal consideration in awarding punishment to a person, and absence of it is often considered an attenuating condition justifying exoneration or at least lessening of the punishment. Thus, contrary to the contention of some modern writers that the inevitability of law of Karma is our assurance for the truth of transmigration (ibid.: 176), the latter becomes a major ground of weakness of the former.

Final Comments

Indian mind's proneness for universality and absoluteness makes it conceive of the law of Karma as inexorable and absolutely infallible and forces itself to back it up with the belief in rebirth as a necessary condition for its unimpeded operation. Since many (perhaps most) of our deserts and sufferings cannot be explained in terms of the result of our actions in 'this' life, a past life (lives) is (are) brought in, to the fore. But the supposition of this is a debilitating working hypothesis as much as the supposition of God in explaining *Esse ist percipii* in Berkeley's philosophy, i.e., in explaining the existence of unperceived reals. (When nobody perceives a table which nevertheless continues to exist, and we have enough reasons to suppose that it does, God is said to do the perceiving). How wonderful it would be—and how much logical—if our favoured theory and law could be explained independently of such weak assumptions! But despite its vulnerability and questionable logic, the belief in transmigration forms so much an essential element of the law of Karma that it, along with the belief in Moksha and Karma, forms a logical trilogy in the sense that anyone of the beliefs can be explained only in the association with the other two. This supposed trilogy and a critique thereof demand a new discourse.

Notes

1. It is to be noted that the word 'Karma' is wider in significance than the word 'Dharma', in so far as Karmas can be 'Dharmas' as well as 'Adharmas', 'Dharmic' actions as well as 'Adharmic' ones, which are both deeds and actions: the former merits rewards and the latter punishments in the 'Karmic' scheme of things.
2. It is immortality of the self, not existence of God, which the higher (eternal) values of life point to, according to these schools.
3. For it was argued that since the results of our past deeds are unconscious (Achetana) factors not known as such because of lack of memory of these actions and of that life, the allotment of the awards to a just and all-knowing God would account for the awards as just and deserved.
4. The spirit of the argument is owed to Hiriyanna (1975).
5. It may also be questioned whether what she said would at all be a case of adultery, for all the while she took the imposter, Indra in disguise, as her husband, Rishi Goutama, who and who alone was in her mind.
6. Mohanty argues that one's Prarabdhas create the necessary situations congenial for their fruition. On this view, described by some as Karmic monism, Jarata's action should be the kind of congenial situation leading to fruition of past actions of all the beneficiaries indiscriminately! To be sure, the last factor lays bare the weakness of Karmic monism stretched to a point of near absurdity.
7. The attempt to disprove past life on the basis of non-remembrance of it, Hiriyanna argues, would be to confound a thing with the consciousness of it. I would however argue, against him and the received view of Karma, that the mere supposition that it exists and even the additional supposition that it helps in explaining the discrepancy between virtue and success of life (as is usually argued by many modern writers, including Hiriyanna), does not and cannot prove that it exists.

Section II

Religion Theorized

6 Rethinking Marx and Religion

Alberto Toscano

In the contemporary study of religion as a factor of social change and political mobilization, Marx is treated as a marginal reference at best, a 'dead dog' at worst.[1] The global impasse, or even reversal, of a secularization process that Marx appears to take for granted; the turbulent rise of explicitly religious forms of political subjectivity; the persistence or resurgence of religion both as a principle of political authority and a structuring presence in everyday life—these current trends seem to militate for the relegation of Marx to a historical moment (that of the European nineteenth century), a political subject (the workers' movement), and a notion of temporality (the one encompassed by notions of progress, development and revolution) which have been inexorably surpassed in a globalized scenario (whether we grasp this scenario through the differential lens of post-colonial critiques, the hegemonic and homogeneous prism of neo-liberalism, or the bellicose culturalism of the infamous 'clash of civilizations'). To compound this state of affairs, which could also be read in terms of a revenge of the sociology of religion against a Marxian 'master narrative'—and with all the apposite caveats regarding the discontinuities between Marx and historical Marxisms, practical and theoretical—we cannot ignore the significance of the religious questions within the so-called 'crisis of Marxism' of the 1970s and onwards. When Michel Foucault (see Afary and Anderson, 2005) in his enduringly controversial reports on the Iranian revolution, stressed the irrelevance of Marx's dictum on religion as the 'opium of the people' in accounting for the role of Islamic politics in the overthrow of the Shah,[2] he was expressing a commonly held rejection of the supposed secular reductivism to characteristic of Marxist theories of social change and prescriptions for revolutionary action. Alongside Iran, the complex entanglement of popular rebellions and religion in the Polish Solidarnosc movement and Latin American liberation theology[3] wrong-footed a theory of revolutionary praxis which took the 'practical atheism' of the proletariat as a sociological datum (Engels, 1987: 143). This situation has been exacerbated today in a context where by the ebb of projects of human emancipation is accompanied the pauperization and brutalization of a 'surplus humanity' living in a 'planet of slums', the catalyst for a twenty-first century 'reenchantment of a catastrophic modernity' (Davis, 2006: 195) in which 'populist Islam and Pentecostal Christianity (and in Bombay, the cult of Shivaji) occupy a social space analogous to that of early twentieth-century socialism and anarchism' (Davis, 2004: 30).

Can Marx's thinking on religion survive the challenge posed by what appear to be the dramatic reversals in the secularizing tendencies and revolutionary opportunities which he identified in the European nineteenth century? And can a Marxian social theory withstand its 'expatriation' into a political scenario in which explicitly Marxist actors, whether states or movements, are weak or inexistent? (Toscano, 2008a). The most economical response, though perhaps a facile one too, would be to indicate the continuing vitality of historical materialism in the study of the socio-political dynamics behind the current religious resurgence, whether in the context of rampant planetary urbanization (as in the writings of Mike Davis, quoted above), or through the analysis of the role of the new imperialism and 'accumulation by dispossession' in fostering the conditions for religious militancy, as in the work of David Harvey (2003).[4] However, rather than merely engaging in a salutary restatement of the virtues of Marxism for a systemic and systematic understanding of the conditions for today's refulgent religiosity, I want to take the aforementioned dismissals of Marx seriously and deal with what we might call the 'subjective' element of religious-political conviction, its mobilizing force, alongside the questions of the explanation of religious phenomena and the supposed secularization of capitalist societies. The aim then is to restore some of the richness of the problems raised by Marx, and even to treat his seeming anachronism as a resource rather than a defect in displacing some of the numerous commonplaces about religion, society and politics that have come to dominate our public and academic discourse. Whilst endowed with their own complex reality and efficacy, appearances—including that of the contemporary centrality of religion to political life—are rarely the whole story. As Marx (1990: 19)[5] puts it, in a mordant description of his method:

> ... the philistine's and vulgar economist's *way of looking at things* stems from ... the fact that it is only the direct *form of manifestation* of relations that is reflected in their brains and not their *inner connection*. Incidentally, if the latter were the case what need would there be of *science*?

We could add that it is such a philistine's myopia for the inner connections that has dominated much recent writing which has sought to explain and to counter the political return to religion by invoking the naturalist and atheist legacy of the Enlightenment.[6] What is striking about the voguish defences of an unfinished Enlightenment project against the delusions and depredations of religious fanaticism is their blindness to the incorporation and radical transformation of the Enlightenment preoccupations, especially in terms of religion, by the emancipatory and workers' movements of the nineteenth century. The impression given by much of the popular literature in defence of atheism is that at an intellectual level—to put it in a nutshell—the 1840s still lie ahead of us. It is indeed to the early 1840s, the only period of sustained writing on the link between politics and religion in Marx's work, that we now turn. Understanding Marx's intellectual intervention into this critical moment in German and European history provides a necessary orientation for examining the way in which the problem of religion, in its various guises, is both addressed and transformed in the further development of Marx's work.

The Criticism of Earth

Glossing over the formidable flowering of radical theory and intellectual activism in the context of which Marx makes his first interventions (see Breckman, 1999; Kouvelakis, 2003), and emphasizing what is 'living' in it today, it is possible to summarize Marx's stance as a 'critique of the critique of religion'. This might seem a very peculiar formulation with which to define a thinker who was not simply a combative atheist (Marx, 1974: 399) armed with an awesome arsenal of anti-religious invective, but a theorist who unequivocally ascribed to the Enlightenment conviction that 'man makes religion'.[7] But as we shall see, everything hinges on how this 'makes' is to be understood.

It is worth noting that Marx's intervention into the politics of religion initially takes place in the ambit of his 'philosophical journalism' (Breckman, 1999: 272). In 'The Leading Article of No. 179 of *Kölnische Zeitung*' (published in 1842 in the *Rheinische Zeitung)* Marx, impelled by a republican and democratic 'élan', confronts the 'German papers [which] have been drumming against the religious trend in philosophy, calumniating, distorting and bowdlerizing it' (Raines, 2002: 39).[8] This 'religious trend', which comprises the works of 'Hegel and Schelling, Feuerbach and Bauer', is under attack in the press for the way it 'rationally' responds to the politicization of religion in the form of the Christian state. As Marx judiciously notes, it is the very attempt by agencies of the state to religiously legitimate politics in a non-theocratic vein, which secularizes religion and opens it to philosophical disputation:

> If religion becomes a political quality, an object of politics, there seems to be hardly any need to mention that the newspapers not only may, but must, discuss political objects. ... If you make religion a theory of state right, then you make religion itself a kind of philosophy. (Raines, 2002: 41)[9]

Marx confronts the anti-philosophical and conformist opinion of his day with the fact that the moment one begins to speak of a Christian state, it becomes impossible to forestall a logic of full secularization. For either the Christian state is equivalent to the reasonable state, in which case its Christianity is redundant and philosophy is fully adequate to thinking through the state-form; or rational freedom cannot be developed out of Christianity, and therefore religion is simply external to the state: 'Answer the dilemma as you like, you will have to concede that the state is not to be constituted from religion but from the reason of freedom' (ibid.: 43). Though this radical democratic secularism can be registered, in a mutated form, in later pronouncements by Marx, it does not exhaust Marx's position.

Initially influenced both by Ludwig Feuerbach's reappropriation for humankind of a species being which had been alienated into the deity, and by Bruno Bauer's unsparing anti-theistic criticism of the baleful effect of religious belief on universality and self-consciousness, Marx's early writings can be understood in terms of the progressive realization that the attack on religion—while a vital spur to undermining the religious legitimation of state power—is always insufficient, or even a downright diversion, when it comes to attain its avowed ends. Repeatedly, atheistic criticism overestimates the centrality of Christianity to the state and treats the state's secularization as an end in itself. The slogan encapsulating Marx's intervention into the fraught 1840s debate over religion and politics is 'from the criticism of Heaven to the criticism of Earth'. The outcome of Marx's philosophical operation is to remove 'the critique of civil society and the state from the broader Left Hegelian campaign against Christianity and [establish] socio-political critique as the object of an autonomous secular discourse of sociological and economic analysis' (Breckman, 1999: 293). The clearest form of this redirection in the aims of 'irreligious criticism' is to be found in a letter (30 November, 1842) to Arnold Ruge, where Marx declares that

> … religion should be criticized in the framework of political conditions (instead of criticizing) political conditions … in the framework of religion … for religion in itself is without content, it owes its being not to heaven but to the earth, and with the abolition of distorted reality, of which it is the *theory*, it will collapse of itself. (cited in Breckman, 1999: 278)

Despite the provocative and problematic declaration that religion is 'without content' of its own—which in turn introduces Marx's belief in the 'withering away' of religion as a corollary of social revolution—it is important to note that, against the image of religion in a certain Enlightenment materialism as a mere delusion or conspiracy, Marx, while never reneging on his militant atheism, affirms what we might term the 'social necessity' of religion as a form of consciousness and an organizing principle of collective life. When Marx writes of religion as a 'theory' of the world, he is making a properly dialectical point: religion provides an inverted picture of the world because the world itself is inverted. Though there is an argument to be made for the idea that Marx draws this 'transformative method', which combines the 'inversion of subject and predicate and exposure of the hypostasized form of both' (ibid.: 286), from Feuerbach, it is also the case that he explicitly refers to the limits of a materialist humanism vis-à-vis religion in order to specify his own position. As he sets out in the fourth of the 'Theses on Feuerbach':

> Feuerbach starts off from the fact of religious self-estrangement, of the duplication of the world into a religious, imaginary world, and a secular one. His work consists in resolving the religious world into its secular basis. He overlooks the fact that after completing this work, the chief thing still remains to be done. For the fact that the secular basis lifts off from itself and establishes itself in the clouds as an independent realm can only be explained by the inner strife and intrinsic contradictoriness of this secular basis. The latter must itself be understood in its contradiction and then, by the removal of the contradiction, revolutionized. Thus, for instance, once the earthly family is discovered to be the secret of the holy family, the former must itself be annihilated theoretically and practically. (Marx, 1998: 570)[10]

To bring religious abstraction 'down to earth' by revealing it to be a distorted projection of human essence is thus insufficient. For Marx, religion possesses a social logic of separation and autonomization (its establishment as an apparently 'independent realm'),[11] whose bases in a really inverted world, so to speak, are the object of theoretical and practical criticism. Marx's critique of the Young Hegelian's critique of religion—and *a fortiori* his views on the insufficiency of the attack on religious delusion in French materialism and the Enlightenment—will persistently take this twofold form: an elaboration of the social logic of abstraction (as a result of the 'inner strife and intrinsic contradictoriness of [the] secular basis') and an elucidation of the necessity for revolution ('the removal of the contradiction') if the real grounds of abstract domination are to be removed.[12] Bluntly put, in order to tackle the endurance of religious abstractions we are to confront the social logic into which they are inscribed, and the dependence of these abstractions on given modes of production and social intercourse. As Marx (1998: 172) writes in *The German Ideology*:

> In religion people make their empirical world into an entity that is only conceived, imagined, that confronts them as something foreign. This again is by no means to be explained from other concepts, from 'self-consciousness' and similar nonsense, but from the entire

> hitherto existing mode of production and intercourse, which is just as independent of the pure concept as the invention of the self-acting mule and the use of railways are independent of Hegelian philosophy. If he wants to speak of an 'essence' of religion, i.e., of a material basis of this inessentiality, then he should look for it neither in the 'essence of man', nor in the predicate of God, but in the material world which each stage of religious development finds in existence.

In the 1844 'Introduction' to the 'Contribution to the Critique of Hegel's Philosophy of Right', Marx had noted that the abolition of religion as the 'illusory' happiness of the people is necessary for their 'real' happiness. To tell them to give up their illusions about their condition is to call on them to give up a condition that requires illusions. Therefore the criticism of religion is in embryo. We might say that the early conviction whereby the struggle against religion is the 'embryo' of true revolutionary transformation, gives way, through Marx's deepening study of the system of exploitation and his own political engagement, to a belief that such an anti-religious struggle might even serve as a detour or a cloak for real political struggle, that is to the idea that the aims of atheism and the Enlightenment cannot be accomplished through a bald affirmation of Godlessness and Reason as matters of consciousness or mere pedagogy. The criticisms of Max Stirner and Bruno Bauer in *The German Ideology* and *The Holy Family* elaborate on this conviction that it is necessary to step outside an obsessive confrontation with 'religious representations', precisely in order to examine and transform the very conditions of possibility for these representations, for their seemingly autonomous, 'spectral' existence. This is the 'Kantian' sense in which Marx provides us with a potent 'critique' of the critique of religion, pointing out both the limitations and the conditions of efficacy of the latter. It would be difficult to underestimate the relevance of this gesture today, when we are confronted with anti-religious arguments, which, whatever the sincerity or nobility of their motivations, often rely on the idealist, asocial view that the sway of religious representations and ideologies over human affairs can be terminated by a mere change of consciousness. Marx indicates that consciousness always takes 'social' forms and these forms are in turn affected by a certain quotient of necessity. His critique of the Young Hegelians asks what the conditions of production of religious representations are, in order to then ask how these conditions themselves might be transformed. The anti-theism of his contemporaries is an obstacle to a consequent political atheism inasmuch as it remains within the ambit of theological reasoning. Marx writes:

> [Stirner] ... shares the belief of all critical speculative philosophers of modern times that thoughts, which have become independent, objectified thoughts—ghosts—have ruled the world and continue to rule it, and that all history up to now was the history of theology, nothing could be easier for him than to transform history into a history of ghosts. (Marx, 1998: 173)

The vision of the struggle against religious domination as a 'fight against [the] thoughts and ideas of the ideologist', where hierarchy is reduced to the 'domination of thought' and the political structure of rule in modern times can be reduced to a 'clericalism' that even includes the likes of Robespierre and Saint-Just, is for Marx emblematic of the dead end of a supposedly radical thought which not only takes religion on its own terms, but succumbs to a generic fight against transcendence, unable to grasp the real conditions for the production of (and domination by) abstraction (ibid.: 186–191).[13]

Aside from this methodological prescription, which in one form or another will accompany Marx throughout his work, there is also something to be learned from Marx's attention to the importance of political conjuncture, as well as historical and geographical specificity, in the criticism of religion. Behind the attack on the Young Hegelian's penchant for remaining at the level of theology, for fighting ghosts with ghosts, lies Marx's estimation that anti-religious mobilization was—despite the necessity of the demand for radical secularization—if not a rearguard, at least an insufficient programme. Confident of a secularizing trend which, spurred by revolutionary politics between 1793 and 1848 'sufficiently announced the direction of the popular mind in Europe', Marx, in an 1854 article for the *New York Tribune* tellingly entitled 'The Decay of Religious Authority', remarked: 'We are still witnesses of this epoch, which may be characterized as the era of democratic revolt against ecclesiastical authority.' But he also indicated the tendency to an ever more opportunistic, non-organic use of religious legitimation for state violence: 'The days in which religious considerations were a governing element in the wars of Western Europe are, it seems, long gone by' (Raines, 2002: 188–189). Some years thereafter, in the 1867 'Preface' to *Capital*, Marx had occasion to note—not without including one of his characteristic jabs at craven clerical authorities—that atheism itself was no longer at the forefront even in terms of its capacity to provoke authorities: 'The Established Church ... will more readily pardon an attack on thirty-eight of its thirty-nine articles than on one thirty-ninth of its income. Now atheism itself is a *culpa levis* [a venial sin], as compared with the criticism of existing property relations' (Marx, 1990: 92). Some might argue that new forms of reactionary or fundamentalist religious politics have reversed this verdict, that Marx remains rooted in a historical moment that is not transposable to our own. To respond to such claims, however, it is necessary not simply to confront Marx's critique of the critique of religion, but to consider the place of reflection on religious phenomena within the wider sweep of his thought, including his mature critique of political economy. In order to do so, I would like to treat in succession what might be seen as three aspects of Marx's thought that speak to contemporary debates on the politics and sociology of religion: the social explanation of religion; the nature of religious-political subjectivity; the process of secularization and the politics of secularism. I will then conclude with some remarks on the idea of a 'religion of Capital'.

The History of a Thing without History

The error of anti-theistic critique—which remains within the ambit of theology, unable to grasp the real social processes that condition the necessity and 'objective illusion' characteristic of religious phenomena—is part and parcel of what Marx regards as the shortcoming of the very Enlightenment tradition of which he is in many respects a proud heir. Whether we are dealing with money or with religion, the crucial error is to treat real abstractions as mere 'arbitrary product[s] of human reflection (Toscano, 2008b). This was the kind of explanation favoured by the eighteenth century: in this way the Enlightenment endeavoured ... to remove the appearance of strangeness from the mysterious shapes assumed by human relations whose origins they were unable to decipher' (Marx, 1990: 186).[14] The strangeness of religion itself cannot be dispelled by referring it to clerical conspiracies or psychological delusions to be cured through mere pedagogy. But does Marx bend the stick too far the other way? After all, there is good reason to feel that the early Marx's position vis-à-vis religious phenomena takes the guise, to borrow a term from contemporary cognitive science, of a kind of 'eliminativist materialism'—a denial of any autonomy or indeed reality to religion. Already in the 'Leading Article' of 1842, Marx had stripped religion of any causal efficacy: 'It was not the downfall of the old religions that brought the downfall of the old states, but the downfall of the old states that brought the downfall of the old religions' (Raines, 2002: 33). In *The German Ideology*, religion, alongside 'morality ... metaphysics and all the rest of ideology as well as the forms of consciousness corresponding to these' is stripped of any 'semblance of independence' (Marx, 1998: 42).[15] Marx even adumbrates a sketch of naturalist psychology whose echoes one could find today in the likes of Richard Dawkins and Daniel Dennett: 'The phantoms formed in the brains of men are also, necessarily, sublimates of the material life-process, which is empirically verifiable and bound to material premises' (Marx, 1998: 42).[16] The notion of religion as a kind of non-being, an 'inessentiality', in the language of the 1844 'Introduction', is also in evidence in the 1843 response to Bauer, 'On the Jewish Question': '... since the existence of religion is the existence of a defect, the source of this defect must be looked for in the *nature* of the state itself. We no longer see religion as the *basis* but simply as a *phenomenon* of secular narrowness' (see Raines, 2002: 49). But as Marx moves beyond this political reduction to the secular basis of the state, into the historical-materialist accounting with real abstractions heralded by the fourth thesis on Feuerbach quoted above, a crucial factor is added to his understanding of religion—a factor which allows him to propose means of explaining, rather than merely explaining away, religious phenomena. It is not enough to 'explain the religious restriction on the free citizens from the secular restriction they experience,' to 'turn theological questions into secular questions' and 'resolv[e] superstition into history', as Marx enjoins us to do in 'On the Jewish Question'. Rather, we are to look to 'the inner strife and intrinsic contradictoriness' of a 'secular basis' (Marx, 1998: 570), to be conceived not in terms of the state but rather in those of 'the entire hitherto existing mode of production and intercourse' (ibid.: 172).

By the time of his mature work on the critique of political economy, we can say that Marx has moved beyond the 'eliminativist' programme, which he polemically counterposed to the theological foibles of the Young Hegelians, to a historical-materialist incorporation of the religious phenomenon into a theory of the social emergence of different modes of 'real abstraction'. Thus, in an important long footnote to *Capital*, Marx suggests—as a corollary to a discussion of a 'critical history of technology' that would be mindful of the role of 'the mode of formation of [man's] social relations'—the possibility of a similarly critical 'history of religion'. His methodological reflections are immensely suggestive for coming to grips with a historical-materialist understanding of religion:

> It is, in reality, much easier to discover by analysis the earthly core of the misty creations of religion, than, conversely, it is, to develop from the actual relations of life the corresponding celestialised forms of those relations. The latter method is the only materialistic, and therefore the only scientific one. The weak points in the abstract materialism of natural science, a materialism that excludes history and its process, are at once evident from the abstract and ideological conceptions of its spokesmen, whenever they venture beyond the bounds of their own speciality. (Marx, 1990: 493–494)

This passage demonstrates the vitality and endurance of Marx's critique of the critique of religion, his opposition to a complacent reduction of religious phenomena to their secular basis (whether this is understood in terms of species being, the state, or even a static notion of economic intercourse), but opens up in a much more forthright manner the possibility of a historical materialist study of religion qua real abstraction, developing 'from the actual relations of life the corresponding celestialized forms of those relations'.[17] In *The German Ideology*, Marx had made the following lapidary declaration:

> '*Christianity' has no history whatever* and ... all the different forms in which it was visualized at various times were not 'self-determinations' and 'further developments' 'of the religious spirit', but were brought about by wholly empirical causes in no way dependent on any influence of the religious spirit. (Marx, 1998: 166)

Notwithstanding the continuity in the denial of independence to the religious phenomenon, *Capital*, shorn of the polemical target of *The German Ideology*, opens up the possibility of a materialist history of religion inasmuch as, whilst denying religion any causal autonomy, it permits us to think of the conditions for its 'real-apparent' autonomization. In her excellent study on the status of religion in Marx and Engels, Michèle Bertrand has elaborated on this methodological suggestion by distinguishing in their work between a path of de-mystification and one of constitution. Commenting on the correspondence of Marx and Engels on Ibn Khaldun and the historical-materialist explanation of the implantation of Islam in the Middle East, she writes: 'Instead of referring religious representations back to the real world that underlies them it's a matter of understanding why the history of real mutations has taken a religious form' (Bertrand, 1979: 82).[18] Or, in the words of *Capital*:

> ... the Middle Ages could not live on Catholicism, nor could the ancient world on politics. On the contrary, it is the manner in which they gained their livelihood which explains why in the one case politics, in the other case Catholicism, played the chief part. (Marx, 1990: 176)[19]

It is not simply a matter of referring the illusory autonomy and separation of religious representations to a material basis, but of showing the socio-historical necessity and rootedness of the 'phantoms' and 'sublimates' of a specific religious form.

If we are to follow Derrida (1994), religion itself can be regarded as paradigmatic of the processes of autonomization mercilessly pursued by Marx throughout the domains of ideology and abstraction. But if the full development of a historical-materialist critique of abstractions, moving beyond de-mystification to constitution, allows us to think of a critical history of religion that would surpass the eliminativist position asserted in *The German Ideology*, we are still faced with the problem of the plurality of religions. Indeed, as Michèle Bertrand rightly notes, is it even possible to speak of 'religion in general'? Though as theory, religion might answer to a relatively invariant human need to render the world intelligible, and as practice, to master it, this still does not tell us why '*this* religion has found a receptive terrain, why men have been sensitive to its message ... . How is a religion born? Why does it gain followers? How does its audience grow?' (Bertrand, 1979: 83). Needless to say, these are questions that the mature Marx, who views religion as a waning force, is not preoccupied with answering (unlike the Engels of *On the History of Early Christianity*). However, we may find in Marx an embryonic theory of the correlation between certain religious forms and institutions, on the one hand, and certain social systems (and more specifically types of alienation), on the other. The outlines of such a theory are tellingly delineated in the chapter on the commodity in *Capital*, where Marx (1990: 172) writes:

> For a society of commodity producers, whose general social relation of production consists in the fact that they treat their products as

> commodities, hence as values, and in this material form bring their individual, private labours into relation with each other as homogeneous human labour, Christianity with its religious cult of man in the abstract, more particularly in its bourgeois development, i.e., in Protestantism, Deism, etc., is the most fitting form of religion.

This 'fit' suggests that, rather than being the offspring of a clerical conspiracy, of a hieratic hierarchy, Christianity is regarded by Marx as bound to capitalism by a certain mode and intensity of abstraction. The autonomization of material production from the communal and the concrete privileges Christianity as its superstructural correlate inasmuch as the latter perceives and presents itself as the religion of autonomy. In *The German Ideology*, Christianity is indeed defined by the manner in which fights against determination by 'heteronomy as opposed to autonomy of the spirit' (Marx, 1998: 272).[20] Hints in Marx's work suggest that the apparent autonomy and abstraction attained by the value-form under commodity production is especially suited by the Christian religion[21]—indeed, inasmuch as religion is both a hypostasis of, and a manner of coping with, not just natural forces but social ones, we could say, paraphrasing Marx's 1844 'Introduction' to the 'Critique of Hegel's Philosophy of Right', that Christianity is in this sense a theory (or logic) of capitalism. In Marx, this insight regarding the affinity of Christianity and capitalism also takes more overtly historical and sociological hues. For instance, in the *Grundrisse*, Marx forwards a thesis which, as Michael Löwy notes, bears a 'parallel (but not identity!) with Weber's thesis' in *The Protestant Ethic*, to wit that: 'The cult of money has its asceticism, its self-denial, its self-sacrifice-economy and frugality, contempt for mundane, temporal and fleeting pleasures; the chase after the eternal treasure. Hence the connection between English Puritanism or Dutch Protestantism and money-making' (cited in Lowy, 2005).[22] But these brief sociological apercus, not necessarily unique or original, must be thought of in the context of Marx's methodological revolution, his formulation of a historical-materialist study of abstractions based on the real abstractions of the value-form, abstract labour etc. Marx's critique can now return to the attack on the personalism, atomism and false equality of the Christian state, which had defined its first moments, on a far firmer footing, whilst losing none of its dialectical bite:

> The development of capitalist production creates an average level of bourgeois society and therefore an average level of temperament and

> disposition amongst the most varied peoples. It is as truly cosmopolitan as Christianity. This is why Christianity is likewise the special religion of capital. In both it is only men who count. One man in the abstract is worth just as much or as little as the next man. In the one case, all depends on whether or not he has faith, in the other, on whether or not he has credit. In addition, however, in the one case, predestination has to be added, and in the other case, the accident of whether or not a man is born with a silver spoon in his mouth. (Marx, 1863)[23]

And if Christianity is indeed the 'special religion of capital', this also means that to the very extent that the society of commodity producers it 'fits' is stamped with a certain necessity—indeed to the very extent that the forms of abstraction and alienation such a society implies prepare the communist socialization of means of production—Christianity is never just a fantasy or a conspiracy,[24] it is also an integral, if contingent and transitory, component of world capitalism. Marx's early intuition that only human emancipation—rather than secularism or Enlightenment pedagogy alone—can snuff out the 'illusory sun' of religion can thus be restated: 'The religious reflections of the real world can, in any case, vanish only when the practical relations of everyday life between man and man, and man and nature, generally present themselves to him in a transparent and rational form' (Marx, 1990: 173).

Protest, Suffering and the Limits of the Secular

Clearly then, Marx holds on to the perspective, evident at the very least since *The German Ideology* and the 'Theses on Feuerbach', whereby only revolutionary praxis can provide the real '*criticism of that vale of tears* of which religion is the *halo.*' In light of the recent theoretical preoccupation with religious matrices of militant political subjectivity (in the writings of Badiou, Negri and Zizek, among others) what can Marx tell us—beyond the historical-materialist explanation of organized religions and institutions—about the political resources of religious subjectivity? More generally, how can we link a 'structural' study of the material bases of religion[25] with issues of belief, passion and agency?[26] These questions are of particular note inasmuch as one of the forms that the criticism or repudiation of Marx's work has taken has been that of describing it as the source for a fundamentally religious subjectivity, if not an outright fanaticism. This 'political religion' approach to Marxism has also relied on the idea that Marxism is somehow the (degenerate) secularization of fundamentally Christian visions of salvation.[27] Such an approach is pre-emptively and categorically repudiated by Marx and Engels themselves, when they condemn any attempt to fashion a 'new religion' to motivate and crystallize social struggles:

> It is clear that with every great historical upheaval of social conditions the outlooks and ideas of men, and consequently their religious ideas, are revolutionised. The difference between the present upheaval and all earlier ones lies in the very fact that man has at last found out the secret of this process of historical upheaval and hence, instead of once again exalting this practical, 'external', process in the rapturous form of a new religion, divests himself of all religion. (Marx and Engels, 1850)

In his own lifetime as a political organizer, Marx was of course faced with various attempts at infusing religion into the socialist politics of the workers' movement. Despite his views on the ambivalence of religious subjectivity, both 'the expression of real suffering and a protest against real suffering'; not just the religion of the state but 'the sigh of the oppressed creature, the heart of a heartless world, and the soul of soulless conditions'—a view poetically summarized in the prescription whereby criticism should not merely aim at plucking 'the imaginary flowers on the chain' of social domination (i.e., religion), but 'throw off the chain and pluck the living flower' (Raines, 2002: 171)[28]—Marx's views on the progressive politicization of religion were bleak to say the least, and not based merely on his 'specific ... aversion for Christianity'.[29] To begin with, there was a sociological judgment about what I have referred to, following Engels, as the 'practical atheism' of the working class, to which we must of course add the desacralizing effects of the epic narrated in *The Communist Manifesto*, in which the bourgeoisie has 'drowned the most heavenly ecstasies of religious fervour ... in the icy waters of egotistical calculation' and 'stripped of its halo ... the priest' (ibid.: 146). On the grounds of these facts and tendencies, the attempt at generating a Christian socialism is showered with scorn.

Even when he had yet to sunder his philosophical allegiance to Feuerbach, Marx already rejected 'the possibility of translating

Christian love into a love of humanity' (Breckman, 1999: 282). In his political interventions, the historical affinity between Christianity and capitalism is not accompanied, far from it, by any faith in the affinity between Christianity and capitalism's transcendence. Though a 'fitting' superstructural correlate of abstract-value and the exchange of commodities between 'equals', Christianity is depicted as a feeble weapon against capitalism at best, and a fig's leaf at worst.

In his scathing piece on 'The Communism of the Rheinisch Beobachter', Marx produces the following tirade on the idea of 'social principles of Christianity' as substitutes for communist revolution, again proving that, when the conjuncture demands it, and notwithstanding the subtlety of his critique of the critique of religion, he is a coruscating foe of religious hypocrisy:

> The social principles of Christianity preach the necessity of a ruling and an oppressed class, and for the latter all they have to offer is the pious wish that the former may be charitable. ... The social principles of Christianity preach cowardice, self-contempt, abasement, submissiveness and humbleness, in short, all the qualities of the rabble, and the proletariat, which will not permit itself to be treated as rabble, needs its courage, its self-confidence, its pride and its sense of independence even more than its bread. The social principles of Christianity are sneaking and hypocritical, and the proletariat is revolutionary. (Marx, 1847)

In passages such as this, Marx seems unequivocal in effecting a separation between politics and religion, in developing his own communist political practice on stringently irreligious grounds.[30] This leads us to a question which is of particular significance in gauging the contemporary relevance of Marx's thinking today: the question of the secular, to be understood both in terms of political secularism and a historical process of secularization.

Now, in his early writings as a radical democrat Marx—chief among them the 'Leading Article' of 1842—strongly advocated a secular 'state of human nature', ingeniously arguing on the basis of Christianity's supposed pioneering of secularism itself. He asks rhetorically: 'Was it not Christianity before anything else that separated church and state?' And he proceeds to chastize Christians that make appeal to a 'Christian state' which thoroughly undermines the mission of the Church: 'Does not every minute of your practical life give the lie to your theory? Do you consider it wrong to appeal to the courts when you are cheated? But the apostle writes that it is wrong.' Marx then goes on, in a manner which could be seen to apply to contemporary political invocations of how the spirit of religion should animate political laws, to dismantle the idea of a non-theocratic state that would somehow express the religious idea. Provoking the advocates of a Christian politics, he writes:

> It is the greatest irreligiousness, the wantonness of worldly reason, to separate the general spirit of religion from the positive religion; this separation of religion from its dogmas and institutions is equal to asserting that the universal spirit of right must reign in the state irrespective of the definite laws and the positive institutions of right. (Raines, 2002: 42)

In Marx's later political career, however, the idea of a secular state voided of its religious character and not interfering in the religious lives of its subjects will no longer be seen as the goal of criticism and emancipation, but merely as a necessary but insufficient 'transitional demand' on the way to an overcoming of the political limits of capitalism, and *a fortiori* of liberalism. This much is evident in the 1875 *Critique of the Gotha Programme*, where Marx (1875) upbraids the intellectuals of the Socialist Workers' Party of Germany for their timid remarks on 'freedom of conscience':

> If one desired ... to remind liberalism of its old catchwords, it surely could have been done only in the following form: Everyone should be able to attend his religious as well as his bodily needs without the police sticking their noses in. But the Workers' party ought, at any rate in this connection, to have expressed its awareness of the fact that bourgeois 'freedom of conscience' is nothing but the toleration of all possible kinds of religious freedom of conscience, and that for its part it endeavours rather to liberate the conscience from the witchery of religion. But one chooses not to transgress the 'bourgeois' level.

The theoretical bases of this political stance were laid more than thirty years before, in Marx's critique of Bruno Bauer's argument on the Jewish question. Bauer chastises Jews who wish to be emancipated as Jews for remaining at the level of religious 'privilege' (the demand for specific religious rights) and religious 'prejudice' (the attempt to maintain what Bauer calls 'the powers of excommunication' consubstantial with the being of religion). But Bauer, in order to eliminate the 'religious opposition' between Jew and Christian, predicates the political emancipation of the Jew (and the Christian) on the 'emancipation of religion', on 'abolishing religion' in the sense of abolishing, which is to say radically privatizing all 'religious privileges'. It is at this point that Marx (Raines, 2002: 48) plants the seeds of doubt:

> Bauer asks the Jews: Do you from your standpoint have the right to demand *political emancipation*? We pose the question the other way around: Does the standpoint of *political* emancipation have the right to demand from the Jews the abolition of Judaism and from man the abolition of religion?

Marx's negative answer, and his unique understanding of secularism, interestingly depends on turning to the example of the 'free states of North America' as the testing ground for investigating what happens when 'the Jewish question lose[s] its *theological* significance and become[s] a truly *secular* question.' Where the state is no longer Christian and religious privilege is not inscribed in legislation it becomes possible to confront Bauer's theses with a situation that supposedly presents their empirical, institutional realization. It is only with reference to the American situation that we can ask, as Marx does: 'What is the relationship between *complete* political emancipation and religion?' The peculiar answer, still reason for much debate and investigation today, is that the politically emancipated North American free states are ones in which not only does religion exist but 'it exists in a *fresh* and *vigorous* form.' Consistently with Marx's overall methodology, the American case allows us to see how persistence of religion, far from being the 'basis' of 'secular narrowness' is its 'phenomenon': 'We therefore explain religious restriction on the free citizens from the secular restriction they experience' (Raines, 2002: 49).[31] The persistence of religion is for Marx the symptom that calls for his distinction between political emancipation and human emancipation, between the secularization of the state, on the one hand, and social liberation, on the other. Thus, 'religious weaknesses' are not to be criticized on their own accord but through a 'criticism of the political state'. It is this step which, according to Marx, Bauer is unable to take, being bound, like his post-Hegelian contemporaries, to a fundamentally theological framework.

In political emancipation, according to Marx's dialectical presentation, religion can persist, and indeed flourish (as it does in the American case), because it is ultimately the state which is 'emancipating itself from the *state* religion', and by the same token separating itself from the very civil society in which it tolerates, or indeed fosters, the continuation of private religion and private interests: '*Political* emancipation from religion is not complete and consistent emancipation from religion, because political emancipation is not the complete and consistent form of *human* emancipation.' A 'state can be a *free state* without man himself being a *free man*,' not just because religion continues to be practised in private but because freedom through the state is itself religious in form: 'Religion is precisely that: the devious acknowledgment of man, through an intermediary' (ibid.: 50). This is the key twist in Marx's argument against Bauer: though it might transcend religious 'content' by separating itself from any confessional determination, the state maintains religious 'form' by embodying the alienated freedom of man in something external to him. As he puts it:

> The perfected political state is by its nature the *species-life* of man in *opposition* to his material life. ... Where the political state has attained its full degree of development man leads a double life, a life in heaven and a life on earth, not only in his mind, in his consciousness, but *in reality*. (ibid.: 51)

The private spirituality of atomized, private individuals in civil society is thus accompanied and compounded by the objective spirituality or transcendence (the real abstraction) of the secular state-form itself. Political emancipation 'neither abolishes nor tries to abolish man's *real* religiosity' because it both perpetuates religion at the level of private law (where it becomes 'the essence of *difference*') and spiritualizes human nature, alienating it into the transcendent domain of state sovereignty. Whence Marx's deeply counter-intuitive dialectical affirmation that true secularization—i.e., emancipation from alien abstractions—can only be achieved through an unsparing practical criticism and overcoming of the liberal secular state, which, through a cunning of reason, turns out to be the formal realization of religious content:

> Indeed, the perfected Christian state is not the so-called *Christian* state which recognizes Christianity as its foundation, as the state

> religion, and which therefore excludes other religions. The perfected Christian state is rather the *atheist* state, the *democratic* state, the state which relegates religion to the level of the other elements of civil society. The state which is still theological, which still officially professes the Christian faith, which still does not dare to declare itself a *state*, has not yet succeeded in expressing in *secular, human* form, in its *reality* as a state, the *human* basis of which Christianity is the exaggerated expression. (ibid.: 54)

Marx, in a quasi-Hegelian vein, thus recognizes the momentous significance of this emergence of the democratic secular state, while simultaneously taking the opportunity to suggest that one must move from the criticism of political theologies to a political criticism of the state-form itself. Is this, to repeat Breckman's (1999: 294–295) criticism, to succumb to a dubious 'metaphoric identification of secular and theological phenomena', to portray liberalism as the bearer of a fundamentally religious form of abstraction, whose apotheosis is to be found in the separation of state and civil society?

Final Comments

As I indicated above, while much of the structure of Marx's critique of the Young Hegelian's critique of religion will feed into his critique of political economy, it is also true that the 'secular basis' will increasingly come to signify the mode of production and social intercourse, and only secondarily the state-form itself. Nonetheless, and by way of conclusion, it is important to tackle Breckman's charge of 'metaphoricity'. For the isomorphy, correlation or affinity between seemingly secular and theological phenomena qua forms of abstraction is not just pertinent to the state-form, it is in many respects determinant for Marx's overall understanding of capitalism. Not for nothing, when Marx tackles the elusive ontology of commodities, 'sensuous things which are at the same time suprasensible or social'; which make it so that 'the definite social relation between men ... assumes, for them, the fantastic form of a relation between things,' he is forced to say that in order to find 'an analogy we must take flight into the misty realm of religion. There the products of the human brain appear as autonomous figures endowed with a life of their own, which enter into relations with each other and with the human race' (Marx, 1990: 165). This autonomy, as Marx's brilliant analysis of commodity fetishism demonstrates, goes much deeper (and in turn conditions) the autonomy of the state which 'On the Jewish Question' had laid bare. Marx leaves behind the critique of the religious form taken by a state in which man contemplates and is dominated by his own alienated species being, to undertake the far more insidious 'religion of everyday life'. In this respect, and in spite of Marx's draining of real autonomy and real history from religion in *The German Ideology*, there is considerable truth to Jacques Derrida's (1994) indication regarding 'the absolute privilege that Marx always grants to religion, to ideology as religion, mysticism, or theology, in his analysis of ideology in general'—if by privilege we understand the necessity of the religious 'analogy', for grasping the process of autonomization that characterizes a society, that of capitalism, in which men are dominated by abstractions. This domination needs to move beyond the state-form and into the everyday of production, consumption and circulation, where men 'have already acted ... before thinking' (ibid.: 181). It is only thus, by tracking the emergence of real abstractions out of social relations, that the tradition of anti-theological criticism whence Marx himself originated may be truly surpassed. This criticism was trapped by a fantasy of omnipotence, whereby the mental critique of abstractions, the impious mastery of ideas, sufficed to dispel them. As Marx (1998: 139) wrote of Stirner: 'He forgets that he has only destroyed the fantastic and spectral form assumed by the idea of "Fatherland", etc., in the brain ... but that he has still *not touched* these ideas, insofar as they express *actual* relations.'

Only a study of the religion of everyday life will realize for Marx the project of moving from the criticism of Heaven to the criticism of Earth. Is this to say that a process of historical secularization of abstractions has allowed capital to replace religion in its function, to transubstantiate religion into commodity relations? This is the perspective wonderfully dramatized in *The Religion of Capital*, the 1887 satirical dramatization by Paul Lafargue, Marx's son-in-law, of an imaginary London Congress where the ruling classes of Europe meet to debate which forms of belief can best pacify labour unrest. The emblematic declaration is voiced by the 'great English statistician, Giffen':

> Now, then, the only religion that answers the needs of the moment is the religion of Capital. ... Capital is the true, only and omnipotent God. He manifests Himself in all forms and guises. He is found in glittering gold and in stinking guano; in a herd of cattle and in a cargo

> of coffee; in brilliant stores that offer sacred literature for sale and bundles of pornographic etchings; in gigantic machines, made of hardest steel, and in elegant rubber goods. Capital is the God whom the whole world knows, sees, smells, tastes. He exists for all our senses. He is the only God that has yet to run into an atheist. (Lafargue, 2006: 13)

This very insight was the object of a brilliant, if beguiling, fragment by Walter Benjamin, precisely entitled 'Capitalism as Religion'.[32] In contemporary theory, it has been consistently advocated, from a Lacanian and *Marxisant* standpoint by Slavoj Zizek, who has revisited the theory of commodity fetishism as the basis for a theory of the 'secular' endurance of *belief*, for instance in the 'faith in money-value' whereof Marx speaks in *Capital* (Vol. 3). In light of Marx's theory of fetishism, Zizek reads the predicament of Western capitalist societies as follows:

> Commodity fetishism (our belief that commodities are magical objects, endowed with an inherent metaphysical power) is not located in our mind, in the way we (mis)perceive reality, but in our social reality itself. ... If, once upon a time, we publicly pretended to believe, while deep inside us we were sceptics or even engaged in obscene mocking of our public beliefs, today we tend publicly to profess our sceptical/hedonist/relaxed attitude, while inside us we remain haunted by beliefs and severe prohibitions. (Zizek, 2006: 93–94)

Zizek's position dovetails quite nicely with Benjamin's conviction that capitalism is a 'purely cultic religion' (the rituals of this purely 'utilitarian' religion include sale and purchase, investment, stock speculation, financial operations, and so on).

But can we treat the 'religion of daily life' as the endpoint and culmination of Marx's development of a historical-materialist critique of religion that would also serve as a critique of the critique of religion, i.e., a critique of the idealist incapacity to grasp actual or real abstractions. While I have tried to explore both the persistence of certain theoretical themes in Marx's confrontation with religious phenomena (chiefly the link between religion and autonomization/alienation) and developments therein (the passage from a denial of religious historicity to the possibility of a critical history of religion; the shift of concern from the 'religiosity' of the state-form to that of the commodity-form), responding to the ubiquitous dismissals of Marx's approach to religion necessitates a further step, one which perforce transcends the bounds of this article. What Marx did not do, for very comprehensible reasons of political and theoretical expediency—respectively, an acknowledgment of the 'practical atheism' of the workers' movement and the conviction that for 'Germany, the *criticism of religion* has been essentially completed'—is the examination of the connection between the 'religion of everyday life' (the forms of actual abstraction, belief and fetishism that populate 'secular' capitalism) and the institutions and subjectivities thrown up by religions in their historical and political existence.[33] Only such an undertaking will allow a critical social theory to come to grips with the present 'reenchantment of catastrophic modernity'.

Notes

1. Though works co-authored and co-ideated with Engels feature in this survey, I will focus specifically on the writings of Marx. From his writings on the German Peasants' war to his later reflections on early Christianity, Engels wrote much more extensively than Marx both on the politics of religious belief (for instance in his account of the conflict between Müntzer's millenarian communism and Luther's conformism to princely authority) and on the link between religion and modes of production. Bertrand (1979) admirably reconstructs the outlines of a theory of religion jointly produced by Marx and Engels, whilst also examining Engels's contribution to this project (for example, his comparison between primitive Christianity and socialism). McLellan (1987) provides an uncharitable but useful survey of Engels's writings on religion, whilst Löwy (2005) presents a sympathetic sketch of Engels's contribution to a Marxist theory of religion.
2. Michèle Bertrand (1979) argues that its common use as an analgesic at the time indicates that opium would have been a less pejorative comparator than it is today, and points out that its use with reference to religion originates in Kant. Löwy (2005) cites its use as a simile by the likes of Heine and Hess before Marx.
3. For an example Marxist engagement with the question of liberation theology, see Löwy (1996).

4. For a potent criticism of the limits of theories of imperialism for a 'geosociology' of religious-political militancy, see Bhatt (2007).
5. Marx to Engels, 27 June 1867.
6. The popular anti-theistic writings of A.C. Grayling, Christopher Hitchens, Richard Dawkins and Sam Harris (among others) belong to this category.
7. We might add that Marx never reneges on the rationalist credo set out in his doctoral dissertation: 'That which a particular country is for particular alien gods, the country of reason is for God in general, a region in which he ceases to exist' (Marx, 1841: Appendix).
8. I am grateful to Roland Boer for pointing out to me the importance of this article.
9. This brief, early phase of Marx's intellectual career has been portrayed by Breckman (1999) in terms of Marx's campaign against the transcendental personalism of the Christian state, a campaign which, picking up on arguments formulated by the Young Hegelians, focuses on the solidarity between the principle of sovereignty, on the one hand, and the atomization and privatization through law and property of the state's subjects, on the other.
10. See the commentary in Bertrand (1979).
11. As Derrida (1994) notes: 'Marx advances that belief in the religious spectre, thus in the ghost in general, consists in autonomising a representation (*Vorstellung*) and in forgetting its genesis as well as its real grounding (*reale Grundlage*). To dissipate the factitious autonomy thus engendered in history, one must again take into account the modes of production and techno-economic exchange.'
12. In this regard, it is useful to keep the following assertion from the *Grundrisse* in mind: 'individuals are now ruled by *abstractions*, whereas earlier they depended on one another' (Marx, 1973: 164).
13. Likewise, in his criticism of Bauer in *The Holy Family*, Marx will declare that when 'we come to the *political* part of the Jewish question we shall see that in politics too, Herr Bauer the theologian is not concerned with politics but with theology' (Marx and Engels, 1975).
14. Marx's move beyond the generic and mental abstractions of Feuerbach is explored in Finelli (1987); Rancière (1989).
15. Pinpointing the place of religion within a Marxist theory of ideology, or of the superstructure, is a task far too intricate for the purposes of this article. Suffice it to say that though Marx clearly indicates religion as an ideological form to which there correspond 'forms of consciousness', some of his political and sociological reflections—evident for instance in the 1854 article 'The Decay of Religious Authority' suggest that he did not regard

religion as a *sine qua non* of capitalist ideology. Michèle Bertrand (1979: 152) makes an apposite point in this respect: 'Religion can be an ideology. But it is not necessarily *the dominant form*, and it is not necessarily to be identified with the *dominant ideology*.'

16. Bertrand (1979) tries to develop these insights in a more psychoanalytic direction.
17. In this regard, the footnote in *Capital* suggests the possibility of applying to religious phenomena the 'scientific method' famously outlined in *A Contribution to the Critique of Political Economy* (Marx, 1970: 206).
18. On Marx and Engels's views on Islam in the context of a comparative sociology of religion, with reference to the 'elective affinities' of different religions to various types of protest and social organization, see Achcar (2007). In his letter to Marx of 18 May 1853, Engels writes: 'Mohammed's religious revolution, like every religious movement, was *formally a reaction*, a would-be return to what was old and simple'. This text is quoted and discussed in Bousquet (1969). Marx also tried, in his articles for the *New York Tribune*, to correlate his understanding of the Indian village system and the Asiatic mode of production to the 'brutalizing worship of nature' in Hinduism and to an 'undignified, stagnatory and vegetative life, that … in contradistinction … rendered murder itself a religious rite in Hindostan' (Marx, 2007: 218). Edward Said famously relied on passages such as these to criticize Marx's 'Orientalism', a view in turn criticized from a Marxian perspective in Ahmad (1994). One of the most glaring lacks in Marx's account is of course a study of religion as a resource (a flag and mask?) for anti-colonial political mobilization (for instance in Indian Wahhabism or the Mahdi revolts in Sudan, to take just two nineteenth century examples). See also Hopkins (1990).
19. Étienne Balibar linked this passage to defence of the concept of 'determination in the last instance' (see Althusser and Balibar, 1997: 217–218).
20. These reflections are indebted to some precious suggestions by James Furner. Needless to say, he is exempted for any responsibility for my argument and its possible flaws.
21. The widespread idea of an elective affinity between Christianity and capitalism has come under important criticism, in, among others, Goody (2007); Rodinson (1977).
22. In the *Contribution*, Marx repeats the same insight in an even more 'Weberian' vein when he writes that 'in so far as the hoarder of money combines asceticism with assiduous diligence he is intrinsically a Protestant by religion and still more a Puritan.' In *Capital* (Vol. 3), the 'fit' between Christianity and abstract value even allows for the deduction of confes-

sional differentiations: 'The monetary system is essentially a Catholic institution, the credit system essentially Protestant. "The Scotch hate gold". In the form of paper the monetary existence of commodities is only a social one. It is *Faith* that brings salvation. Faith in money-value as the immanent spirit of commodities, faith in the mode of production and its predestined order, faith in the individual agents of production as mere personifications of self-expanding capital. But the credit system does not emancipate itself from the basis of the monetary system any more than Protestantism has emancipated itself from the foundations of Catholicism' (cited in Raines, 2002: 202). I will return to this idea of faith in the mode of production later.

23. A historical narrative of this correlation can be found in the *Grundrisse*, where Marx tracks the manner in which the 'imposition by the Popes of church tax' can be linked to the emergence of money as the universal equivalent and the corrosion of any 'absolute values, since value as such is relative to money.' This is a situation in which the '*res sacrae* [holy things] ... do not exist before money—as all are equal before God.' Marx characteristically concludes: 'Beautiful, how the Roman Church in the Middle Ages is itself the chief propagandist of money' (Marx, 1973).
24. Though Marx is particularly caustic, in *Capital* among many other places, regarding the hypocrisy and brutality that frequently accompanies religious allegiance. See his denunciation of the hypocrisy of the British ruling class, combining supposed piety with the compulsion of 'Sunday labour' for the working-class ('The orthodox parliament will entertain no complaint of Sabbath-breaking if it occurs in the "process of valorisation" of capital'); or his reflections on the 'Christian colonial system'. 'Even in the colonies properly so called, the Christian character of primitive accumulation was not belied. In 1703, those sober exponent of Protestantism, the Puritans of New England, by decrees of their assembly set a premium of £40 on every Indian scalp and every captured redskin ... .' (Marx, 1990: 375).
25. It belongs to the peculiarity of Marx's materialism that these 'bases' comprise realities that we may regard as abstract, notional or indeed ideal: the value-form, the commodity-form, abstract labour, etc.
26. One crucial question which this article does not tackle is the Marxian response to the idea of an ineliminable anthropological basis to religious phenomena, which no amount of social transformation will ever dissipate. Important indications in this regard can be found in Bertrand (1979); De Martino (1977); Virno (2003). In a far more 'transcendental' vein, Derrida will speak of an 'irreducible religiosity' that no revolution or secularization can displace (Sprinker, 1999).
27. See Stevens (2004). His exacting critique of Gareth Stedman Jones's reading of the *Manifesto* also provides a useful introduction to the political

religion thesis and its contemporary uses. For a popular, liberal-conservative version of its use against Marx and Marxism, see Gray (2007). A positive account of Marxism as the 'historical successor of Christianity,' can be found in MacIntyre (1971). Derrida (Sprinker, 1999: 255) discusses the Judeo-Christian specificity of Marx and the 'messianicity' within his thought.

28. It is interesting to note that in his sympathetic account of the 'spiritualization of politics' during the Iranian revolution, Foucault (Afary and Anderson, 2005: 255) tries to play off the idea of a religion of protest qua 'spirit of a world without spirit' *against* that of religion as the 'opium of the people'.
29. Marx to Lasalle (16 June 1862), See http://www.marxists.org/archive/marx/works/1862/letters/62_06_16.htm. This aversion might also explain why, unlike Engels, Marx does not produce any accounts of conjunctures in which religion may play the role of a flag, a mask or a screen (to use some of Engels's own metaphors) for forms of emancipatory or communist politics. Marx is also unconcerned for the most part with what Gilbert Achcar (2007: 58) calls 'the *incitement dimension* of religion'.
30. This does not mean that Marx believes that the object of politics should be the abolition of religion (though this seems to be a welcome corollary of communist emancipation). From a tactical point of view, he would presumably have countersigned Engels's pronouncement (whose spirit is also present in Lenin's critiques of anarchist anti-theism): 'the only service, which may still be rendered to God today, is that of declaring atheism an article of faith to be enforced' (cited in Achcar, 2004).
31. As noted above, in Marx's early writings this 'secular basis' is still understood in primarily political rather than socio-economic grounds.
32. See the excellent discussion of Benjamin's text, alongside Weber, in Löwy (2006).
33. Some useful indications for a comparative Marxist sociology of religion are to be found in Achcar (2007); Siegel (2005).

7 Nietzsche and Religion

Håkan Sandgren

When Friedrich Nietzsche (1974) places the phrase 'God is dead!' in the mouth of the madman in his book *The Gay Science* he makes certain that he will be remembered, if for nothing else, then for that particular phrase. The phrase has been interpreted by many commentators and the interpretations have led to a number of conclusions as to what Nietzsche really meant. This article will discuss on what Nietzsche based his statement that God was dead, as well as discuss what he meant. It is as important to understand what influenced Nietzsche early in life as it is to understanding his later works in order to decipher his claim about God's death. His writings as well as his biographical information will be examined to find examples that make it possible to understand what he meant. Another angle on Nietzsche's writings that will be discussed here is Nietzsche's atheism. It is often considered that he is an atheist. However, while he speaks about atheism, it is a different atheism to that understood by most people. Nietzsche's atheism is the consequence of him perceiving the Christian God as being a misrepresentation of godliness and not a reaction to theism as such (Roth, 2002). As Nietzsche writes so prolifically and eloquently, it is the intent to let him speak for himself wherever possible rather than rely on commentaries, apart from when they add a new dimension to the discussion.

Nietzsche has written some of the most influential works in the history of philosophy during the 1870s and 1880s. A sign of his importance for Western philosophy is the numerous responses to his work that have been written by those ranging from his greatest admirers to his fiercest critics. Nietzsche writes extensively on the topic of religion and in particular Christianity, which he considers a force that has totally corrupted the intentions of Christ as well as having developed into a religion that he views with utter contempt. However, he acknowledges the usefulness of Gods and in some instances sees a place for religion as, for example, when he, in *The Birth of Tragedy*, invents an anti-Christian counter-doctrine, which he names Dionysian based on the Greek God Dionysus. This counter-doctrine stands for the values that he sees Christianity as having corrupted (Nietzsche, 2000). His view that it is detrimental to follow any authority, without critically assessing the doctrine and thinking for oneself, makes him very critical of any institution either secular or religious, such as the Church. He sees that these organizations create a group that blindly follow a set of rules and conventions.

When Nietzsche writes a new introductory section as a preface to the second edition of *The Birth of Tragedy* (published in 1886, fourteen years after the first edition) he names the introduction 'Attempt at a Self-criticism' and attempts to address the shortcomings of this early work. In the introduction to his translation of this second edition, Douglas Smith (2000: xxv) notes that: 'In retrospect, it [*The Birth of Tragedy*] also seems to fail to identify what should have been its real targets—Christianity and modern science, the religious and secular forms of the belief in a single and exclusive truth,' which is an apt description of Nietzsche's sentiment in his new introduction. A single and exclusive truth is what Nietzsche vehemently opposes and sees as the total enslavement of those that believe in it. His view is that the philosophers are those who are meant to think about and express thoughts about truth, thus, taking away the power from science and religion to make way for discerning and thinking individuals, uncorrupted by religion and science.

The Origins of Nietzsche's Thoughts

Nietzsche's father and grandfather were Lutheran clergymen, as were many of his relatives. From an early age Nietzsche felt the expectation that he should follow in his father's footsteps. His father died when Nietzsche was only five years old and it then became even more expected that he was to become a clergyman. Though he feels a growing unease as regards to his faith, he enters the University of Bonn to study theology where he wins the university preaching prize (Fraser, 2002). He writes in *Ecce Homo*: '... I am merely my father once more and, as it were, his continued life after an all-to-early death' (Nietzsche, 1967: 228). Nietzsche acknowledges the influence that his early exposure to Christianity has on him when he writes:

> I have tried to deny everything. Oh, it is easy to tear down, but to build up! And even tearing down seems easier than it is: these impressions of our childhood, the influences of our parents, our education determine us to our innermost depths, so that those deeply-rooted prejudices are not so easily weeded out by rational grounds or sheer will. (cited in Mette, 1934: II)

As is argued by Giles Fraser (2002), Nietzsche's paradigm as regards to the question of God is largely a paradigm built on influences from his childhood and, in particular, on Martin Luther's way of understanding what God is. As a child, youth, young man and theology student, God was portrayed to Nietzsche using Luther's understanding. Luther sees God as distant and hidden and God's revelation in words, the Bible, as indirect and concealed. Comprehension of God is dangerous and should not be attempted. Blind faith is the response to God that will assure that the followers will be rewarded with eternal life after death (Bowker, 2002). After dropping his studies of theology for studies in classical philology, Nietzsche discovers the philosophy of Arthur Schopenhauer. Schopenhauer's atheistic vision of the world, which forms a platform for Nietzsche's own thoughts on religion, particularly captures Nietzsche's interest, even though he later rejects many of Schopenhauer's ideas (Wicks, 2007).

Nietzsche's Views on Christianity and Religion

It is clear that Nietzsche has distinguished between different kinds of Christianity and that he particularly dislikes the German Lutheran Christianity. In other kinds of Christianity there were also, as Nietzsche sees it, utter corruption of the original ideal and an enslavement of the followers. About 'free-thinking' German people Nietzsche writes that generations have dissolved their religious instinct so that they no longer know what religion is good for. They merely register its presence in the world with a kind of dumb amazement and they have simply no time left for engaging in real religion. When it is required, they perform religious customs with patient and modest seriousness without much curiosity, though they are, in fact, according to Nietzsche, enemies of the customs (Nietzsche, 1989). As regards to religion in northern Europe as a whole, Nietzsche (1989: 62–63) writes: 'We northerners are undoubtedly descendants from barbarian races, which also shows in our talent for religion: we have *little* talent for it.' Italian and French Christianity are not seen in such a negative light. About the French, Nietzsche (cited in Mann, 1939: 15) writes:

> One cannot but allow to the French that they have been the most Christian people on earth—not in that faith of the masses has been greater there than elsewhere, but because the most difficult Christian ideals have turned into men, and have not remained mere images, attempts, half-creations.

Here he has judged the various types of Christianity according to the individuals they foster, which is, it is suggested, what he has done as regards to everything he has encountered. When Nietzsche attacks religious and secular organizations and authorities, it is as a result of what he perceives them to have done in regard to human individual freedom. In judging the religions Nietzsche, among other things, examines the priests and their work. The Christian priests do not fare well under the examination, as they use guilt and punishment as tools for enslavement (Nietzsche, 1968) and neither do priests of other traditions, for example, Brahmins whom Nietzsche accuses of providing cures that were worse than the original disease (Nietzsche, 1967). Nietzsche perceives a ladder of religious cruelty connected to the loss of individuality. He describes the three most important steps as sacrifice of human beings to God, the sacrifice of one's strongest instincts, one's nature, and the sacrifice of God himself as worship of the stone, stupidity, gravity, fate and, what Nietzsche called, the nothing, referring to Eastern traditions where the goal is nirvana, or emptiness (Nietzsche, 1989). Here it is evident that he does object to the way God or the concept of a God is treated rather than dismiss the existence of God or the concept, which is an argument against the view that Nietzsche is an atheist.

Another concept that Nietzsche despises because it takes away the individuality of humans is the concept of loving man for God's sake. When he writes about it, there is a sense that he cannot believe that such a concept could ever have been considered seriously, let alone been made an important concept in Christianity. About the concept and the person that first seriously expresses the concept, Nietzsche writes:

> To love man *for God's sake*—that has so far been the noblest and most remote feeling attained among men. That the love of man is just one more stupidity and brutishness if there is no ulterior intent to sanctify it; that the inclination to such love of man must receive its measure, its subtlety, its grain of salt and dash of ambergris from some higher inclination—whoever the human being may have been who first felt and 'experienced' this, however much his tongue may have stumbled as it tried to express such *delicatesse,* let him remain holy and venerable for us for all time as the human being who has flown highest yet and gone astray most beautifully! (Nietzsche, 1989: 72)

As regards to morals, Nietzsche sees Christianity as the most thorough working through of morals yet undertaken. In fact, he sees Christianity as wanting to be exclusively moral. This has the consequence that all kinds of art are exiled and condemned to the realm of lies. Art is not discarded, according to Nietzsche, but it is *used* by religion and science in a manner that exclude all spontaneity and life force, thus it has been exiled from its true place in humanity. He writes about this non-artistic type of art while also referring to the possibility that the movement away from the previous conformity, present in his time, can change the position of art. He poses the question:

> Will the net of art which is cast over existence, whether under the name of religion or science, be woven ever more tightly and delicately or is it destined to be torn to shreds in the swirling restlessness and barbaric turmoil which now calls itself the 'present'? (Nietzsche, 2000: 85)

He describes the attitude to art by religion and science as being hostile to and showing disgust for life and he writes: 'Christianity was from the very beginning essentially and fundamentally the disgust and aversion felt by life towards itself, merely disguised, concealed, and masquerading under the belief in an 'other' or 'better' life' (ibid.: 9). After observing the Christian view of morals Nietzsche concludes that the first few centuries of the religion had been shaping Christianity into the way he observes it in Germany. He points out how Christianity responded to part of the Greek world-view:

> It was this appearance of 'Greek serenity' which so outraged the profound and fearful natures of the first four centuries of Christianity: to them this feminine flight from seriousness and fear, this cowardly complacency in comfortable pleasure appeared not only contemptible but also as the specifically anti-Christian mentality'. (ibid.: 64–65)

He further writes about the fear that pessimism has fostered following the response to the Greek world-view, which is the fear that the inner strength of man will not be able to face the truth. He writes:

> It is the profound, suspicious fear of an incurable pessimism that forces whole millennia to bury their teeth in and cling to a religious interpretation of existence: the fear of that instinct which senses that one might get a hold of the truth *too soon*, before man has become strong enough, hard enough, artist enough. (ibid.: 1989: 71)

Nietzsche describes ancient Greek religiosity with great respect. He writes: 'What is amazing about the religiosity of the ancient Greeks is the enormous abundance of gratitude it exudes: it is a very noble type of man that confronts nature and life in *this* way.' However, there were to be changes in the Greek religion and he continues: 'Later, when the rabble gained the upper hand in Greece, *fear* became rampant in religion, too—and the ground was prepared for Christianity' (ibid.: 64).

This shaping of the religion that, coupled with blind faith, has become Christianity makes Nietzsche write: 'From the start, the Christian faith is a sacrifice of all freedom, all pride, all self-confidence of the spirit; at the same time, enslavement and self-mockery' (ibid.: 60). Nietzsche experiences the religions as exhausted because the foundations of the religions have degenerated into 'religions for scholars'. Therefore, he experiences that myth, which he sees as vital in religions, has been paralyzed. He writes:

> There is nothing more fearful than a barbaric slave class which has learnt to regard its existence as an injustice and is preparing to take revenge not just for itself but for all generations. In the face of such threatening storms, who dares to call calmly on our pale and exhausted religions, whose very foundations have even degenerated into religions for scholars? This is to such an extent that myth, the necessary presupposition of every religion, is already everywhere paralysed and even this religious domain has succumbed to the domination of that optimistic spirit which we have just characterized as the seed of our society's annihilation. (Nietzsche, 2000: 98)

The optimistic spirit Nietzsche refers to here is the faith in the Holy Spirit and the promise of a better life after death, which leads to a society devoid of individuality and which keeps the members enslaved in positions favourable to the rulers.

As a consequence of his study of the development of religions, Nietzsche sees much to judge. He cannot see anything but danger in religious following. He concludes:

> Wherever on earth the religious neurosis has appeared we find it tied to three dangerous dietary demands: solitude, fasting, and sexual abstinence. But one cannot decide with certainty what is cause and what effect, and *whether* any relation of cause and effect is involved here. The final doubt seems justified because among its most regular symptoms, among both savage and tame peoples, we also find the most sudden, most extravagant voluptuousness which then, just us suddenly, changes into a penitential spasm and denial of the world and will—both perhaps to be interpreted as masked epilepsy. (Nietzsche, 1989: 61)

Thus every thought, ritual, act, rule and moral reified under religion has led to a kind of apoplexy of being and ruined a natural balance and grace of thinking and feeling.

The Death of God

The claim that God is dead does not mean that Nietzsche feels that there is no God or that the concept of there being a God or Gods is a false or useless concept. However, he feels strongly that the Christian God as offered to people has been corrupted and is without value. That he is particularly addressing the Christian God in his statement is clearly evident: 'The greatest event—that 'God is dead' that the belief in the Christian God has ceased to be believable—is even now beginning to cast its first shadow over Europe' (Nietzsche, 1968: 447).

He, however, does not only feel that God is dead but that God has been killed. In fact, the madman declaring that God is dead also declares that 'we' killed him. We, in this case, stand for those following northern European Christianity, which Nietzsche finds utterly wanting, and those who has accepted the Christian way of understanding God. Therefore, Christianity and Christians have become the targets as the perpetrators of the killing of God. Nietzsche sees in the writings of the Jewish *Old*

Testament a God that he can understand and some descriptions of events and person's that he can recognize as being real. He even notices the style as superior to texts in other traditions: 'In the Jewish "*Old Testament*", the book of divine justice, there are human beings, things, and speeches in so grand a style that Greek and Indian literatures have nothing to compare with it' (Nietzsche, 1989: 65). However, his criticism of the *New Testament*, which he sarcastically labels as having a 'true-believer and small-soul smell', is thoroughly developed.

Nietzsche particularly finds Paul's writings objectionable in the sense that he sees those writings as directly leading to priestly power over the followers of the recently established Christian faith. Nietzsche writes about Paul: 'His need was for power; in Paul the priests wanted power once again—he could use only concepts, doctrines and symbols with which one tyrannizes the masses and forms herds' (Nietzsche, 1968: 618). Writings like Paul's letters make Nietzsche see Christianity in particular and religion in general as a means to gain power and rule over the religious followers. In this instance he continues by criticizing Islam for having adopted the Christian attitude of priestly power: 'What was the one thing that Mohammed later borrowed from Christianity? Paul's invention, his means to priestly tyranny, to herd formation: the faith in immortality—*that is, the doctrine of the "judgement"*' (Nietzsche, 1968: 618). In Paul's introduction of a hierarchy in the early Christian communities, Nietzsche perceives and criticizes one of the tactics of religion, the use of splendour and beauty to infuse colour into the colourless existence of many of the followers, which is also a tactic of religions in general. Dazzled by the splendour, the ruled, according to Nietzsche, do not mind being ruled. However, those ruled are not, in Nietzsche's eyes, without blame as they let themselves be ruled and, furthermore, see religion as an opportunity to gain power and become one of those who rule in the future (Nietzsche, 1989). That the *Old Testament* and *New Testament* have been combined to form the Bible has incurred Nietzsche's criticism. For the 'Christians of "educated" Christianity' whom he describes as only knowing 'the needs of domesticated animals' and, therefore being unable to fathom the *Old Testament*, he writes:

> ... perhaps he will find the *New Testament*, the book of grace, still rather more after his heart (it contains a lot of the real, tender, musty true-believer and small-soul smell). To have glued this *New*

> *Testament*, a kind of rococo of taste in every respect, to the *Old Testament* to make *one* book, as the 'Bible', as 'the book par excellence'—that is perhaps the greatest audacity and 'sin against the spirit' that literary Europe has on its conscience. (ibid.: 65–66)

However, it is not only people that are following a religion that has become Nietzsche's targets but every institution that makes people follow and become engaged in a herd mentality, like blind political following, and their followers are targets. He even notices some, if somewhat sarcastically, value in religion as: '… religion can even be used as a means for obtaining peace from the noise and exertion of *cruder* forms of government, and purity from the *necessary* dirt of all politics' (ibid.: 73).

The Late Writings

Nietzsche's critique was at first controlled (a northern European like myself may even say normal), but became more and more stinging, uncompromising and without frills. In his best known work *Thus Spoke Zarathustra*, Nietzsche (1978) outlines most of the themes that will be recurring in later works. Towards the end of his time of writing, the criticism in his writing often became furious, seemingly bordering on the insane at times. It is understandable that outburst like the ones in *The Antichrist* would make some conclude that Nietzsche is insane. His verdict on Christianity in the book is: 'I condemn Christianity. I raise against the Christian Church the most terrible of all accusations that any accuser ever uttered. It is to me the highest of all conceivable corruptions.' Further, he writes:

> The worm of sin, for example: with this distress the church first enriched mankind. The 'equality of souls before God,' this falsehood, this *pretext* for the rancor of all the base-minded, this explosive of a concept which eventually became revolution, modern idea, and the principle of decline of the whole order of society—is Christian dynamite. … I call Christianity the one great curse, the one great innermost corruption, the one great instinct of revenge, for which no means is poisonous, stealthy, subterranean, *small* enough—I call it the one immoral blemish of mankind. (Nietzsche, 1968: 655–656)

In 1886, when Nietzsche writes the new introduction to *The Birth of Tragedy,* he is in the beginning of the phase of his life which brings him to insanity. The works that follow become increasingly direct and sometimes ferocious in their criticism of Christianity. His last productive year, 1888, produces the works *The Wagner Case, Twilight of Idols, The Antichrist, Ecce Homo* and *Nietzsche contra Wagner*. After being certified as insane, he has to spend the last decade of his life in mental institutions totally oblivious of his earlier life and the impact he has had and will continue to have for generations to come.

The books Nietzsche writes in 1888 have often been disregarded as written when he is already insane. It is suggested here that what he writes in 1888 is similar or, in most cases, identical to what he has already expressed in a much gentler fashion in earlier works. Furthermore, it is argued here that the ferocity seen in Nietzsche's late works is not an expression that can be equated to insanity. Rather, it is an expression of helplessness at being, in his eyes, entirely misunderstood. He starts his preface to *The Antichrist*, a book that by many is regarded as entirely affected by raving lunacy, with the passage:

> This book belongs to the very few. Perhaps not one of them is even living yet. May be they will be the readers who understand my *Zarathustra*: how *could* I mistake myself for one of those for whom there are ears even now? Only the day after tomorrow belongs to me. Some are born posthumously. (Nietzsche, 1968: 568)

He continues by describing the qualities, such as becoming indifferent, having courage for the forbidden and being predestined for the labyrinth as well as the reverence and love of oneself and, further, unconditional freedom before oneself that is necessary to understand his work. About those who do not possess those qualities Nietzsche writes: '... what matter the *rest*? The rest—that is merely mankind. One must be above mankind in strength, in *loftiness* of soul—in contempt' (ibid.: 569). These are, it is suggested, the words of a sane but entirely separated man with little confidence that his words will be heard and understood.

In earlier works Nietzsche has discussed the Christian concept of God, as when he writes in *Thus Spoke Zarathustra* that 'God is the thought that makes crooked all that is straight, and makes turn whatever stands' (Nietzsche, 1978: 86). In *Will to Power* Nietzsche outlines how the only way God could survive as a concept is if God is seen as a 'highest power' from which everything follows rather than a 'driving force' (cited in Small, 2001). This is one of the instances where Nietzsche indicates that it is not the concept of God that he is opposing but certain particular ways of understanding the concept. In this case, as discussed by Robin Small (2001) it is the concept of minimal guidance in an extreme form that Nietzsche presents and, though there are only a few other mentions of this particular way of understanding the concept of God in Nietzsche's writing, it is a valid way of understanding his thoughts. With Nietzsche's contempt for any organization that curtails the freedom of the individual, it is not a large step to take to adopt the concept of minimal guidance as the way to give the individual both the incentive to think for him or herself and to create a working social order. The above writings are controlled and persuasive. However, later, Nietzsche becomes disillusioned with his audience.

The style of *The Antichrist* initially reflects an author who believes that explaining is useless. It does not present an argument but statements that the reader is invited to accept or reject. However, it does not take Nietzsche long to abandon the style that has made him state in the beginning of the book: 'What is bad? Everything that is born of weakness' (Nietzsche, 1968: 570) to a discourse on pity as one of the weaknesses of the modern age brought about by Christianity. He continues this theme to critique all of the aspects of Christianity that he sees as detrimental to human beings. About the Christian God he writes:

> … when he degenerated step by step into a mere symbol, a staff for the weary, a sheet-anchor for the drowning: when he becomes the God of the poor, the sinners, and the sick par excellence, and the attribute 'Savior' or 'Redeemer' remains the end as the one essential attribute of divinity—just *what* does such a transformation signify? what, [sic] such a *reduction* of the divine? (ibid.: 584)

Later he continues to venture his contempt for the Christian concept of God of which he writes:

> … God as God of the sick, God as a spider, God as spirit—is one of the most corrupt conceptions of the divine ever attained on earth. It may even represent the low-water mark in the descending development of divine types. God degenerated into the *contradiction* of life, instead of being its transfiguration and eternal Yes! God as the declaration of war against life, against nature, against the will to live! (ibid.: 585)

Having thoroughly placed Christianity in the realm of the negation of life, Nietzsche writes about Buddhism comparing it to Christianity:

> Buddhism is a hundred times more realistic than Christianity: posing problems objectively and coolly is part of its inheritance, for Buddhism comes after a philosophic movement which spanned for centuries. The concept of 'God' had long been disposed of when it arrived. Buddhism is the only genuinely positivistic religion in history. (ibid.: 586–587)

However, though he praises Buddhism in the above passage, he recognizes that there are some problems remaining in that religion as well:

> Perhaps nothing in Christianity or Buddhism is as venerable as their art of teaching even the lowliest how to place themselves through piety in an illusory higher order of things and thus to maintain their contentment with the real order, in which their life is hard enough—and precisely this hardness is necessary. (Nietzsche, 1989: 73–74)

Piety is one of the qualities that he singles out for criticism as one of the expressions of religiosity that hide, or even avoid discovering, reality:

> Piety, the 'life in God,' seen in this way, would appear as the subtlest and final offspring of the *fear* of truth, as an artist's worship and intoxication before the most consistent of all falsifications, as the will to the inversion of truth, to untruth at any price. (Nietzsche, 1989: 71)

After reading the passages about Buddhism that includes praise of Buddhist philosophy as well as thoughts on lack of revenge, antipathy and resentment in Buddhism and further thoughts about practices and prayer, it is obvious that Nietzsche is not, nor sees himself as, a Buddhist. However, it shows that he is not attacking and rejecting religion per se but that he objects to the forms of religion that takes away the freedom and power of the individual. Nevertheless, it is difficult to imagine a religion of which Nietzsche would approve.

Nietzsche's Atheism

When Nietzsche is labelled as an atheist by commentators, it is suggested that it is, as is often the case in commentaries on Nietzsche's work, reductionism at work. Commentators fail to see the complexity in Nietzsche's writings and conclude that since he, in this case, obviously despises God he must be an atheist. As has been seen so far, Nietzsche's contempt for many forms of Christianity cannot be seen as proof of Nietzsche being an atheist. To be without a theist God is not necessarily to be without religiosity or a God. As his statement 'God is dead!' specifically referred to the Christian God, it is also inadmissible as proof of atheism in this case. Nietzsche frequently writes about Gods other than the Christian God, such as Dionysus, and it is clear that it is theism and the systems theism has produced that he despises. Therefore, as discussed by Robin Alice Roth (2002), a-theism is a suitable term for Nietzsche's point of view. Roth (ibid.: 62) writes: 'Simply put, his use of a-theism is his term for rejecting every theism that he regards as corrupt. One might say that in this sense Nietzsche is an a-theist with respect to any theism based on the ascetic ideal.' When Nietzsche discusses atheism in his discourses it is often as a critique of Schopenhauer's 'honest scientific atheism'. Nietzsche sees Schopenhauer's atheism aligned with the ascetic ideal that he has attacked for its illusory faith in absolute values (ibid.: 2002). Nietzsche explains the fact that atheism was gaining popularity in northern Europe towards the end of the 19th century. About European theism, he writes: 'It seems to me that the religious instinct is indeed in the process of growing powerful—but the theistic satisfaction it refuses with deep suspicion' (Nietzsche, 1989: 66). He connects this development to the philosophers at the time when he writes: 'Modern philosophy, being an epistemological scepticism, is, covertly or overtly, *anti-Christian*—although, to say for the benefit of more refined ears, by no means anti-religious' (ibid.: 66). Nietzsche also connects the state of God, as he sees it, to the upturn in atheism:

> Why atheism today?—'The father' in God has been thoroughly refuted; ditto, 'the judge', 'the rewarder'. Also his 'free will': he does not hear—and if he heard he still would not know how to help. Worst of all: he seems incapable of clear communication: is he unclear? (Nietzsche, 1989: 66).

For Nietzsche atheism is not a rejection of God or the concept of God followed by hopelessness and emptiness. Instead it is an outcome of unconditional morality where, in this case, the Christian God has been exposed and devalued. Thus, atheism is a positive outcome that enables a new beginning with a possibility for a different meaning to the concept of a God and transcendence.

Final Comments

Nietzsche's writings have been discussed and commented on since their publication and it is the strength of his writing, displaying total commitment to being true to himself and his views that has called forth this engagement. His views on religion and Christianity have been critically assessed by many and the mistake that has often been made is that commentators have used reductionism to equate his views on religion with his views on Christianity and vice versa. But it is not possible to understand Nietzsche in that way. While immensely critical of religion as a whole and Christianity in particular and, furthermore, while it is difficult to imagine a religion that Nietzsche would embrace, he has assessed religion and Christianity on the impact on human freedom and expression of being that he has perceived them to have at the time in which he lives. He does not bolt the door to keep religion out but keeps it slightly ajar as he sees a possibility of a life affirming, vibrant religiosity, like the one he perceives to have been present in ancient Greece. The atheism Nietzsche has experienced growing around him is, in his view, a logical outcome of Christianity that does not fulfil the need for religiosity in the society. Atheism is an opportunity to find a new meaning for the concept of God. The frustration, he feels when his writings are not understood, makes them more and more direct and intense towards the end of his productive time right up to the time he becomes insane. It has been argued in this article that Nietzsche is sane when he writes the last works but runs out of patience with his audience. The connection between this separation from humanity and madness is not explored here but did become a central theme in the existential movement that was growing in Europe at the time. Though Nietzsche's last works were written nearly 120 years ago, no one reading them now can be untouched by how contemporary they feel and the conviction, honesty and vigour they display. As long as there are thoughts on religion, it is suggested, Nietzsche will be read with interest for he has insights and poses questions about the role of religiosity in society and for individual that are still being explored today.

8 Durkheim and the Sociology of Religion

Swapan Kumar Pramanick

Durkheim, while analysing the origin and nature of social institutions, followed a methodology which we can conveniently regard as sociologism. This is a combination of positivistic methodology and a theory of social primacy. Individual behaviour in society is not the result of his choice and discretion—it has reference to an external system of control. When an individual performs his duties as a family man, he does it because they are defined and regulated by society. Hence, social norms regulate the behaviours of individuals and it is with reference to them only that individual behaviour can be explained. As regards positivism, Durkheim, like Comte and Saint Simon, believed that social sciences should adopt the methods or schemes of the physical sciences (see Durkheim, 1982). Elina Osipova (1989: 217) iterated:

> … he continued the traditions of positivism, in the sense that he systematically examined the rules of the gathering of initial empirical data, of examining the relations empirically established between them and the evidence for hypotheses put forward. He shared the naturalistic principles of positivists, striving to build sociology on the example of the natural sciences … .

So Durkheim believed that systematic generalizations and conclusions can be reached, only by empirical observations. Sociology, as an empirical science, should not be based upon any philosophical presuppositions but rather such philosophy should be constructed only after scientific investigations (see Gross and Jones, 2004). This methodology was applied by him throughout his major writings. His conclusions regarding the nature and utility of religion also were based on this empirical methodology.

Unlike Max Weber, whose study of religion was profoundly historical and comparative, embracing the course of the entire civilization, Durkheim's study was predominantly analytical and structural and it was based exclusively on his minute study of the religious practices of a single primitive Australian tribe (Durkheim, 1912). As he believed this tribe to be entirely primitive, he was of the opinion that the early forms of evolution of this tribe can be traced by studying its religious beliefs and practices. Like other nineteenth century sociologists, Durkheim's interest in religion rose out of four cardinal beliefs:

- First, religion is necessary as an integrating and unifying mechanism. The non-rational precepts of religion create a myth which holds society together.
- Second, religion is a source of social change. This can be clearly proved with reference to Protestantism which gave birth to individualism and secularism.
- Third, the essence of religion lies in its social character. All aspects of religion create in men a sense of membership and a sense of belonging together.
- Fourth, there is an unbreakable relation between religion and the origins of human language and thought. It is in this sense prior to, and the source of, human rationality.

Thus, Durkheim's sociology of religion was based on its unique importance on the origin, continuation and change of the essential features of human society.

The Primacy of Social

Durkheim's theory of religion is to be found essentially in his *The Elementary Forms of Religious Life*, published in 1912 and based on study of the people of Tierra del Fuego, an aboriginal and primitive tribe of Australia. It was an intensive analysis of the religious beliefs and practices of the Australian tribe. This methodology was quite uncommon in his days when there was the wide currency of comparative method and the major trend was to delineate a unilinear line of evolution. Durkheim was led by the belief that the religious practices of the tribe under investigation were the simplest to be found in the world. Not only that, in line with his evolutionary thought, Durkheim believed that the essential ingredients of any institution can be analysed by observing its primitive and simple form. With this aim in mind Durkheim analysed the fundamental and essential elements of a religious system. These, according to him, are the distinctions between the sacred and the profane, the cult and the positive and negative rites—which are to be found equally in the simplest and the most complex religions of the world. Prima facie, religion is a 'unified system of beliefs and practices relative to sacred things, that is to say, things set apart and forbidden—beliefs and practices which unite into one single moral community called a church, all those who adhere to them' (ibid.: 47).

As regards the relationship between religion and society Durkheim thought that religion is always a reflection of society. For according to him '[t]he sacred principle is nothing more nor less than society transfigured and personified' (ibid.: 347). Rather it is a product of man's absolute dependence upon society and upon its symbolic representations. Durkheim (1912: 347) explained:

> ... social life ... moves in a circle. On the one hand, the individual gets from society the best part of himself, all that gives him a distinct character and a special place among other beings, his intellectual and moral culture. If we should withdraw from men their language, sciences, arts and moral beliefs, they would drop to the ranks of animals. So the characteristic attributes of human nature come from society. But, on the other hand, society exists and lives only in and through individuals. If the idea of society were extinguished in individual minds and the beliefs, traditions and aspirations of the group were no longer felt and shared by the individuals, society would die.
>
> ... the effect of the cult ... is to recreate periodically a moral being upon which we depend as it depends on us ... this being ... is society.

At bottom, it is nothing more than man's respect for society carried to a superlative degree of symbolic intensity. It is a symbolic representation of society itself. A believer in religion believes in the existence of a moral power upon which he depends and from which he receives all that is best in him; and this power is nothing but society. It is a system of ideas which also holds society together (Barnhardt, 1977). It is sustained by the belief that outside us there exists something greater than us—the society. Durkheim said that the communal and corporate aspects of religion are far more important than its individual aspects. And in this respect religion is a 'social' fact which acts as a mechanism for regulation of individual conduct in society. Some people living together must have certain strong beliefs and these beliefs ultimately take on a religious character. So he (1912: 10) wrote in *The Elementary Forms of Religious Life*:

> The general conclusion of the book which the reader has before him is that religion is something eminently social. Religious representations are collective representations which express collective realities; the rites are a manner of acting which take rise in the midst of the assembled groups and which are destined to excite, maintain or recreate certain mental states in these groups. So if the categories are of religious origin, they ought to participate in this nature common to all religious facts; they too should be social affairs and the product of collective thought.

The Dichotomy: Sacred and Profane

The processes or structures through which religion acts as the basis of all institutions and functions as a 'symbolic representation' of society itself, are the distinctions between the sacred and the profane, the religious cult and the religious rites. The foundation of religion lies in the distinction between the sacred and the profane. Religion, reduced to its essentials, is a society's classification of 'some' things as sacred and of other things as profane. It is not a distinction between the good and the evil. A sacred thing, by its very nature, is superior to profane things in dignity and power and this is particularly true in its relation to man himself. Man looks upon the 'sacred' with an attitude of awe or reverence and feels a sense or dependence or inferiority in relation with it. Osipova (1989: 242) analysed:

> The sacred (1) had a taboo character, a separateness from earthly phenomena, and was an object of aspiration, love, and respect. The

> sacred was thus simultaneously a source of constraint (taboo) and respect (authority). In Durkheim's view, that indicated the social nature of the sacred, since only society had such qualities: it was at once a source of authority, love and adoration, and source of constraint.

But for Durkheim (1912: 87–88) '[s]ince neither man nor nature have of themselves a sacred character, they must get it from another source.' He continued '[a]side from the human individual and the physical world, there should be some other reality, in relation to which the variety of delirium which all religion is in a sense, has a significance and an objective value' (ibid.: 88). Here he justified the existence of cult.

The distinction between the sacred and the profane is most profound which surpasses the boundaries of time and space. Religion is constituted of the fact that men belonging to it think in the same way in regard to the sacred world and its relations with the profane world and these common ideas are transmitted into common practices. Similarly, every specific institution derives its authority with regard to this idea of the sacred. For example, the notion of right of property comes from the sacredness originally diffused in things and fixed by rituals. The idea of reverence and awe which man has towards the sacred things is a reflection of his similar feelings towards the social order and thus it is vitally related to the society.

The Cult and the Totem

If the origin of the sacred is to be found in the immeasurable value man has always tended to place upon the social order, then the most elemental form of collective representation of the sacred is the cult which is the social molecule of religion. The totemic cult is the basis of religion in its most primitive form. Durkheim (ibid.: 63) explained:

> In reality, a cult is not a simple group of ritual precautions which a man is held to take in certain circumstances; it is a system of diverse rites, festivals and ceremonies which all have this characteristic, that they reappear periodically. They fulfil the need which the believer feels of strengthening and reaffirming, at regular intervals of time, the bond which unites him to the sacred beings upon which he depends.

The origin of religion lies in society, in man's dependence upon society and in man's consecration of the social bonds. The earliest manifestation of this dependence is the totem: the plant, insect, bird etc.[1] But the totemic entity is not worshipped as such. The totem has no intrinsic importance at all; it becomes an aspect of the sacred only in so far as it has been taken over as a symbol of the unity and indestructibility of the group. Durkheim (ibid.: 206) wrote:

> Thus the totem is before all a symbol, a material expression of something else .... But of what? From the analysis to which we have been giving our attention, it is evident that it expresses and symbolises two different sorts of things. In the first place, it is the outward and visible form of what we have called the totemic principle or god. But it is also the symbol of the determined society called the clan. It is its flag; it is the sign by which each clan distinguishes itself from the others, the visible mark of its personality, a mark borne by everything which is a part of the clan under any title whatsoever, men, beasts or things. So if it is at once the symbol of the god and the society, is that not because the god and the society are only one? How could the emblem of the group have been able to become the symbol of this quasi-divinity, if the group and the divinity were two distinct realities?

Thus, the essence of totemism is the use of something external as the visible symbol of the social fabric. In Durkheimian analysis all cults are essentially functional in nature. By the mere fact that their apparent function is to strengthen the bonds attaching the believer to his God, they at the same time really strengthen the bonds attaching the individual to the society of which he is a member, since the God is only a figurative expression of the society. As Durkheim (ibid.: 206) said 'the god of the clan, the totemic principle, can therefore be nothing else than the clan itself, personified and represented to the imagination under the visible form of the animal or vegetable which serves as the totem.'

The essence of religion is not to be found ever in the individual, but only in the community of believers. Though the individual has a faith and devotion in him, behind his faith lies the cult. For Durkheim, anyone who has really practised religion knows that it is the cult which gives rise to those impressions of joy which are, for the believers, an experimental proof of his beliefs. It is not simply a system of signs by which the faith is outwardly translated; it is a collection of the means by which this is created and recreated periodically. Religion is community—cult—or it is nothing but a precarious assemblage of impressions and words with no power to integrate.

Every cult presents a double aspect—negative and positive. Both of them flow from the all-important separation of the 'sacred' and the 'profane'. The function of the negative cult is to free man from contamination by the profane in order that he may be put in position to achieve the sacred. This is the value of self abasement and religious asceticism. The positive cult is expressive of the relationship of God and man which is a reciprocal one. Since the Gods are but manifestations or personifications of society, they cannot do without their worshippers any more than these can do without their Gods. In his view here we touch the solid rock upon which all the cults are built and which has caused their persistence ever since human societies have existed. Thus, the cult is cellular to religion and constitutive to society as a whole. The religious ceremonies multiply the relations between group's members and make them more intimate with one another and by this very fact, the content of their consciousness is changed. When the cult exists and rituals are celebrated, men's thoughts are centred upon their common beliefs, common traditions, the memory of their ancestors and the collective ideas of which they are the incarnation; in a word, upon social things.

Rites: The Visible Manifestations

The religious rites are crucial in that they are the visible manifestations of a communion of spirits.[2] Two essential rites are sacrifice and imitation. The first symbolically bridges the gap between the sacred and the profane and the second, by focusing upon an ideal conception, be it totem or God, supplies the means whereby men may emulate the ideal and thus be spiritually and morally elevated. Beyond these are two other types of rite, which Durkheim calls, representative and piacular. The primary function of representative rites is to commemorate the group's continuity with past and future, emphasizing through sacred observances—the links each living member has both with history and with posterity. These representative rites also subsequently generated aesthetic and recreational activities which have gradually separated them from the religious matrix. This process constitutes one important aspect of the secularization of culture. Piacular rites, on the other hand, introduce another element: the notion of sadness, of fear. All the other rites have one thing in common: they are all performed in a state of confidence, joy and enthusiasm. But the rites which are performed in a spirit of uneasiness and of apprehension are the piacular rites—expiatory rites—which are the ritual cleansing of man from his sins or his affronts to the sacred powers. Between the joyful rites and the piacular, there is a deep affinity. The two poles of religious life correspond to the two states between which society must oscillate.

Final Comments

The functional value that Durkheim gives to sorrow in individual life is noteworthy. Only in his oscillation between sorrow and joy is man made human. So it is with the oscillation between ritual states of spiritual deliverance and spiritual abasement that man satisfies his psychological needs: each is necessary to the other: both are necessary to religion and to society.

Thus, between religion and society, there is a functional interplay. Just as religion can only be collective in nature, so society also depends upon a non-rational, supra-individual state of mind that can only be called religious. The majesty of society is expressed to the individual through religious rites and rituals. It is in this way that we can analyse the proper reason and logic of religious beliefs and sentiments.

Notes

1. Hans Mol (1979) believes that Durkheim imposed 'his own totemic or ordering principle on the interpretation of Australian religion'. According to him, Durkheim did not analyse the tensions existing between different segments of tribal society.
2. For a detail analysis of the importance of rituals, see Giddens (1972).

9 Max Weber

The Sociology of Religion

Kathleen A. Riddell

The influence of Max Weber across the disciplines of the humanities and social sciences persists, despite numerous scholastic and cultural advances, nearly one hundred years after his death. His legacy is not only a result of his wide breadth of knowledge and study, but his insistence on the need for objectivity and his keen attention to methodological processes and applications. Max Weber's perception of sociology was an inclusive science of social action. His main objective was to explain how Western society had evolved, distinct from the East, and become dominated by goal-oriented rationality. In his vision of history, he concluded that the best perspective of modern, Western society could be understood through characteristic shifts in human action.

In an attempt to understand the motivation behind action, particularly within an economic sphere, Weber revolutionized the social-scientific study of religion. He did this by shifting the influence of religion from an 'other-worldly' to a 'this-worldly' sphere, notably that of the Protestant ethic. Through an understanding of how religious motivation may have contributed to the development of capitalism in the West, he provided both an alternative and more significant role for religion. Weber maintained that Karl Marx had proposed a theory which was inadequate in accounting for the complexity of causation (Weber, 1999: 455–56).[1] Marx proposed that the rise and fall of civilizations or societies, were dependent upon a change in, or lack of, productive resources, while Weber put greater emphasis to ideas, values and changing rationalizations in forming shifts in action.

Weber's work is still widely used. He laid down a foundational theory and orientation to understand the motivations and values that inform the actions of individuals. Although there are inaccuracies in his work on Eastern society, the breath of his study (and contrast of Eastern and Western society) was important to the development of comparative study. Weber began his work on the sociology of religion with what was originally an essay, 'The Protestant Ethic and the Spirit of Capitalism'. Other important works of Weber are: *The Religion of India: Sociology of Hinduism and Buddhism (1958), Ancient Judaism (1967)* and *The Religion of China: Confucianism and Taoism (1968)*. He intended to write on further aspects of Judaism, Christianity and, eventually, Islam, but this was interrupted by his death in 1920 (Turner, 2000: xviii). His primary interests were the following: the influence of religious ideas on economic activity, social stratification and religious ideas, and the characteristics distinct to Western civilization.

During the late nineteenth and early twentieth century 'Orientalism' was a popular subject of study. Weber, however, had a different perspective; he was interested in the differences between the Occident and the Orient. Many of his contemporaries portrayed the Occident as civilized and superior to the 'savage' and 'primitive' Orient whereas his goal was more evolutionary in nature.[2] In the following quotation Weber explained the purpose of his approach:

> Anyone who is heir to the traditions of modern European civilization will approach the problems of universal history with a set of questions, which to him, appears both inevitable and legitimate. These questions will turn on the combination of circumstances which has brought about the cultural phenomena that are uniquely Western and that have at the same time ... a universal cultural significance ... . (Weber, 1978: 200)

Puritan and, more generally, Christian religious ideas were found by Weber to have a major role in the development of Western economic systems. Also important in this development was the increasing rationalization present in the Protestant religious orientation. Latently, this orientation contributed to scientific advancements, economic and bureaucratic developments and industrialization. A consequence, however, of this progress was de-humanization or the 'disenchantment of the world': a distinguishing aspect of Western civilization.

This article will provide an overview of Weberian sociology of religion. While it is not possible to account for the breadth of his study, the main points of each work will be discussed in relation to his primary objective to explain the unique aspects of the Western world and how they developed.

The Protestant Ethic and the Spirit of Capitalism

This work (Weber, 2006) was an attempt to apply the 'Protestant Ethic', as viewed following the Reformation as a causal factor for the development of capitalism in the West. The 'Protestant Ethic', in Calvin's formulation, was known as the doctrine of predestination. Within this doctrine lay the absolute omnipotence of God. Consequentially, humanity could know neither why nor to whom God would extend his grace. In order to ease the burden, which among the Calvinists was the possibility of an eternity in hell, followers looked for ways in which they could determine the direction of divine will. As a result, a devotion to one's vocation, in their worldly life, occurred. A lapse of devotion would once again put one's soul in doubt. In much the same way that earlier Christian ascetics deprived themselves, Calvinists turned this asceticism to their worldly vocation. All profit was invested, rather than an expenditure of the benefits of their labour. The Protestant method of continual investment resulted in the most rapid accumulation of capital. In response to critics who insisted that 'highly developed capitalist enterprises existed centuries before Calvin', Weber said that previous capitalist enterprises were, in many ways, held in disdain by the dominant religious order rather than embraced by it. The Puritan's religious convictions allowed them to conceive of their economic success as in accordance with the divine will of God. They may have perceived their investment as fulfilling religious obligations or burdens, but it nonetheless helped to create the structure of modern economic life. In the following quotation from the *Protestant Ethic* Weber provided his definition of capitalism, or the action of increasing the capital:

> We will define a capitalistic economic action as one which rests on the expectation of profit by the utilization of opportunities for exchange, that is on (formally) peaceful chances for profit … . Where capitalistic acquisition is rationally pursued the corresponding action

> is adjusted to calculations in terms of capital. This means that the action is adapted to a systematic utilization of goods or personal services as means of acquisition in such a way that, at the close of a business period, the balance of the enterprise in money assets (or, in the case of a continuous enterprise, the periodically estimated money value of assets) exceeds the capital, i.e., the estimated value of material means of production used for acquisition in exchange. (Weber, 2006: xxxii)

Weber's conception of how the 'Protestant ethic', or specifically Calvinism, contributed to the acquisition of values (money) for the purposes of increasing capital is seen in an inward sublimation of piety, both toward God and secular vocation (another effect of the Reformation). Subsequently, this discipline of frugality led to the investment of the capital and increasing opportunities for exchange rather than an expenditure ('The Spirit of Capitalism'). Through dedication to their earthly vocation, Protestants also saw opportunities for salvation, hence their extreme discipline.

Weber addressed the paradox and its resolution that led to the development of capitalism, in that Protestants, during the aftermath of the Reformation, were encouraged to place piety and devotion into a secular vocation; they were not encouraged to use its profit for the purchase of luxurious and excess goods. The solution was to invest this capital and work to increase its worth by utilizing increasing opportunities for exchange. The paradox within this model was that normally religious Puritanism discouraged an increase of wealth, or excess of any kind, hence the resolution involved its investment rather than its expenditure. Weber (2004: 29) explained how he came to identify these values and motivations and attributed significance to them:

> And even this result is only seemingly possible, since every perception discloses on closer examination an infinite number of constituent perceptions which can never be exhaustively expressed in a judgment. Order is brought into this chaos only on the condition that in every case only a *part* of concrete reality is interesting and *significant* to us, because only it is related to the *cultural values* with which we approach reality. Only certain sides of the infinitely complex concrete phenomenon, namely those to which we attribute a general *cultural significance*—are therefore worthwhile knowing. They alone are objects of causal explanation.

Essentially, Weber was able to attribute the 'Protestant Ethic' to Puritans, and, in turn, the basis of Western economic structure. The Puritans accomplished this through the normative value of investing as an expression of devotion and restraint in God's name. Weber acknowledged that the actions of a community were not based, solely, on one specific motivation or principle, but the overriding value to which one attributed a high level of cultural significance, such as the Protestant ethic, as a satisfactory causal explanation.

After the Reformation, Weber believed that there was a mass action, in sociological terms, that causally led to nascent capitalism or the drive to invest and increase the capital. The cultural reality apparent in this situation was the resolution of Puritan asceticism, a culturally significant value. This was done through increasing dedication to an earthly vocation as an attempt to gain God's favour. And so, becoming a value-concept of predominant cultural significance, a drive to increase capital took place on a mass scale. As time progressed, Weber hypothesized that the Puritans' rationalization of the Calvinist doctrine grew to be incompatible with the original motivations—an attempt to save their souls. For Weber, value-oriented rationality is characterized by striving for a goal, which in itself may not be rational. Such an example is Puritan asceticism. It is an avoidance of condemnation, but nonetheless pursued through rational means, or, in this case, the investment of profit. Weber acknowledged that locating these mechanisms could be problematic and so this is not the only explanation, but the one which has the greatest cultural and rational significance: 'Empirical reality becomes "culture" to us because and insofar as we relate it to value ideas.' Theorizing the action of individuals is an essential component of social scientific analysis because without an understanding of why people do what they do, we cannot have any greater knowledge of the actions in which they engage on a larger scale (Weber, 1968: 15).

This method of locating 'essential value-concepts', was frequently used by contemporary and subsequent scholars (such as Emile Durkheim) in an attempt to locate the mechanisms which drive the ethos of a culture or society. Understanding the meaning of the action for an individual or group of individuals was important for the overriding conception of the greater purposes of such action (Schutz, 1967: 7). Within a 'Hegelian Dialectic', Weber would be the antithesis to Karl Marx. Weber located the societal and economic drives within religious morale, whereas Marx saw religion as a product of society, more specifically, the alienating aspects of class and economic structure.

Overall, this work, within sociology, would be termed an explanation of functional reality in that it is an attempt to explain social action or the predominant social action. The most well-known translator of his work, Talcott Parsons, was heavily influenced by this school of thought, with his most notable work dealing with both the structure and theory of social action. Significant interpretations of Weber's writings were produced by Parsons, along with American sociologist C. Wright Mills.

Aside from *The Protestant Ethic and the Spirit of Capitalism*, Weber wrote three additional books concerning the sociological aspects of religion: *The Religion of India: The Sociology of Hinduism and Buddhism (1958), Ancient Judaism (1967)* and *The Religion of China: Confucianism and Taoism (1968).* After the completion of *Ancient Judaism* he had intended to complete a study of Psalms, the Book of Jacob, Talmudic Jewry, early Christianity and Islam, but he died in 1920 (Bendix, 1977: 285). Structurally, these works are concerned with an analysis of the relationship between religion or religious models and people's orientation to the economy or a work ethic. Religion is a plausible, causal explanation because of the predominant cultural significance. In the following quotation Gerth and Mills (2000: 286) explain why religious world-views, in the approximation of Weber, are suitable ideas in which to anchor causal mechanisms of social and historical change:

> Weber is convinced that intellectually cultivated world-views can be, and often are decisive forces of historical development—because ideas serve to anchor values, which in turn induce dispositions of action leading to the patterning of cultural life, and in this fashion the course of historical evolution takes its peculiar direction. As he explains on one occasion, 'The rational elements of a religion, "its doctrine", have an autonomy … . The rational religious pragmatism of salvation, flowing from the nature of the images of God and the world … under certain conditions had far-reaching results for the fashioning of a practical way of life.'

In addition to the interests described above, it is said that the primary motivation of his work was to explain the elements of Western civilization that were distinctive through a study of differences and similarities between the Occident (Western civilization) and the Orient (Eastern civilization). The culmination of his eventual desire to make contrasting claims between the Orient and the Occident was particularly apparent in the last of these works: *Ancient Judaism*.

Ancient Judaism

Ancient Judaism (1967) was the fourth, and last, of his major works on the sociology of religion. In this work, Weber attempted to explain the historical differences between the Western and Eastern religiosities and expanded his Protestant ethic thesis. An additional, but equally important, concern was the task of contextualizing the rationalization of the modern world within the context of universal history (Turner, 2000: 173). It provided another framework for his previous works on the sociology of religion, but also contributed to his vision of history. *Ancient Judaism* did this by an attempt to explain, in an evolutionary manner, the differences between the Occident, or the West, and the Orient, or the East (Weber, 1967: 3–7). Among the more obvious of differences is the asceticism cultivated in Western Christianity with that of a mystical reflection, such as in India. In some respects, Weber noted that Christianity sought to overcome worldly imperfections rather than withdraw, or accept them, as in many Eastern religions. For example, Confucianism encouraged adaptation to the world, rather than a desire to continually improve upon, or, overcome imperfection, whereas the Puritans approached life with restraint and reason in preparation for an afterlife. This distinction was a result of Christianity evolving out of Judaism, more specifically Jewish prophecy. In the following quotation, Weber explained the reasoning behind this conclusion:

> For the Jew ... the social order of the world was conceived to have been turned into the opposite of that promised for the future, but in the future it was to be overturned so that Jewry could be once again dominant. The world was conceived as neither eternal nor unchangeable, but rather as being created. Its present structure was a product of man's actions, above all those of the Jews, and God's reaction to them. Hence the world was a historical product designed to give way to the truly God-ordained order .... There existed in addition a highly rational religious ethic of social conduct; it was free of magic and all forms of irrational quest for salvation; it was inwardly worlds apart from the path of salvation offered by Asiatic

> religions. To a large extent this ethic still underlies contemporary Middle Eastern and European ethic. World-historical interest in Jewry rests upon this fact .... Thus, in considering the conditions of Jewry's evolution; we stand at a turning point of the whole cultural development of the West and the Middle East. (ibid.: 4)

From examining the fall of the United Monarchy, the dividing period of confederacy since the exodus and the eventual settlement of the Jews in Canaan, Weber saw this as a basic template of how the prophetic movement came to serve as a foundation for the Western civilization in the future. After a discussion of the organization of early confederacy, the Israelites' relation to God, the influence of foreign cults and the struggle of priests against idolatry (which would be carried into Rabbinical Judaism following the fall of the second temple) Weber found that Judaism had not only a profound effect on the other two Abrahamic religions, Christianity and Islam, but was decisive in the rise of the Western civilization as a whole. This was primarily the result of Jewish life being based on an organization surrounding Talmudic law. As seen in the Rabbinical writings, the discussions among the rabbis were a rationalization and negotiation of their social circumstance, and a way in which they could engage in the world while still being in accordance with the Will of God. Weber believed that this process, within Judaism, was instrumental in developing Western rationalization. It was also a key factor in why it, as well as industrialization, did not develop as quickly, or to the same extent, in the East.

In the following two sections, the orientation of Eastern spiritualities will be examined. The discussion is not for comparative purposes in the religious sense, but in order to understand how the ethos, compared to that of the Protestant ethic, did not produce the same religious motivations tied to industrialization and a capital economy.

The Religion of China: Confucianism and Taoism

The Religion of China was Weber's second major work on the sociology of religion. Along with a contrast of Chinese society with the West, specifically Puritan values, he wanted to gain an understanding of why capitalism did not develop in China (Weber, 1968: 247). This, he believed, was the result of the lack of a particular kind of religious ethic that acts as a motivating force. *The Religion of China* was meant to be seen within a larger context, specifically the work of Weber on religious value systems as an influence on socio-economic systems.[3]

The early Chinese state, around the period of 200 BC developed into a united empire. Previously, it had consisted of an informal federation of feudal states (Bendix, 1977: 98–99). Early Chinese cities were centres of small cottage industries; however, citizens did not benefit from the political autonomy or privileges. The strength of this arrangement was laid in the bond of, what is most often termed, kinship ties.[4] In turn, these ties were derived from the religious belief in ancestral spirits. The following quotation, from Weber's *The Religion in China*, describes this belief and practice:

> In any case, in general, it may be said that the orthodox Confucian Chinese, but not the Buddhist, performs his rites for the sake of the fate of the world—for long life, children, wealth, and to a very slight degree for the good of his ancestors, but not at all for the sake of his fate in the 'hereafter'. (Weber, 1968: 144)

The 'Confucian orientation is distinctly 'this-worldly' in comparison to the Puritan emphasis on gaining merit, during this life, which will be of benefit later (ibid.: 226–49). Weber understood Confucianism as a 'religious ethic'. A natural order, or law, of nature existed, in the form of sacred ceremonies, with duties directed toward ancestral spirits. In the religions of China, practice of custom and tradition was of greater importance than a rational calculation of means to achieve a desired afterlife. Religious motivations aside, the Western world or Occident had a basis for rationalization in Roman law, which, notably, was the product of an urbanized business life. In China, the guilds used to compete against one another, but not collaborating to fight for civil and legal rights. For this reason, among others, the Chinese never developed a separate status class, as was common among residents of European cities (Bendix, 1977: 98–99). In other words, advocacy of rights, in the Western sense, was absent.

A number of popular cults existed alongside Confucianism, but without any effort to systematize them into religious doctrine. In turn, this encouraged toleration as well as adjustment to the world. In Europe, however, the Church discouraged deviations in religious observance, and all were united under one rule. The cultured members of Chinese society, or the literati,[5] were deterred from pursuing wealth, though not wealth itself. Rank in China was given more often on the basis of office, or education. As a result of this, those who served in a civil capacity were granted a much high status than a businessman. Consequentially, it can be understood why Chinese society did not develop a capital market in comparison to the Western world (Bendix, 1977: 99–100).

In contrast to Europe, where the Church occupied the domain of secular and state rule, Chinese civilization maintained a plurality of religion, tolerated by the emperor. The ethos of Confucius, the founder of the philosophy, 'lacked the notion that men are differently qualified in a religious way, and beyond these reasons Confucianism was indifferent to religion' (Weber, 1968: 146). Condemnation of folk practices would only disrupt the natural order—a detriment to the whole community.

Religions of China in Comparison with the Western Religions

In his study of Taoism and Confucianism, Weber came to several conclusions. These are:

- Technical or production-oriented inventions were, for religious reasons, opposed. Eastern spiritualism stressed on adjustment to the world rather than overcoming it, as in the Western world.
- Kinship groups often protected its members against economic difficulties, such as the repaying of debts, and in turn, discouraged the development of many important elements of capitalism, such as the rationalization of work.
- Kinship groups hindered the development of a metropolitan status-class along with the development of legal institutions.

For Weber, Confucianism and Puritanism represented a rationalization of one's life order in accordance with the religious beliefs. Though this emphasis was expressed in a different manner, both stressed on the importance of self-control as means to certain ends. The outcome of the rationalization was an accumulation of wealth. In Confucianism it served the purpose of a cultured position of status, such as the literati, which was also an expression of the Confucian values of education, self-perfection and familial piety. In contrast, Puritans used rationalization and its benefits in order to serve God and to take control of what could also result in deviance, the expenditure of wealth on luxury. The intensity of belief and action present in Puritan ethic differed from Confucian values which emphasized on ascetic well-being. The prevailing drive of the Puritan in the West led to the establishment of the economic market of capitalism, and lack of such intensity to channel a similar drive resulted in the absence of this type of market in the East (Bendix, 1977: 126–27).

The Religion of India: The Sociology of Hinduism and Buddhism

Hinduism, as discussed in *The Religion of India,* presented a unique view in the sense that traditional Indian society was segregated on the basis of a caste system, supported by the dominant religious order. Within a caste system, religious beliefs and social status were determined by the caste into which one was born. This system was described by Weber (1958: 29–30):

> Caste, that is, the ritual rights and duties it gives and imposes, and the position of Brahmins, is the fundamental institution of Hinduism. Before anything else, without caste there is no Hindu ... 'caste' is and remains essentially a social rank, and the central position of the Brahmins in Hinduism rests primarily upon the fact that social rank is determined with reference to *Brahmans*.

Essentially, the caste system determined the economic, social and religious function of each individual. In many ways, a caste was similar to a 'status group' in traditional India. A status group was an expression, or absence of, social honour. It differed from a 'class' in that class was normally determined on the basis of one's economic position. For example, the highest caste, known as the Brahmins (the priestly caste), maintained the highest status while also maintaining the greatest religious purity. The caste system was mentioned only once in the Vedas, Hinduism's oldest and most sacred text (ibid.: 29). Despite this, Hinduism was completely dependant upon the Brahminical institution, and the position of each caste could be understood only in relation to the Brahmins.

While modern India has evolved from this traditional economic social structure, the Brahmins, for a long period of time, prevented the development of an urban class. There was little social or economic mobility, as caste was the largest determinant of one's social and economic position in life. In other considerations, Weber concluded that the traditional caste system, supported by religion, served to slow economic development and industrialization. If in Hinduism, the end goal was to escape the cycle of death and rebirth, known as Samsara, and devalue, to a large extent, the benefits of material wealth, then it is understood why it was not the ideal climate for which capitalism to take hold. The Western rationalization of increasing the capital, which developed out of the Puritan notion of investment of monetary goods as a sign of restraint, was not accorded the same spiritual merit in Eastern religions.

Similar to China, Weber observed that intellectuals in the more mystical traditions of India and the Far East tended to be apolitical in orientation, with the greatest division between those who were or were not educated. The uneducated tended to maintain religious beliefs closer to magic and, unlike those in the Western world, lacked any Messianic notion or promise of eternal redemption. Religious belief in the West allows any individual, regardless of class or status, to achieve a desired position in the afterlife, mainly on the basis of virtue, piety and correct practice. In contrast, Hinduism structurally prevented this possibility, while in Buddhism enlightenment was available only to a select, and very dedicated, few. Weber felt that the notions of Messianic prophecy in the Near East prevented Western countries from following the direction of China and India. His work, *Ancient Judaism,* was an attempt to develop this theory further.

Weber and Modernity

Weber identified various forms of rationalization. Rationalization is the process by which one increasingly relies on calculations of efficiency in social actions, rather than motivation derived from custom, tradition or emotional considerations, as common in many traditional cultures (Brubaker, 1984: 1–2). In traditional cultures, actions were guided by customary habits of thought and by reliance on the 'eternal yesterday', that is by custom or ancestral guidelines. The process of rationalization implies an abstraction and calculation of action, or actions, in order to achieve the desired or predicted result (Rheinstein, 1954; Schluchter, 1981).

Rationalization has come to characterize a key aspect of modernity and has largely been associated with the vast number of technological advancements in the twentieth century. Many problems that currently plague humanity, such as isolation due to technology, the resulting de-humanization and the environmental epidemic were predicted over a hundred years ago by intellectuals such as Frederich Nietzsche and Max

Weber. Weber was concerned about the consequences inflicted upon human culture as a result of the processes of rationalization and bureaucratization. Rationalization also led to the weakening of traditional forms of religious governance and moral authority.[6] In some ways, his views are comparable to Marx's notion of alienation and Durkheim's notion of anomie.

In the Marxist sense, Weber felt that alienation[7] was the result of bureaucracy, rather than a direct result of capital economy (Weber, 1978). With regard to actions of greater social significance, agency became associated with larger organizations, rather than at the level of the individual or individuals. Where the interests of a select few outweighed those of the general population, individual motivations became secondary to those that could benefit the organization, or the select few who controlled the organization. Weber pointed out that an important consequence of bureaucratization and increased rationality was de-mystification. For him, de-mystification led to the systematic, logical and reasonable elements in social life which were devoid and emptied of spiritual meaning and moral significance (Koshul, 2005: 12). As outlined in *The Religion of China*, Puritanism became devoid of references to traditional forms of mystical or magical spiritualism, even in its symbols. 'Folk' religion was discouraged in the Western world and seen as a deviant heresy to the higher and rational order of Protestant faith. An example of this would be the witch hunts that took place in Europe and isolated parts of North America following the Reformation. Any practice of 'magic' or irrational behaviour became associated with deviance. Forms of magic and traditional practice in Eastern religions were retained and practiced much longer, not only for their civil and economic benefits, but also due to the Eastern notion that stressed adjustment to the world.

Weber's 'disenchantment of the world', the 'iron cage of reason' and Nietzsche's (1974) parable of the 'Madman' in *The Gay Science* warn that, as a consequence, if 'God is dead' responsibility and the burden of power lie in humanity. This is due to no longer having to project the power onto an other-worldly God, or conception of a God or Gods. Such tropes have as much meaning, now, as they did during the time they were written. In a perhaps fatalistic sense, some have argued that rationalization must lead to de-humanization as it gradually results in the elimination of concern for human values. Industrialization is a process affecting every area of society, the macro and micro, the public and private spheres. Rationalization is both a necessary and inevitable part of this process. As a result, society continues to question traditional and customary ways of being, calculating more efficient and rational ways to conduct its lives.

But this area of Weber's work, disenchantment and modernity, has become debated. Earlier interpretations in the humanities and social sciences imply a negative connotation to some aspects of a completely rational modernity. Such is the case in his (Weber, 1978) *Economy and Society* that indicated an eventual 'polar night of icy darkness', in which increasing rationalization trapped individuals in an 'iron cage' of rule-based, rational control. Weber's vision of the future, then, is not one of complete prediction, but rather of values or sets of values, whose outcome is determined a priori. In his writings on authority and bureaucracy Weber further detailed the effects of rationalization and some of these de-humanizing aspects.

Final Comments

Through an overview of Weber's writings on religion, one can see that he traced economic developments through a world-view informed by a religious ethic. In each of the works *The Protestant Ethic and the Spirit of Capitalism, The Religions of China, The Religions of India* and *Ancient Judaism*, it can be seen that the way a society rationalizes its religious belief has served as a causal mechanism or influence for economic and institutional organization. In the West, Weber theorized that Calvinist devotion to God manifested in an 'economic austerity' by a desire to overcome worldly imperfections. Rather than an expenditure of earnings, one continually wanted to invest. This change in orientation, where one must rationalize his relationship to one another, to his vocation, and to intuitions, has become a foundational aspect of modernity.

In contrast to the West, Eastern society delayed the development of capitalism. This was primarily the result of the Hindu, Taoist and Confucian religious ethic of adjustment to, and balances within, the world. Scholars debated Weber's motivation in conducting his Eastern studies. A consensus, however, lay in his desire to contrast Western society, with the East, where capitalism did not develop. In doing so, he further supported the causal significance of Protestantism. Although factors relevant to the development of capitalism were not entirely absent in the East, there was a unique character to Western rationalism. It was through his Eastern studies, that Weber sought to elucidate the unique character of Western society. Later scholars, some of whom were critical of Weber's work on Eastern civilizations, claim that the failure of capitalism to develop in China was the result of economic factors. While Weber did not altogether disregard this aspect, his work relied more on cultural analysis as factors of influence.

While more could be said about the motivations of Weber's study of China and India, and a large body of work related to its reception, he wrote primarily in support of, and in contrast to, his work on the historical evolution of Western society, particularly its unique aspects. In Eastern civilization, one could see both the socio-economic outcomes that occurred in the absence of Calvinist doctrine and, alternatively, the cultural and economic developments which occurred in its absence.

Weber has been referred to as both an 'inheritor' of the Enlightenment, and a 'Father' of modernity. He has served as a bridge between the two, continuing the growing momentum of the Enlightenment reason, and placing it into the context of modernity. Reason and rationality have come to prevail over magic and enchantment: 'emptying' and 'de-mystifying', in the words of Weber, the modern world. In simple terms, reason and magic, have separated the East and the West and have resulted in a transference, or projection of, enchantment onto the 'Orient'. Neither the East nor the West, at least conceptually, has any ontological stability; however, the ideas of Weber and those whom he has influenced, continue to influence the way we understand the world.

The 'disenchantment of the world' has been described as having its 'ideological origins in the Enlightenment critique of religion' (Casanova cited in Koshul, 2005: 1). While it is evident that Weber has been influenced by the Enlightenment, his relationship to religion is not entirely hostile, and, at one point, he notes that 'only a hairline separates faith from science' (ibid.: 1). Western rationalism is not entirely devoid of 'supra-rational' elements and any 'scientific inquiry' must be based on an 'unscientific ground'. The relationship between science and reason, and religion and enchantment becomes one of interrelation rather than contrast.

One of the most famous examples Weber provided of the complex and intertwined relationship between religion and reason was the 'iron cage'. As a metaphor in *The Protestant Ethic and the Spirit of Capitalism*, it symbolized the methodical order and control in which a Puritan lived. In this instance, a Puritan would rationalize his or her own faith into a mode of existence in which a by-product of economic gain resulted, yet still remained in good spiritual standing. The term often implied a sense of imprisonment, in this case, by one's own reason (Swedberg, 2005: 132). The 'iron cage' was not the actual term used by Weber to describe this condition, rather it was the one chosen by Talcott Parson, the first translator of the work (ibid.: 132). The original intention, and from which the connotation 'iron cage' arose, was that of a figurative description of the Puritan: to wear 'his worldly goods "like a light cloak which can be thrown aside at any moment"—but … this light cloak has today become an "iron cage"' (Weber cited in Swedberg, 2005: 132).

Another way Weber characterized the relationship between religion and reason, or modernity in general, was through his discussion of the disenchantment of the world: 'The fate of our times is characterized by rationalization and intellectualization and, above all, by the "disenchantment of the world"' (Gerth and Mills, 2000: 155). This phrase explains the notion by which people no longer relies upon religion and forms of enchantment, such as magic, to explain their every day lives, but relies on their own reason and rationalization. It has the same 'limiting potential' as the iron cage, particularly when discussed in relation to themes of secularization and the technological revolution, because individuals become distanced from one another and institutions, as their lives become a process of 'routinization'. The 'disenchantment of the world' also captures the way humanity considered, and captured, the world.

Weber's vision of history, and the use of the Protestant ethic as an exemplar, distinguishes an important break in sources of knowledge and the rise of intellectualization. Scaff (1989: 241) describes this problem: 'The sense of expansive discrepancy, of an increasingly radical tension between this world and the thought to be inviolable self seems to be at the basis of our most serious and austere responses to a disenchanted fate.' Ultimately, humanity should be able find a 'way to experience wonders and marvels while avoiding enchantment's potential to beguile' (Saler, 2004: 139). In doing so, we are neither depriving ourselves of, nor limiting ourselves to, sources of knowledge.

Overall, an important characteristic of his work is the relationship between interests and ideas and this is particularly developed in his sociology of religion (Swedberg, 2005: 121). Historical action is not simply the result of an idea, but motivation by the interests of the group. Puritans may have developed the 'idea' of capitalism, but it has resulted in a motivation to fulfil their devotion to God. It may be said that Weber's greatest merit is that he critically studied other influential thinkers of nineteenth century European thought—namely Karl Marx and Friedrich Nietzsche. In doing this, he created a methodology and a body of knowledge dealing with the sociology of religion, economics and the sociology of political parties, small group behaviour, and the philosophy of history. His work continues to inspire scholarship, while also finding modern applications.

Notes

1. Weber was particularly critical of the Marxist notion that economic factors determine what occurs in society.
2. For a more detailed discussion of the evolution of such scholarship, see Said (1994).
3. For more information, see Kalberg (1999).
4. Weber described kinship groups as being concerned with in-group interests. Members of kin groups may expect to inherit from one another. The interests of kin groups, in the estimation of Weber, were contributing factors to the reasons why rational capitalism did not develop in the East.
5. The literati were respected high-ranking members within Chinese society, well educated in literature and traditional arts. From this position, they were seen to be the 'rational administrators of intelligence' (Weber, 1968: 107–109).
6. For more detailed discussion of the relationship between rationalization and its effect on culture, see Schluchter (1981); Weber (1993).
7. Weber used the term de-personalization, rather than alienation, to describe these phenomena.

10 Interrogating Religion

A Critique from the Enlightenment Perspective

Soumyajit Patra

Certainly we know very little about prehistoric religions, but it is sure that some of the early human cultures 'have contained traces of religious orientation' (Hultkrantz, 1982: 22). The Peking man, who lived about half a million years ago, for example, had developed their own religious practices. The Neanderthal man also had some concept of religion. They buried dead body with some particular rituals and ceremonies and had some belief in life after death. Hultkrantz (ibid.: 25) writes that it is with the emergence of the *Homo sapiens* (about 30,000 years ago) the 'religious patterns which we could glimpse in earlier periods' took a definite form.

The existence and consolidation of religion for such a long period of time in the history of human civilization definitely justify the theory of 'fear' concerning its origin. This fear can be explained from two aspects, first, the fear of uncertainty of life and nature, and second, the fear of limitations of human ingenuity and control over the events in concrete situations. These two important and related issues, however, give rise to different reactions so far as the question of God-man relationships is concerned. Sometimes, God is believed to exist in and intermingled with every major and minor events and relations, and thereby the believers can take a relief from their tensions. As God is there in every phenomenon and with everyone, they believe, He will save them from all dangers and undesirable events. Thus, the identification with someone, who is all-powerful and generous, known as God, reduces the fear of dealing with things alone. Even among some tribal communities this kind of feeling is prevalent. Robert Brow (1982: 31) says that this 'high god' of the tribal people 'is no longer worshipped as he is not feared.' The opposite reactions are also found, even among the believers of the same religion: this is to consider God as living in a sacred world, quite distinct from that of the humans. From there He watches and governs the course of the events of the whole universe. What He does obviously is beneficial for the mankind: His own creation. It is not difficult to explain that both notions are embedded in the theory of predestination and providentialism.

One positive, direct or indirect, consequence of explanations of all real sufferings, frustrations and failures, in terms of God's Will, is that the subjects in the true sense have been able to vanish from the scenario that reduces their mental agony and external pressures. This may be termed as the 'strategic need of religion' that till now helps. So despite the emergence of rational thoughts that reject the existence of spirit or supernatural world among a section, the influence of religion, though gradually decreasing, exits with varying degrees among a large number of population. The obvious question, is that in what sense then the God is dead?

So far as the Enlightenment philosophy of eighteenth century, with all its emphasis on reason, attacked providentialism that believes in 'God's care for the world after its creation' (Lyon, 1999: 7), the earlier hegemony of religion started declining. As a result of the shift in the emphasis from providence to reason, the notion of progress on the basis human ingenuity and human initiative, as opposed to divine intervention, came into being. This change in explanations had far reaching consequences on the all-embracing influence of religion. The almighty religion, in course of time, in all modern democratic set-up, has been reduced to a matter of choice ensuring the virtual death of God.

Secularism, as the new paradigm having what Kar (2006–2007: 70) says 'no visionary speculation concerning supra-empirical transcendental sense of divinity', not only became the fashion for the eighteenth and nineteenth century social scientists, but it percolated rationality in every aspects of life in such a way that dependence on God had largely been reduced. In philosophy also the medieval ways of looking at things exemplified in the writings of Thomas Aquinas and others were questioned and ultimately relegated. There were also strong reactions among a section of social scientists against this type of what may be called the Enlightenment archetype, and as a consequence a conservative predisposition that sought for the revival of tradition and spirituality was found.

Religious excellence had been elevated by these so-called critics of the Enlightenment thought to a level beyond all this-worldly munificence, and its association with Gods, who were believed to possess the qualities that cannot be attained by the human beings, was believed to be the cause of its omnipotence. As Nietzsche (1986: 61) critically pointed out '[t]he religions were thus—such was the assertion of all opponents of the Enlightenment—supposed to express sensu allegorico,[1] having regard to the understanding of the masses.' The arguments of the theists, however, have been severely criticized.

First, following Feuerbach's (1957) analysis that man himself attributes divinity to some socially created values and passed it on to religion, it has been said that as what man considers good have been attributed to the God, those qualities are very much this-worldly and man-made. Second, God is all-knowing and all-powerful is a false assertion which becomes evident from day-to-day ailing-experiences of common people. That means God is either non-existent or imperfect. Thus, the dominant and mainstream thought of the Enlightenment celebrating the triumph of reason ultimately survived. Religion, in course of time, was not only considered as a false consciousness, but also regarded as a hindrance to scientific development which was evident in Schopenhauer's declaration that religion never contained a truth.

All-too-human: A Note from Nietzsche

Having lost all his faith in traditional beliefs and practices, Nietzsche tries to analyse critically the origin of religion from a what may be called all-too-human antispiritual point of view. What particularly attracts his attention is the lack of 'any conception of natural causality' of the primitive people (Nietzsche, 1986: 63). In such 'religiously productive primitive cultures' every natural phenomenon is considered as the action of 'conscious and volitional beings' and is characterized by 'tremendous complex of arbitrariness' (ibid.: 63). Nietzsche (ibid.: 63) writes:

> Becoming ill and dying never occur naturally; the whole conception of a natural occurrence is lacking—it first dawns with the older

Greeks, that is to say in a very late phase of mankind, in the conception of a moira (fate) enthroned above gods.

Man tried to control this 'dreadful, mysterious nature' with the help of the sorcerers. Nietzsche believes that 'the sorcerer is older than the priest' (ibid.: 65). What is important is that Nietzsche here points to a very much this-worldly cause in his analysis of the origin of religion. He analyses: 'the believer in magic and miracles reflects on how to impose a law on nature: and, in brief, the religious cult is the outcome of this reflection.' He is happy, however, that man's cognitive power has increased and he no longer believes these.

Emphasizing on the importance of critical reasoning and scientific analysis Nietzsche renounces traditional religions on the ground that though religion has what he calls a 'narcoticizing effect' in the sense that it helps find out pleasure in pain, it reverts our attention from the true, this-worldly and all-too-human cause (source) of the pain. He (ibid.: 60) clearly opines:

> The more a man inclines towards reinterpretation, the less attention he will give to the cause of the ill and to doing away with it; the momentary amelioration and narcoticizing … . The more the domination of the religion and all the arts of narcosis declines, the stricter attention men pay to the actual abolition of the ill … .

He thinks that traditional religions have lost its usefulness. Nietzsche's celebrated announcement of God's death endorses his basic philosophical standpoint. To him the death of God has mixed consequences. It is at the same time a 'cultural disaster and a philosophical blessing' (Clive, 1965: x). Nietzsche who time and again has advocated the importance of 'cognition' and 'rigorous quest for the way things are' (ibid.: xxviii), is sure that the death of God is a clear insinuation of the real spirit of his time, a spirit that celebrates reason. He simultaneously feels that the true significance of religion has not been realized by the Enlightenment thinkers. He believes that man cannot live only by reason, a theoretical stance that has been developed later by Max Weber. Nietzsche here acknowledges the importance of myths and illusions. Interestingly, in a unique analysis he declares that art will be the substitute of religion to '*post-Christian* Western man' (ibid.: xxiv emphasis added).

Alternative Expressions: Beyond the Primacy of Spirituality

The analysis of 'religion as belief' as opposed to 'religion as ideology' brings about the issue of its actual effect on social and political life to the fore. In other words to what extent the legitimacy of the principles of religion could be kept intact when it is judged from the perspectives and practices of the believers in actual situation has been doubted and questioned. In fact, in a pluralist cultural tradition 'a segment, a caste, a religious category—carries not only social bonds' but also exhibits 'animosities and antagonism, directed at other segments' (Saberwal, 2001: 201). The reason behind this paradox lies in the fact that though every religion, in theory, contains some integrating and moralizing principles, in practice, as Beteille (2001: 306) thinks, it leads to 'the tendency to define itself in opposition to other religion … .' This tendency denies the primacy of spirituality and takes different forms depending upon the situation.

In his classic analysis of democracy in America, Tocqueville (1954) has attributed the success of democracy in that country to the flexibility of religion that incorporated the spirit of liberty in its own ideological foundation. It is implied that the basic principles of religion honoured individual rights in such a way that an environment favourable to cultural pluralism had developed slowly in that part of the world. Tocqueville had in mind that the appeal of religion was so strong in America that without its support true democracy in civil society was impossible. What he could not foresee was that religious fundamentalism and the spirit of liberty could coexist. Even that kind of fundamentalism, as an alternative expression of the 'theoretical' spirituality, could be evidently supported or at least taken for granted, by what may be called the silent majority. Giddens (1993: 483) has rightly observed that 'the growth of fundamentalist religious organizations in the United States is one of the most notable features of past twenty years or so. Christian fundamentalism is a reaction against liberal theology and against in-church secularization … .' As a consequence 'fundamentalism is much more prominent in the United States today than in other industrialized countries' (ibid.: 485).

Despite the fact that Americans have some sense of equality, some skills and technical knowledge, American society is not free from religious fundamentalism. Here lies the danger of 'religion as faith'. It seems that every religion in the world has some elements which can give rise to religious fanaticism and destructive dogmatism, latent or manifest. Examples of this kind of ethnocentric aberrations can be found in India, Pakistan and in the states of Middle East.

In fact, beyond the primacy of spirituality and transcendentalism, there is an apparently indiscernible insider-outsider categorization in every religion that ultimately creates, if not encourages, a feeling of distrust and enmity. It is often erroneously said, following some of the classical sociologists, that the social expression of religion is also spiritual that increases solidarity. This is true so far as the insiders or the followers of the same religion are concerned; with regards to the 'others' the animosity sometimes takes violent forms. Saberwal (2001: 201) correctly says that where 'identities which lay claim to sovereign truth are caught in antagonistic relations the ensuing conflicts can be devastating.'

It is interesting that the emphasis on reason through the introduction of cause-effect frame of reference in the analysis of social and natural phenomena and in philosophy, the popularity of anti-religious materialism in the writings of, for example, Denis Diderot and other Enlightenment thinkers weakened the spiritual dimension of religion, but religion as a source of identity formation remained important as before.

When the dialectic between reason and faith, in the process of secularization, puts religion in its own domain separated from other areas of life, for example, polity, education and economy, religious sentiments and religious identities are often tactfully used for political mobilization. The so-called safronization of politics in India is a case in point. If we think that there are spiritual reasons behind the agenda of some political parties to campaign explicitly in favour of what is called cultural nationalism, it would be erroneous. This cultural nationalism will be based on Hinduism, the religion of the 'majority' in India. Unfortunately, a significant portion of the masses too supports this agenda. Beteille (2000) here reminds us that Hinduism, as an ideology, never encourages assimilation. The tension between 'religion as an ideology' and 'religion as a belief and practice' is increasing and a logical interpretation of this discrepancy puts a significant note of interrogation on the existence of God. Austin Cline has put forward a fundamental question that seems very much relevant here:

> If there are any gods, why don't they act to eliminate it [evils]? The absence of substantive action against evil would be consistent with the existence of evil or at least indifferent gods, which is not impossible, but few people believe in such gods. Most claim that their gods

are loving and powerful; the suffering on earth makes their existence implausible.[2]

From Maturity to Movement

Immanuel Kant, in his famous article 'What is Enlightenment?' has put forward the idea that as rationality was prioritized during the Enlightenment man had subsequently come out of his dark age of infancy and reached its adulthood (cited in Gandhi, 1998: 30). Reason per se, became the ethos of every explanation of social, physical and natural phenomena that ultimately paved the way for advancement of human civilization. That was, as Kant described, the reflection of the maturity human being reached at.

In the evolution of human thought this transformation brought the humans to the centre stage negating the earlier belief in the invisible hands of the Gods in creating history. Modern secular humanism simply promotes values that have nothing to do with divine sanctions. This stance further strengthens the 'No-God thesis'. The sharp divergence in the world-views, from supra-empirical spiritualism to practical rationality, is being found among the common people also. A 2001 estimate[3] says that the average increase in the number of atheists in every 24 hours in the world is 1200.

Modern secular humanism, a direct corollary of the Enlightenment thought, also has become, in course of time, the creed of different atheist movements throughout the world, that, realizing the harmful consequence of blind faith, superstition and irrational dependence on God, have started campaigning for intransigent scienticism in the explanations of all social and natural phenomena.[4] This has received responses from different sections, and secular humanism has become a ready frame of reference for many.

To popularize the materialistic interpretation of the world we live in, Marxian analysis also plays a significant role. That historical transformation is not the function of God's Will, rather it is the dialectic hidden in the economic infrastructure, has been the basic proposition of a group of thinkers and the atheist movements are strongly supported by them.

In an era of globalization the importance of God has remarkably been decreased. Lyon (1999) has correctly identified the basic feature of a globalized culture: the continuous insistence on possession and an urge for hedonism. The difference with the principles of religion is thus sharp and fundamental. Consumerism is characterized by a thrust to possess more and the emphasis is on what Habermas calls 'instrumental reason'; religion on the other hand, is characterized by a thrust to sacrifice more and the emphasis is on blind faith.

Final Comments

Philosophical paradigm that distinguished the Enlightenment thoughts from all sorts of its earlier versions was distinct in the sense that it, perhaps for the first time in the history of mankind, inundated providentialism in a very organized and logical manner. Reason per se, being in its core, became the ethos of every explanation of social, physical and natural phenomena that ultimately brought cause-effect reference framework to the fore. That new and radical change in what may be called world-views had not only far reaching influence on scientific discourses, but also initiated an era of declining religious influence. The notion of progress on the basis of human ingenuity, instead of God's Will, slowly but steadily won over spiritualism, and dependence on God was reduced that gradually weakened the earlier hegemony of religion. Growing rationality and the diminishing significance of religion were so prominent that Nietzsche announced the death of God. For Nietzsche (1986) '[p]eople whose daily life appears to them too empty and monotonous easily become religious: this is understandable and forgivable; only they have no right to demand religiosity of those whose daily life is not empty and monotonous.'

Notes

1. This means that a sense of allegorical representation is implicit in the philosophical framework of religion as if religious characters are symbolic representation of the reality.
2. See his arguments against the existence of God in http://atheism.about.com/od/aboutatheism/p/whynotbelieve.htm
3. See www.bible.ca/global-religion-statistics-world-christian-encyclopedia
4. The proclamation 'God is dead' made by Nietzsche (1974) has been the inspiration of these movements. This famous statement first appeared in his *The Gay Science*.

Section III

The Local and the Global

11 Understanding Tribal Religion

The Garos in Bangladesh

Zahidul Islam and S.M. Arif Mahmud

Religion is such a term that itself leads to many emotional responses. It is a phenomenon as old as the history of mankind itself. 'Even since the primitive religious views were published by E.B. Tylor in the late nineteenth century, no ethnographer has reported any primitive society without touching religious beliefs and practices' (Hasnain, 1983: 58). During the course of the development of human thought it has not only attained varied meanings but also led to multitudes of thought, beliefs and practices. Religion is often defined as supra-sensory phenomenon constituting human relations to the supernatural. The 'world-view' conception of religion 'implies all the beliefs and ideas by which a person, or, a culture, perceives, orders and reacts to the powers of the universe and natural phenomena, including the human body (Maloney et al., 1981: 1). In a similar way, after pronouncing the theory of 'animism', Tylor (1958: 23) defines religion as 'the belief in the supernatural powers lying behind natural objects.' He continues '... among the lower races, the development of animism; that is to say, the doctrine of souls and other spiritual beings is general.' However, one thing is clear that 'fear' is very important in all primitive religions. Be it fear of material loss or disaster, or, of loss of crops, attack of the enemy, of being preyed upon by wild animals in the forest or solitary caves, of scourges, epidemics and death or of fear of damnation and eternal torment in the hereafter (Sattar, 1975: 17).

In India, studies have been conducted on different aspects of tribal religion in particular and tribal culture in general. The pioneers of these studies were mostly the European travellers, missionaries, natural historians and some of the administrators during the British India (Troisi, 1978: 9). Perhaps the first detailed monograph on the Garos, a tribal community, was written by Major Playfair in 1909. Various census reports also contain some ethnographic records on different aspects of tribal religions and their beliefs and practices in Bangladesh.

However, this article is based on an empirical and in-depth anthropological research among the Garos living in Andharupara village of Sherpur district in eastern Bangladesh. This village accommodates some other groups like the Muslims, Hindus and Koch (a tribal community) etc. The purpose of the present study is to focus on the religious values, beliefs and practices of the Garos, living in a multicommunal as well as multicultural setting. The issue of change in their traditional religious faiths and values and the problem of their accommodation as a part of the mainstream religion in Bangladesh have also been addressed.

The Garos and their World of Religion

The Garos have their own religious beliefs and rituals. Fear of the supernatural seems to be the foundation of their religion. Their traditional religion is known as Sangsarek, which derives its name from all those fears that frequent them and are manifested in their beliefs and related weird cults of animism and ancestor worship. But according to Zangcham (n.d.: 58), the Sangsarek religion seems to be related with animism but it also has belief in spiritual content like others. In fact their religion has no written record; the Garos only depend on memory for the preservation of their traditional myths. So their mythology varies with change of places and circumstances (Dalton, 1847: 28). Different groups among the Garos have different Gods, Goddesses and spirits. A few of them have common spirits too, but they have different names in different places. Therefore, it is difficult to say that the Garo religion is totally animistic. The Garos believe that it is the supernatural power that has created the earth and the human beings, the best of all his creations.

Fatalism is also found among them like the Muslims and Hindus who believe in 'Takdir' and 'Adrista' respectively (Maloney et al., 1981: 32). Whereas fatalism gives solace, it also generates inaction and stands on the belief that the events of nature and human life have a mysterious relationship. It may be seen as an irrational but the shortest process of peace to mind. The Garos believe that luck (Bhaigya) is determined by God and it has a significant place in their life. They also believe that whatever happens in one's life is determined by the Ishar (God) and it is not changeable. Even sickness and diseases are considered as the results of the sinful deeds. Their belief in luck is also expressed in their belief in God as the creator and destroyer of the world.

As it is seen the Garos express some philosophical and secular attitude towards religion. Most of them describe their religion as 'Christian Dharma-Ba-Namma', 'Sangsarek Dharma-Ba-Namına', and 'Ghismic Mandharang Ishlani Bisha'. It means every religion is good. We are all sons of God whether we believe in Sangsarek or Christianity. In terms of religious beliefs and practices these people express negative attitudes. This is definitely rooted in their socio-economic conditions. Perhaps their poverty has induced some sort of alienation from religious beliefs and practices. Interestingly, Church Father of Baromari Mission iterates that the Garos (Christian and Sangsarek) are not interested in rigorous religious practices, and they do not visit church regularly and do not observe some religious ceremonies due to their economic handicaps.

It should be mentioned here that the impact of Christianity on these tribal community has been enormous. Actually, Christianity in Mymensingh district of Bangladesh was popularized by the Christian missionaries during the British rule. Perhaps the first Christian mission was established at Mymensingh in 1837 (Majumdar, 1906). The name of the mission was 'The Australian Victorian Baptist Foreign Mission' (ibid.: 44). However, in course of time, about eight different Catholic church missionaries were established in the Garo area of Mymensingh. With the missionary intervention the Garos came into close contact with Christianity and eventually some of them adopted Christianity. Such religious conversion is still going on.

Transmigration of Soul and Rebirth

The Garos believe in transmigration of soul and rebirth. They think that the soul turns into ghosts or insects and beasts after death, especially if it happens to be the soul of a sinner (Hamilton, 1820: 95). Burling (1963: 54–55) has rightly observed that they think that 'these spirits are present everywhere—in the sky above, on the earth, beneath the depth of the waters, trees and bamboo groves.' Rivers and lakes, mountains and hills, trees and shrubs, sticks and stones are also some important dwelling places of the spirits. Similarly, as per Garo religion the stars, the sun and the moon are all associated with some spirits which are immortal (Sinha, 1966: 48).

Good Spirits and Evil Spirits

The concepts of good and evil spirits are important in Garo religion, but both types of spirit are known as deity. The names of the deities are remarkable and, in some cases, they bear the teknonymous affixes for father or mother (Sangma, 1981: 221). The principal names of Sangsarek Garo deities are Tatara (Rabuga), Saljon, Nostu (Nopantu), Chorbudi, Geora, Kalkame, Susime, Asim (Dingsma), Tongrengma and Nawang. All the mites among the Garos represent different beliefs and functions. Playfair (1909: 80) explains:

> ... the numerous deities among the *Garos* are composed of both benevolent and malevolent deities. Some of them were regarded as the creator of man, the world, and all that is therein, as controllers of natural phenomena, while others as the shaper of destinies of man from birth to death. It is because such powers have been attributed to them that they offer sacrifices to propitiate them.

They are afraid of the evil spirit or Nawang which creates diseases such as pain in the stomach, vomiting and diarrhea. This evil sprit often comes at a man's death bed to devour him when he is dead.

Worship of Natural Phenomena and Human Sacrifice

Once the Garos practised human sacrifice. The death of Nokma often called for a sacrifice. It was based on the belief that a rich man should have a servant during the journey to the land of the spirits and such immolation of slaves and captives was a frequent occurrence. For such sacrifices they captured a slave and if a slave was not found, raids were made on the plains to procure one. When the victim was brought in, it was customary to lay the body on a funeral pyre (Ganchi) around which the people danced. The body was then decapitated and the hands and feet were cut off. Though at present human sacrifice has been replaced by the sacrifice of a fowl (Gohain, 1977: 36; Playfair, 1909: 103).

However the Sangsarek Garos are very religious and God-fearing people. They believe that all physical ailments, accidents and unnatural deaths are due to the wrath of one or the other malevolent spirits. Sacrifices of animals and birds must be offered to the deities to appease them as well as to invoke their blessings (Sangma, 1981: 223). So when they are sick they throw themselves entirely on the mercy of the God, who, they consider, has been for some reason, incensed against them. And they consequently endeavour to appease his wrath by smearing his alter with the blood of a sacrifice (Dalton, 1847: 24). They also worship the natural phenomena like thunder, lightning, earthquake, eclipse, wind, rain and shooting stars. Frazer writes in this context:

> ... the worship of nature is based on the assumption that natural phenomena, whether animate or inanimate, are living personal beings analogous to men in their nature though often far superior to him in power. In short the worship of nature is based on the personification of nature. (Frazer, 1926: 19)

These natural phenomena per se are not the object of the worship or sacrifice, but since each of these events is controlled by a spirit, sacrifices must be offered to those spirits to have their favour. Thus, sacrifices are offered to the God of rain when rain is required and to the God of sun when sunshine is needed (Sangma, 1981: 235).

The Garo Religion: Some Comparative Discussions

The Garos lived in their villages for centuries with their traditional religious beliefs, values and practices. But the changes that have occurred in their religious practices have become a point of discussion. Some important issues are highlighted here for a comparative understanding of this tribal religion.

Existing Religious Festivals and Practices

Saint Leo Catholic Church was established in Andharupara in 1942. The jurisdiction of this church is confined to the village only but its practical influence spreads to the neighbouring villages as well. On the basis of their religion the Garos in Bangladesh may be classified into three groups: Sangsareks, Christians and Hindus. But Andharupara consists of only the Christians and Sangsareks. The Christian Garos are guided by Christian beliefs and practices and celebrate its socio-religious festivals. Some of these are Christmas Day, Easter Day and Good Friday in which they take good food, wear new clothes and attend the church congregation. On the other hand, the Sangsarek Garos maintain their traditional beliefs, practices and organize different festivals of their own. The main festivals of the Sangsarek are primarily related to farming, sowing and harvesting. Two important festivals which they observe are Rongchugala and Wangala.

Before harvesting any crop they celebrate a thank-giving ceremony in which they offer their first fruit to the spirits known as Rongchugala (Rongchu means 'preparation of rice boiled until dry' and *Gala* means 'to throw'). Eating, drinking and playing of songs at every household of the village follow this, but generally they do not dance on this occasion. On the other hand, Wangala, celebrated in connection with the Jhum cultivation, is the most important of all festivals and this is performed with great pomp and grandeur after the harvest. The Garos observe it to honour and offer sacrifices to their greatest God called Saljong (the Sun God) and seek its blessings for the future.

For the Sangsarek Garos there are no specific places of worship in the village while the Christians have the Saint Leo Catholic Church. The Garo Christians have the pictures of Jesus Christ (popularly known as Zisu) and mother Mary in their own houses. They treat Jesus as the God of the Christians who devoted his life to humanity and peace. This reflects a detachment of the Christian Garos from their traditional religion.

The Sangsarek Garos often cannot celebrate their traditional festivals because their population is small and celebrations of such festivals require lots of money which they cannot afford. They also have some annual religious festivals related to natural events such as droughts, calamities and misfortune. These include A'Songtata for ill person, Wachikrita for rain and drought, Salak So'a for excessive rain and sunshine. Apart from these, they also celebrate some ceremonies related to birth, marriage and death, like others.

The Role of the Priest

Those who follow Sangsarek, the animistic Garo religion, have a priest known as Kamal. The selection of the Kamal is neither hereditary nor confined to a particular clan or Mahari. Anyone can become a Kamal, if he has enough knowledge about religious traditions. He should be able to prescribe the name of particular God or Goddess to be appeased or worshipped on particular occasion. A Kamal is aware of the nature of sacrifices to be offered and knows the words to be recited at the time of sacrifices and worships (Dalton, 1847: 24). Andharupara also has a Kamal. He is an elderly person of that village.

The Kamal performs certain rituals on the occasions of naming a child, wedding and funerals etc., for which he is paid with little remuneration. However, he commands respect and prestige and plays a significant role in community life. The Christian priest in that Garo village, on the other hand, is the Church Father. Where there is no church, the villagers themselves organize and make their own church and appoint Christian priest. These Garo people have a church in their village where everyday in the morning and evening the priest evangelizes and performs Christian rituals. As a whole the Christian priest is the most prestigious man both in and outside the village.

Garo Religion: The Current Scenario

It is evident that these tribal people are no more able to retain their traditional religion as such as they are facing changes that affect even their core religious issues. At this point it is interesting to note the impact of Christianity and other factors on their religious beliefs, practices and values. Before the advent of British the Garos had a closely knit democratic socio-political set-up, characterized by the absence of private property, existence of mutual exchange of labour and yearly allotment of communal land (A'king). They depended on shifting cultivation with regular cycle of social ceremonies and festivals. There were no individually performed sacrifices or worshipping. Another important feature was the inheritance of property from the mother to the chosen daughter or Nokna (Kar, 1967: 92). However, after the advent of the British in 1756 changes took place.

The British, through the adventurers, easily came in close contact with this tribal community. They found that in comparison to the

Muslim and Hindu population of the then Bengal (present Bangladesh), the Garos were ethnographically different and less civilized. So to bring them within their fold, foreign missionaries were invited. Accordingly, 'The Australian Victorian Baptist Foreign Mission' appeared in the field in 1837. This Christian Mission started an extensive evangelization and proselytization—from traditional religion Sangsarek to Christianity. At this point the British authority intervened and encouraged elementary education for the Garos. During 1930s, Catholic churches were established in different areas of present Bangladesh. These churches provided some facilities and established schools, hospitals, cottages, industries, etc. The missionaries also developed scripts for the Garo dialect (first in Bengali script and then in Roman). They translated the Bible, wrote text books for schools and started journals for the Garos.

These missionaries also have brought modern amenities such as electricity, clean drinking water, etc., to the people. In course of time traditional folk music and dance of the Garos were replaced by Christian hymns and Western dances. Even they have become habituated to cut their hair by barber in the village market and dress their hair with comb to which they were not familiar earlier. The changes are also evident in their dress pattern. Males wear shirts, shorts and Lungi (long loincloth) along with different Western ornaments and females wear saris with blouses. Christianity has infringed even upon their traditional marriage practices. But despite these changes their basic matrilineal social structure, kinship pattern, customs related to succession and inheritance of property remained almost unaffected.

Diffusion of Bengali Culture

The Garos live alongside the Bengalis in Bangladesh. Kar (1967) has argued that their dresses, intelligence and education, sophisticated way of living, shrewd transaction motives, knowledge of wet cultivation and kitchen gardening, techniques of house building, arts, music and dances—are largely influenced by and patterned after the East Bengal (now Bangladesh) culture. Now the Garo children, educated in Bengali language are to be integrated with greater Bengali culture.

Eventually these people have composed Zisu Gits (song of Jesus Christ) in Bengali. They also sing Kirtan (a type of song) with the help of traditional musical instruments of Bengali Vaishnavas. The Garo folk songs and dances, Jatras (traditional open air opera) and theatres are composed in Bengali, and they participate in different national programmes of Bangladesh. The Bengali cultural influx is one of the significant factors of change in the life of these people.

Islamic Mission

In recent times another external force has started working with the establishment of Islamic Foundation of Bangladesh by the Government. In 1982, this foundation undertook the project of 'Amalus Saleh Mission' and accordingly took a decision to establish 25 missions in different parts of Bangladesh. In 1983, one such mission was opened at Haluaghat Upazila (upgraded Police Station), a Garo inhabited area in the district of Sherpur. The main objectives of this mission are to evangelize the ideology of Prophet Mohammad and to popularize Islamic culture. It also tries to provide medical, educational and other services to the people. However its impact on the Garos has not yet been so significant as that of the Christianity.

Final Comments

This article throws light particularly on the changing aspects of religion of the Garos living in the village Andharupara of the district Sherpur in Bangladesh. The major issues that can be pointed out from the above discussion are now summarized below for a precise understanding.

- The Garos seem to have departed from their traditional religious practices, beliefs and values. Most of them have adopted Christianity and do not generally follow their traditional religious practices as such. Even those who are clinging to their traditional tribal religion do not celebrate their festivals and other rituals with much enthusiasm. There are two factors lying behind this: first they are very few in number, and second due to their poverty they cannot spend much on such occasions.
- The Christian Garos observe Christian rituals on various occasions whereas the traditional Sangsarek Garos observe their own traditional rituals. But the traditional Garo priest has lost much of his religious authority today. The Christian Church Fathers, on the

other hand, are taking over a dominant place in the socio-religious life of the Garos.

- Both the Christian and Sangsarek Garos have faith in fatalism but there are some differences also. While to the traditional Garos fatalism is simply a matter of belief in the mysterious relationship between man and nature, it has a wider meaning that God is the creator and saviour of mankind to the Christian Garos.
- In short, it is Christianity that has replaced, to a significant extent, the traditional socio-religious beliefs and practices of the Garos. It has also brought them in the new orbit of dynamism inculcating a quite alien value system.

12 Understanding Punjabi Folk Religion

Grappling the Field and Framework

Harvinder Singh Bhatti

Religion is a very complicated phenomenon in Punjab (India) where it always has been a point of contention. The history of Punjab which is at least five thousand years old is replete with religious controversies, conflicts and the emergence of new religious movements. The scholarly interest in this aspect of Punjab is also as old as Punjab itself. It is also believed that the Vedas, the world's oldest scriptures, were also composed on the banks of the rivers of Punjab. No doubt that this aspect of Punjabi religion is quite developed and a large body of literature concerning it has been produced. But there is another aspect of Punjabi religious life which has remained neglected and unnoticed. Despite the development of various religious movements, the common people of Punjab have been sticking to certain forms of religion which have not been touched by the ever occurring religious changes. These popular forms of religion do not fit into the sectarian confines of various religious movements of Punjab. These are largely based on oral traditions as there is hardly any written literature available on these popular traditions of Punjabi religion. Some scholars like Coomaraswamy (1971) and Divedi (1961) while commenting on other aspects of ancient history have mentioned about the various forms of popular religion of Punjab and North India. The British officers and collectors of folklore

The initial version of this paper was presented at a conference on 'Punjabi culture' at University of California, Santa Barbara on 29 May 2004.

have also recorded various forms of popular worship (Bedi, 1994; Crooke, 1968; Rose, 1970; Temple, 1969). Recently, some scholars have tried to analyse and understand the structure of the dense symbolism of folk traditions of Punjab (Bhatti, 2000; Gill, 1975; Singh, 1981). It is a well-known fact that for centuries, Punjab has been a battle ground for the new ideas and invading armies. The ancient forms of religion survived and blended with the new forms of religion. The earliest form of religion in Punjab may be a primordial form of present day Hinduism which is known as Sanatan Dharma. Later on Buddhism and Jainism became popular. The movement of Nath Yogis around the tenth century was also popular before the advent of Islamic forces. Islam came with the Muslim invasions and influenced large sections of Punjabi population. Particularly the Sufi saints, who preached a non-conformist version of Islam blending it with local cultural traditions, became very popular. In fifteenth century a new religion, Sikhism was founded by Guru Nanak. And Punjab became the birth place of this new religion.

In the past Yaksha and Naga cults, mentioned in the legends and epics, were parts of the religious life of the people (Agrawala, 1981). Academically and intellectually these traditions pose a number of conceptual problems for the scholars who try to understand the realm of religion in the context of great and little traditions or as a deformed version of the other institutionalized religions. Perhaps it is one of the main reasons that this tradition has been neglected by most of the scholars who considered it as obscure and irrelevant. The evidences available suggest that the folk tradition has always been very strong and deep-rooted in this region. It represents the folk conceptualizations of the religious, cultural and social universe on one hand and the explanation of problematic existential experiences on the other. Being a non-discriminatory and all-inclusive tradition it has been a source of integration and confluence of various differing traditions. To locate and analyse various facets of folk religion of Punjab is certainly an uphill task, particularly in the present situation in which the Punjabi community is geographically scattered and culturally fragmented.

However, in the following discussion of folk religion the reference point is present eastern Punjab. The information is primarily based on field observations, early records of the British officers and census reports. The account is intended to be descriptive to facilitate the comparison with institutionalized religious traditions of Punjab.

Present Punjab (India) is overwhelmingly a Sikh-dominated province. Around 62.95 per cent of its population believe in Sikhism while 34.46 per cent believe in Hinduism. There are also very small percentages of Muslim (1.18%) and Christian (1.11%) populations (*Statistical Abstract of Punjab*, 2002). Interestingly, the census questionnaires have no separate provision for the folk religion. Thus, census puts the variety of people into some stock classificatory categories, neglecting the diversity and plurality of their beliefs. Even within the fold of institutionalized religions like Hinduism, Sikhism and Islam there is a variety of sects. In census reports all believers are clubbed together as followers of one or another institutionalized religion, which do not reflect the reality. But at the practical level a large number of people practice folk religion. Every visitor comes across a number of shrines of Muslim Pirs or other shrines, which are growing in size and splendour alongside the highways of Punjab. Despite the transfer of almost entire Muslim population to western Punjab, the popularity of these shrines is gradually increasing.

Punjabi Folk Religion: Intriguing Simplicity and Complexity

Punjabi folk religion provides a broad canvas of belief systems according to which the believers modify the practices of the institutionalized religions and transform the symbolism to integrate various mutually opposing traditions. Religious preachers and reformers have noticed this all-pervasive presence of folk religion and its sway over the minds of the people, but, however, it has escaped the eyes of the scholars. It has generally been viewed as an unwanted deformity of institutionalized religions or at the most a crude attempt of the illiterate minds to comprehend the sophisticated complexities of religions experience. There had been an element of systematic neglect and contempt towards this religious and social reality (Oberoi, 1994). This may be due to the ambiguity and complexity of this type of religion. The complexity increases when we look at it as a deformed version of other institutionalized religions. A closer and incisive look may reveal the logic, creativity and richness of collective mind working behind the development of folk religion. It may also reveal its fundamental differences from the formal scriptural and institutionalized religions.

Following is an account of the unique characteristics of Punjabi folk religion. It may be helpful for analytical purposes to have a comparative look at both domains of religion. The 'other' religions, practised in Punjab namely Hinduism, Islam, Sikhism and Christianity hereafter will be referred to as the 'institutionalized religions'. The whole attempt is to present an objective analysis by bringing the folk religion of Punjab into focus which otherwise has been relegated to the invisible margins.

The Shrines

There are approximately 12,000 villages in the present-day Indian Punjab. Almost all these villages have a number of shrines which do not fit into the well-known framework of institutionalized religions. Usually these shrines are located at the peripheries. Generally, these are non-descript and ordinary structures of bricks or small round mounds painted with white colour, sometimes with a small flag atop. These shrines may be divided into various categories according to the deities or according to the nature of functions.

In the first category there are shrines of major folk deities which exist almost in every village. Among these folk deities the prominent ones are Gugga Zahir Pir, Sakhi Sarvar, Seetla Mata Khwaja Pir and Khera (Bhatti, 2000). Khwaja Pir is also known as Khwaja Khizar. He is primarily a Muslim water deity, who is worshipped before digging new wells or at the time of the installation of other water sources like tube wells and hand pumps. His shrines are usually located near the natural sources of water like rivers, streams and ponds. Traditionally he was invoked by the sailors for safety and smooth sailing. Khera is a protective deity of the village who is supposed to save the villagers from outsiders and other calamities. Khera is also known as Bhumia and Khetarpal.

The second category includes the shrines of the ancestors of different families, lineages and clans. These shrines are found in all villages and may be divided into two categories: the shrines of the ancestors of clans or lineages and the shrines of village ancestors. The shrines of lineage or clan ancestors, known as Jathere or Vade Vadere, are worshipped by the clan members during some important occasions. The clan members may not be residing in the same village. The other category is of the village ancestors whose descendents reside in the same village. These ancestors are mainly family ancestors. Such shrines at many places are referred to as the places of Shaheed, the persons who sacrificed their lives while protecting the village or community from the outside invaders.

The third category shrines are built on the graves of Muslim Pirs commonly referred to as Mazar. These Mazars belong to a variety of Muslim saints ranging from Sufi saints to local ancestors or other miracle men. The fourth category is associated with Singh Shaheed. These are the shrines of the Sikh fighters who laid down their lives while fighting against the invaders or for the protection of the community. The shrines of some of the village ancestors are also called Shaheed.

There are shrines of Sati Mata which are associated with a Rajput custom. According to this, the wife burns herself on the pyre of her husband after his death. The legends associated with these shrines tell the stories of the dispersion of Rajputs and their skirmishes with the Muslim invaders. There are a number of such shrines in the rural areas of Punjab. The reverence for these shrines is equal to the shrines of the ancestors. Interestingly these shrines are similar to the temples of mother Goddesses of the Hindus.

Apart from these shrines of local or regional folk deities there are a number of places, trees, ponds, etc., which are believed to possess some special spiritual powers. The important thing is that the cremation grounds are always associated with the domain of power. Some scholars have discussed these aspects of folk worship (Bedi, 1994; Bhatti, 2000).

Generally, the folk religion of Punjab is without any central shrine, scripture or organization. The structure of the shrines, related to various deities, is also different. Though the shrines exist in all the villages, some of these are more famous and exert more influence on the believers. However, there is a central shrine of the cult of Gugga Zahir Pir at Garh Dadrera in Rajasthan. In Punjab the important shrines of this deity are at Chhapar and Pamah villages of Ludhiana district and Naina Kaut village of Patiala district. These shrines are considered more important than other village level shrines. At the time of crisis these shrines are visited and the respective deities are worshipped.

Different legends are narrated to highlight the importance of these shrines. The central shrine of Sakhi Sarvar is located at Nigaha. But its smaller shrines are scattered all over, in both parts of Punjab falling in India and Pakistan. There are some other important local shrines of Sakhi Sarvar designed according to the pattern of the shrines associated with Gugga Zahir Pir. The interesting point to note is that the central shrines have no control over the local shrines. The managements of the local and central shrines are different and independent. The shrines of other folk deities are very much localized. For instance, there is no central shrine of Seetla Mata, Khera or Khwaja Khizar; they are worshipped at the local level. The shrines of these deities are small brick-made structures and have some common patterns. However the shrines of Seetla Mata are small structures of bricks, grouped along with the seven sisters of Seetla Mata. Usually these shrines are located near the ponds around the villages. The shrines of the deity Khera, being the protective deity of the village, are either located at the borders or at the entrances of the villages. While the shrines of Khwaja Khizar, being a water deity, are located near the sources of water like wells, ponds and streams.

The Scriptures

Unlike fully institutionalized religions, the folk religion of Punjab does not have any scriptures. Some written versions of the legends about the folk deities known as Kisse are available in vernacular languages. But these are not treated as sacred nor these are worshipped anywhere. Mostly such Kisse are about the cult of Gugga Zahir Pir. The cults of Sakhi Sarvar, Seetla Mata, Khwaja Khizar and Khera are based on oral traditions. It is surprising that without any written word, these cults are surviving for centuries. Perhaps it is because of its symbolic appeal to the collective mind of the people. The figures of folk deities are portrayed in the minds of the people. There are hardly any legends or stories about the origins of the deities. Only a few local legends about the power and nature of these deities are available. The legends have different versions in different areas. Most of them are similar to the traditional Hindu mythology and in some cases the mythical figures are modified according to the needs of these legends. At the time of annual worship the praise songs, locally known as Sohle, are sung by the traditional singers.

Lack of Central Organization

One important feature of the folk religion of Punjab is its informal and loose organization. It becomes apparent when we compare it with the organized or institutionalized religions. The institutionalized religions are usually organized around a central scripture and a central shrine. These are propagated and managed through the central organizations. Classical sociologists like Durkheim (1926) defined religion on the basis of a central organization of the believers like church. They differentiated religion from magic on the basis of such organization and a community of believers.

In sociology, organization is considered as one of the defining qualities of the religion. The type and nature of religious organizations had been an area of interest for long. A complete typology of Christian religious organizations was developed by Troeltsch (1971). The institutionalized religions employ the principle of organization at various levels. At one level the believers organize themselves into church-like organizations; at the other level the central shrines in these religions play the role of administrative and religious centre for the community of believers. In Christianity the church and the institution of Pope, in Islam the shrine of Mecca and in Sikhism the Golden Temple and Shiromani Gurudwara Parbandhak Committee (SGPC) are central. These central organizations play an important role in the standardization of practices and ceremonies.

The notion of organization in folk religion operates entirely at a different plane. The festivals and fairs associated with various cults of the folk deities are organized by the devotees. Usually, these are organized according to the lunar calendar which is the hallmark of peasant societies. The organization, if any, is usually spontaneous, temporary and casual. Generally at the local shrines, there are no regular priests or worshippers and there is no supervision or control over the beliefs, practices, ceremonies and rituals. The whole process of worship is dictated by tradition passed on from generation to generation. Where there are regularly attached priests, they act as full-time priests only at the time of annual worship; otherwise they remain busy with some other part-time occupations for their livelihood. For instance the priest of Gugga Zahir Pir at Pamah village in Ludhiana district is basically a farmer. He also works as a carpenter at the shrine of Naina Kaut village in Patiala district.

Non-discriminatory Nature

The essence of folk religion lies in its non-discriminating nature. Discriminations if they ever occur in the framework of folk religion are qualitatively different from the existing notions of discrimination. These discriminations, unlike the socially prescribed discriminations, are temporary and contextual. On the contrary the institutionalized religions thrive on distinctions and discriminations. The institutionalized religions impose a strict code of conduct upon its believers which encompasses their entire way of life. There are at least three spheres of religious activities in which discriminations are made. These are as follows:

The Identity

The institutionalized religions always try to establish a distinct identity of its believers. The emphasis remains on the separateness through carefully constructed religious boundaries (Oberoi, 1994). The believers are supposed to follow an explicit and distinct way of living which differentiates them from others. The institutionalized religions enforce the classificatory systems which provide the models for the discrimination between sacred and profane, religious and secular, and between private and public domains. The classification of time according to different calendars and of space with the notions of sacred geography is also common to almost all institutionalized religions. The emphasis is put on the differences from the non-believers and the followers of other religions. In fact, the differences between the believers and non-believers become central in these cases.

Such separate religious identity gradually becomes the fundamental rallying point and organizing principle of the religious community as such. At times this overemphasis upon religious identity becomes the source of sectarianism, fundamentalism and communalism. Folk religion in his context is qualitatively different from the organized religions in the sense that there is no question of the separate identity of the believers. Though in some legends the devotion and the allegiance to a particular deity are emphasized, the notion of separateness or opposition of believers is almost absent. As in one of the legends of Sakhi Sarvar, a devotee named Dani Jatti was compelled by her husband to worship Guru Nanak. Sakhi Sarvar punished her husband and family through his spiritual agent and compelled the whole family to follow Dani Jatti (Bedi, 1994). Such competition among various spiritual agencies is shown in some other legends as well, to highlight the spiritual power of a particular deity. But in principle all deities are considered as manifestations of the same spiritual power and the believers or devotees are treated equally. Often the religious identity is used at the time of annual worship. During annual fairs and festivals some devotees tie a thread around the wrist known as Gana or tie a cloth around the head to mark their identity as the pilgrims. But as soon as pilgrimage or annual worship is over this identity mark is removed. So religious identity as such is not important in folk religion.

The Membership

In the absence of an organized community of believers there is no formal procedure of membership. Practically everyone is eligible to invoke the power of the deity and can seek favour or blessings without any consideration of caste, religion and status. The identity of the pilgrims during the annual worship as has been mentioned earlier is established by tying a thread or piece of cloth of special colour. The worship of a folk deity is practically open to everybody. The 'notion of separation' works entirely at a different plane in case of folk religion. The area of the shrines is separated through symbolic actions of the devotees. For instance, while entering the area of shrines during the annual worship devotees may remove their shoes and scoop the earth five times before entering the domain of the deity. These rituals mark the area of deity and separate it from the rest of place. Often the period of worship is considered as the period of a particular deity. In case of Gugga Zahir Pir, the lunar month of Bhadon (August/September) is devoted for worshipping.

The Clergy

Another significant feature of folk religion is that there is no priestly class which otherwise is very important in institutionalized religions. There are certain social groups which may have special relationships with particular deities. Such relationship exists between Gugga Zahir Pir and Chuhras, (a lower caste group) and between Sakhi Sarvar and Bharais (Muslim). It seems strange that in a country like India where the priestly class of Brahmin has played a prominent role for centuries, the folk religion is surviving without a regular class of priests. It has also been noticed that in case of the most of the cults of the ancestors of various Jat clans, the Brahmins have been prohibited from acting as priests. They are substituted by the lower caste groups of Chuhras and Mirasis who are preferred as priests (Rose, 1970).

The criteria followed for the recruitment of the priests at various shrines are also very arbitrary and irregular. Spirit possession and state of trance of various devotees play an important role in case of appointment. During annual worship some devotees get possessed and act almost like oracles and make prophesies about the future of devotees and answer their questions. They are often selected as priests. At the central shrines of folk deities particularly at the shrines of Gugga Zahir Pir and Sakhi Sarvar the priesthood is determined on the basis of heredity but at local and less important shrines the rules about the priesthood vary according to the local needs of the situations.

Level of Operation

Folk religion largely works at the subconscious level. Its efficacy particularly in cases of faith healing is dependent upon the context of social reproduction. The role of socio-cultural milieu in determining the responses to symbolic stimulants is very important. The common impression is that folk religion is mainly the religion of rural peasants but some urban people also believe in the power of folk deities. In many cases urban people also participate in the annual worship. They want the support of the folk deities during the time of a crisis. For instance in case of snakebites they worship Gugga Zahir Pir or in case of smallpox they seek the blessings of Seetla Mata. Often they donate land or money for the development and upkeep of the shrines.

Institutionalized religions insist on the explicit expression and declaration of faith and provide a doctrinal explanation of the rituals, ceremonies and practices. The operation of folk religion is largely at subconscious level because it operates through traditional symbolism. But the devotees may not always be aware of the power of these symbols. They respond to these symbols at the subconscious level. The devotees may not even be aware of the cause of their ailments which is diagnosed by the priest as the displeasure of the deity. They come to know about it only when they are 'chosen' by the deity which is euphemistically referred to as 'kindness', or when the priest, during the spirit possession, reveals that the deity is displeased with them. After such discovery they are directed to appease the deity through the prescribed rituals. The other forms of religion almost overemphasize the role of conscious faith and attempt to develop a logical system of explanation of the extraordinary experiences of the devotees. The folk religion depends upon the power of symbolism which is deeply embedded in the 'collective unconscious'. It remains invisible and in a dormant state till the devotees violate its code and face a crisis. The ailments and other misfortunes are considered as the reactions of the deities. The offended or enraged deities may punish the devotees through various symbolic ways. The priests and the believers hardly make any attempt to logically understand and explain the nature of the reactions of the deities. Rather such questioning is discouraged. The whole focus is on the unpredictable nature and the will of the deities. The symbolism used to invoke the power is deep-rooted and operates at various levels of consciousness.

The Notion of Power

The notion of spiritual or supernatural power is essential to any religion but it is conceptualized differently in various traditions. Usually, God is the ultimate source of power. In polytheistic traditions there may be plurality of agencies of such power. The domains of sacred power and secular power are usually well demarcated and well defined. The ultimate supremacy of spiritual power is emphasized over the secular power.

The notion of power in Punjabi folk religion differs from the common religious notions of power in many ways. Power in other religious traditions is normally conceptualized as positive and benevolent for the devotees. The operation of this power is almost predictable if it is invoked through prescribed rituals and ceremonies. But in folk religion the power of folk deities is described as most unpredictable and mysterious. Thus, the elements of fear and awe are quite pronounced along with the element of devotion and faith. The folk notion of power is essentially all-inclusive as it includes good as well as evil, sacred as well as mundane sphere. The important historical personalities are conceptualized as manifestations of spiritual power. No wonder that local heroes like bandits, legendary fighters, lovers, renouncers, saints, etc., are treated as manifestations of power. The power is believed to be all-pervasive and it can manifest itself through human beings and a number of other agencies. For instance various animals, plants, springs, birds or insects may be the mediums of power as well. Certain places are also considered as powerful and endowed with spiritual power. Though some culturally prescribed ways to acquire this power like worship, devotion or Yogic techniques are recognized, normally this power depends upon the blessings or the kindness of the deities. The symbolism used to describe this power is usually ambiguous and mysterious. Usually in the legends the conflict between worldly power and spiritual power becomes a central theme. The worldly power is represented through physical strength, political power or through the power of wealth, while the spiritual power is represented by the spiritual being—a spiritually oriented hero, Yogi, saint or a deity. The spiritual being is ultimately shown as victorious in conflicts and the supremacy of spiritual power is established over the worldly power. The deities are shown as the masters of the specific domains of power. For instance, mother Goddess Seetla can protect people from smallpox or Gugga Zahir Pir can protect his devotees from the snakes. Similarly, these deities are believed to be the cause of smallpox and snakebite when they become angry.

Thus, the notion of power in folk religion is markedly different from that of the institutionalized religions. It is more ambiguous and inclusive in folk religion as compared to the institutionalized religion. Power in folk religion includes both the positive as well as negative aspects and its operation remains mysterious and unpredictable.

Pragmatic and Concrete

The nature of the institutionalized religions is usually other-worldly as these are concerned with the higher and absolute goals. The main purpose of these religions is spiritual advancement and ultimate salvation. The chief goal of Christianity, Islam, Hinduism, Sikhism, Buddhism and Jainism, despite their internal differences and variations, is ultimate freedom from the worldly and material bondages. It is described differently as regaining the lost paradise, freedom from cycle of rebirths or Moksha from worldly desires, but the preoccupation remains almost the same. Such spiritual and intellectual preoccupations are not found in folk religion who perceives the folk deities as the granters of their worldly wishes like the cure of some ailments, etc. The emphasis of folk religion is upon concrete and existential problems of day-to-day life. In the face of the material and practical problems of the rural people, the abstract problems like salvation and doctrinal explanation become irrelevant. Folk religion grapples with the worldly preoccupations of survival like the mysteries of fertility, death and disease.

In various legends the deities are shown facing the problems which common man faces during his or her life time. These common problems are barrenness, the absence of male child in a patrilineal society, stigmatization, family division or division of ancestral property, property disputes, jealousy and treachery of kinsmen and the problems of scarcity, etc. The power of the deities is also shown over the immediate natural processes. They can alter or change the natural course of the events in favour of their devotees. But this power is limited and inadequate in the face of the challenge. They go through various ordeals but ultimately either with their own spiritual power or with the help of some other spiritual agency they turn out to be victorious. This pattern is also found in the folklore in which various folk heroes are shown as spiritually oriented or associated with some spiritual being. For instance the legend of Heer Ranjha is replete with such situations in which Ranjha is shown as a spiritual hero (Temple, 1969).

Place of Reason

In folk religion, reason and logic have hardly any relevance. The myths and legends, rituals and ceremonies, and beliefs and practices tend to neglect logical explanations. This aspect is further confounded by the multiple changes occurring in the Punjabi society in the recent past. Punjabi society has always experienced upheavals caused by the outside invasions or internal conflicts. The partition of Punjab and consequent large scale transfer of population have brought some irreversible changes. The younger generations have got modern education and have hardly any direct experience of the traditional and composite folk life. The pace of urbanization and the changes occurring in agriculture and in rural areas are influencing their attitudes and outlook. The traditional folk symbols are disappearing. The ignorance of the cultural heritage has led to mystification of folk religion and its symbolic world. For instance, the lunar calendar, according to which the traditional peasant life once revolved, is totally unknown to the younger generation.

Thus, the earlier explanatory systems of folk symbolism have either been lost or distorted. The survival of the folk religion is dependent on uncritical faith in the power of deities. The need of logical explanation is not felt because the power of deities is considered all-inclusive and unpredictable. The emphasis remains not on the reason, logic or explanation but on mystery, symbolism and uncritical acceptance. All other religions tend to develop an integrated system of myths, legends, beliefs and practices. This integrated system ultimately provides the explanations of the varied experiences and events to the believers. The absence and the lack of logical and reasonable explanatory systems highlight the fact that the folk beliefs are so deeply embedded in the 'collective unconscious' of the believers that these do not require any additional explanatory system.

Unifying and Integrative

As folk religion ignores and transcends social and sectarian boundaries, it acts as an integrative principle for various sections of society. The believers are not categorized on the basis of caste, class or any other stratifying principle. Folk religion emphasizes on the unity of human beings. Usually, it does not work as a divisive principle for organizing the group. The organization associated with folk religion is temporary and transitional. Generally, it ignores the differences and neglects the social hierarchy. Even in some cases the existing hierarchy is completely inverted upside down to create a symbolic balance. In the legends also religious distinctions are blurred and confused; the mythical characters or deities of one religion are shown to be associated with another religion without bothering their origins. It is clear from the legends, rituals and practices that the folk religion not only negates the social and cultural distinctions but it also reverses these to create new meanings. It treats these distinctions as symbolic categories to organize a counter symbolic order.

Symbolism

The universe of folk religion is a symbolic universe. It is replete with social and cultural motifs of rich symbolic import. In rituals and other practices the materials used have symbolic value for the people. For instance the case of barrenness of the royal couple, which is a common theme in the folk legends, is depicted as the barrenness of land or the withering of the gardens or drying up of wells and other water sources. This barrenness is cured by the symbolic blessings of a spiritual agency in the form of grain of rice or some other form of seed. In the story of Gugga Zahir Pir, the Yogi gives blessings for the male child and gives ashes of his fire pit to the queen. Symbolically ashes stand for death and negation of life. These motifs in the legends and myths and the materials being used at the time of worship make hardly any sense for an outside observer. But for the believers these are very significant. The symbolism used in the folk religion is different from the symbolism of the institutionalized religions.

Another aspect of the folk religion which baffles many observers is the inversion of symbols or the creation of counter symbols. The figures of folk deities sometimes are described exactly as the opposites of the accepted images of the deities of the institutionalized religions. The figure of Seetla Mata, for instance, is described as ugly and repulsive. 'Her face is hideous, teeth are projecting, ears are large, eyes huge and mouth wide open. She rides on an ass and carries a broom in her hand' (Bhatti, 2000: 141–158). The entire symbolism in this cult is inverted. The cleanliness is replaced by the dirt; even the offerings which are usually the valuable materials are replaced with the stale food. The vehicle of the Goddess is an ass, the opposite of lion, bull or horse.

The shrines of the folk deities are located on the boundaries of the villages, not in the village centres like the shrines of institutionalized religions. The offerings at some of the shrines are also symbolic counterpoints of the institutionalized religious patterns. At some of the shrines of the ancestors like the shrine of Kala Mehar, the ancestor of Sandhu clan of Jats, Brahmins are prohibited from entering the shrine, and wine or liquor is offered as an offering (Rose, 1970). Otherwise Brahmins are traditional priests and liquor is considered as a polluting element in religious ceremonies. There are a number of such instances of the inversion of the established practices and symbolism. The institutionalized religions emphasize on a particular type of religious morality based on the differentiation of good and evil or right and wrong. Folk religion does not bother about such distinctions, perhaps it addresses to some deeper psychic and symbolic needs. The institutionalized religions preach and impose a specific way of life based on an ideology and expect complete conformity to it. Folk religion primarily depends on symbolism. The structure of the rituals and practices also emphasizes on the symbolic submission of devotees before the deity. Folk religion instead of promoting any specific ideology emphasizes on the symbolic supremacy of the spiritual power over the material and worldly power. In certain cases it also emphasizes on the primacy of nature over culture. The natural and cultural objects are interchangeably used as symbols.

Principle of Inclusion

Folk religion is based on the principle of inclusion. The legends associated with the folk deities indiscriminately refer to the Hindu, Muslim and Sikh religious traditions. A predominantly Hindu God may ultimately be transformed into a Muslim deity. In the same way a Muslim saint may become a common deity. The legends and folklore of Punjab are replete with such examples in which the hero is shown seeking the blessings of both Hindu and Muslim deities. In some legends the Sikh Gurus are also presented as folk deities.

Sometimes the shrines are treated as common sacred places by all rural communities. Gurudwara Haji Rattan at Bathinda city of Punjab is one classic example of such confluence of different religious traditions. The legend associated with this shrine is that Rattan, a Hindu prince, was a spiritually oriented person who renounced his kingdom and became a Yogi. Later on he converted himself into Muslim and went on a pilgrimage to Mecca. Such pilgrimage is locally known as Haj and the pilgrims are referred to as Haji. Thus, prince Rattan became a Haji and became popular as Haji Rattan. He became a prominent saint of that area and stayed at Bathinda till his death. A shrine was constructed by the devotees to commemorate and to worship him. Later the tenth Sikh Guru, Guru Gobind Singh visited the place and performed some miracles. A Gurudwara was also constructed to commemorate the visit of the tenth Guru. Now the shrine is known as Gurudwara Haji Rattan and has become a common sacred place of all religious communities.

The Absence of the Other

The emergence of fundamentalism and communalism in the recent past as forms of political discourse has compelled the scholars of various fields to reframe and reformulate the existing conceptual frameworks. Consequently, the term 'construction of the other' has gained currency in social sciences. The ideology or belief systems are explained and understood in terms of their definition of the perfect opposite, the 'other'. The threat to the religious or ethnic community is perceived in the form of the otherness of the groups. The opposition between two mutually opposing groups is presented as irreconcilable and permanent, thus legitimate. No doubt in theory every religion preaches the idea of universal brotherhood and the unity of mankind, but this brotherhood and unity is defined by every group in its own terms. The diagnosis presumes the remedy also, thus every group identifies the obstacles in the way of its progress in its own terms. The root cause of these problems is often found in the existence and definition of the 'ugly other'.

In the domain of folk religion the existence of such 'ugly other' is almost absent. Though some legends portray the fight between the deity and his opponents as a fight between good and evil or the fight between just and unjust, after the victory of the deity, the opposition is considered resolved and the notion of the hostile 'other' is not invoked. It is interesting to note that at some shrines of Gugga Zahir Pir, the maternal cousins of the deity are also worshiped, though in the legends they are shown as enemies. This instance highlights that good and evil coexist within the same framework of folk religion. Folk religion neither imposes on its believers any particular code of conduct nor is there any concept of conversion or re-conversion.

Final Comments

In Punjab there has always been a strong vernacular tradition of folk religion along with other changing religious traditions. This tradition is based on the principle of inclusion and the recognition of the plurality of faiths. In this particular domain religious sphere is not viewed as divided or fragmented into various mutually opposing categories punctuated with 'either' 'or' choices. It can be said that on the one hand folk religion represents a symbolic dialectic between nature and culture while on the other it is a multivocal dialogue between various religious and cultural traditions of Punjab.

13 Education for Experience

One View of Tibetan Tantric Initiation

Brian J. Given

The purpose of this essay is two-fold. I want to offer a brief ethnographic description of some aspects of a Tibetan Tantric[1] initiation cycle held during 1980–81 at Puruwala in Himachal Pradesh, Northern India called the Lam Dre' (Lobsche form). The ritual cycle was previously offered in this form about 55 years ago in Tibet, prior to China's invasion of that nation. Such a major initiation cycle represents one of a number of possible comprehensive statements, recognized by Tibetan Buddhists, regarding the nature of Tantra and Buddhist views of mind and reality. Secondly, I would like to address three issues relevant to the study of rituals of initiation and to the study of ritual in general.

The Anthropology of Experience

Scholars have tended to omit from our theoretical discussions of rites of passage detailed investigations of the altered phenomenology that they are often designed to engender. I would like to add my voice to those of Bourgignon (1973), Eliade (1964), Harner (1980), Katz (1982, 1984), Laughlin et al., (1979) and others in emphasizing that for many of our

---

This article first appeared in the *Journal of Ritual Studies* (1993), 7(2): 91–115. I would like to thank Regna Darnell and Jerome Barkow for their comments on an earlier draft of this manuscript. Their help and encouragement have been essential. This research was conducted under a grant from the Social Sciences and Humanities Research Council of Canada. I am deeply grateful to the Council for their support.

informants, rituals are, above all, about generating specific states of mind which may, in turn, be about generating long-term changes in world-view and experience. In 1936, Firth (1936: 422) was calling for a detailed study of 'the reaction which the initiation ceremonies produce in the person who is the focus for them ...' and Victor Turner's (1970) explorations of symbols' multivocality gave us an appropriate set of conceptual tools. However, at least with regard to descriptions of the experience of non-ordinary awareness engendered by ritual, we have sometimes been remiss. The analysis contained herein extends the concept of multivocality to encompass ritually-derived non-ordinary states of experience.

The ritual cycle I will allude to here, the Lam Dre', is certainly the expression of a highly complex culture and epistemology that has been preoccupied with the exploration of consciousness for more than thirteen centuries. I remind the reader, however, of Bourgignon's (1973: 418) documentation of institutionalized forms of dissociation, which I would consider to be one form of altered state of consciousness, in 437 societies or 89 per cent of those for which data were available.[2]

I join Katz, Laughlin, Lex, Bourgignon and others in pointing to the fact that most non-Western cultures recognize more than one state of mind in which it is possible to apprehend knowledge. In Laughlin's (1979) terms, Western societies tend to be 'mono-phasic' (a term originally coined by John Cove) in acknowledging only the 'normal waking state' as that in which one can know 'reality'. The majority of societies with which anthropological fieldwork is conducted recognize one or more other states of mind as domains of experience in which knowledge can be developed. Examples would include various dream states, a variety of states which those without experience of them may homogenize under the label 'trance' states, including the experiences facilitated by different techniques of meditation.

There is clear evidence that most of the cultures we study possess institutionalized strategies which are designed to produce, for the initiate, the experience of what my Tibetan teachers would call 'extraordinary' reality. In many cases a variety of such strategies, designed to produce a corresponding variety of extraordinary experiences, are in evidence. For example Tibetan Buddhists recognize 32 major kinds of meditation and delineate hundreds of carefully defined experiences to be derived from meditation practice. I suggest that where our informants' cultures incorporate sophisticated taxonomies of ritual technique and experience result, it behoves the ethnographer to attend to the full range of these experienced cultural categories, even where a minority of culture members (ritual specialists, Shamans, Tantrics, etc.) may experience them. Such experiences with reference to more limited taxonomies under such glosses as 'trance', 'vision', or 'fit' diminish the complexity of our informants' strategies for learning and teaching about the world and the richness of experience upon which their pedagogies and epistemologies are based. The Lam Dre' ritual cycle employs multiple strategies for the attainment of meditative states. Collectively, these techniques and their experiential consequences constitute a pedagogical programme which is a major component of that culture's epistemology. It is arguable that an exploration of such a ritual based pedagogy requires an appropriate use of its own lexicon. Any eventual translation into terms of the researchers' language must come much later. When our informants tell us that the cognates associated with that lexicon can only be accessed through the appropriate use of ritual we have little recourse but to examine with great care the extent to which our participant observation methodology addresses the experiential dimension of ritual. We must theorize the concept of participation with reference to our experiential involvement in the rituals we study.

Asking Relevant Questions

At a methodological level asking insightful questions about non-ordinary states of consciousness is likely to be difficult for a researcher who has been unable to experience them (Tart, 1969, 1975). It will be even more difficult if he or she does not recognize that such questions may address the crucial aspects of the institution under study from the perspective of the informant. The danger here is that, as researchers, our positivist enculturation and professional training may tend to preclude our asking questions about other ways of knowing. Further, Western cultures' de-emphasis of ritual as a strategy for knowing, and our resultant unfamiliarity with ritually altered experience, may render us incapable of asking appropriate questions about ritual based pedagogies.

The Question of Time Frame

It seems likely that in those cases where initiates are introduced to ritual practices and instructions which are believed to alter their experience as a result of much repetition (e.g., Katz, 1982, 1984), the process of initiation must be thought of as including both the formal introduction to and the subsequent public or private practice of those techniques. Katz (1982), Laughlin et al., (1984), Reichel-Dolmatoff (1971) and my Tibetan teachers emphasize that the events of the few days or months during which formal initiation ceremonies are held can only be properly understood in the context of the initiates' mental preparation and subsequent practice of the rituals. Several aspects of the Tibetan Sakya Lam Dre' initiation cycle present a challenge to our models for the understanding of initiation rites.

Lam dre': A Buddhist Tantric Initiation Cycle

Sakya is a principality of central and eastern Tibet. Prior to the Chinese invasion, Sakya's 2100 square miles had a population of about 17,000 (Cassinelli, 1964). The two largest monasteries of Sakya housed and educated about 500 monks. The Sakya monks were respected throughout Tibet for their depth of study and skill in debate. The Sakya lineage is now based in Rajpur in the state of Uttar Pradesh in Northern India as a result of the Chinese occupation of Tibet and suppression of its Tantric meditative traditions.

The Buddhists believe that through the practice of 'right actions of body, speech, and mind' they can build good Karma, which can be conceptualized as a sort of psychic inertia, such that they can gain a good rebirth in a good family with a comfortable life and with exposure to the religious teachings that will allow them to build even better Karma with which to again enter the Bardo states between death and rebirth (Evans-Wentz, 1960).

Tibetan Buddhists believe that 'all sentient beings' will eventually attain Buddhahood. However, this might take us three Kalpas. A Kalpa is a 'countless eon'. It is taught, however, that one may choose to embrace the Vajrayana (or thunderbolt path), also referred to as Tantra Yana or simply Tantra. Tantra has come to mean the practice of esoteric techniques to promote rapid enlightenment. Through the practice of Tantra an individual of exceptional ability might gain Buddhahood during this lifetime or at the moment of death. Tantric practice is thought to ensure that even an individual of very poor ability will gain Buddhahood within only a few lifetimes.

The Initiation

The Lam Dre' Tantric ritual cycle is described by the Lamas who taught it, as a 'complete teaching'—that is, it contains both basic and advanced information, conjunctive with mental training techniques necessary to attain enlightenment. As such, Lam Dre' is considered by the high Lamas of the Sakya lineage to be an encapsulation of Sakya philosophy and Tantric esotericism. The present discussion is based upon several years of work as a participant observer in the role of initiate-practitioner studying a variety of Tibetan Tantric ritual and meditation practices in North American culminating with a four month Lam Dre' initiation cycle in Northern India. All of the high Lamas of the Sakya lineage must be present for the Lam Dre' to be offered in this form. Most of the instruction was given by five high-ranking Lamas with His Holiness Sakya Trizin[3] presiding and, through initiation, becoming the initiates' Root Guru.[4] Each of the main teachers gave some of the Wang Kurs or initiations that comprise the core of Lam Dre' although the Wang Kurs that were described as the most important were given by His Holiness. All of the main teachers, as well as several monks who offered less central instruction, made constant reference to the importance of our 'connection' with the high Lamas. Several Lamas commented positively about the high levels of meditative and scholarly attainment of the other Lamas and it was made clear that, with reference to both written texts as well as oral tradition, they believed that they had received a shared canonical version of this ritual complex.

The Lam Dre' was held in the village of Puruwala in Northern India—a refugee community of 300 people and 25 four-room houses which is now an important spiritual centre for the Sakya lineage because the highest teachings have been offered there. A new traditional temple was built in Puruwala for the occasion of these initiations that were received by about 800 people, most of whom were monks.

The initiate is expected to receive initiation and instructions for each successive phase of the initiation cycle and is then supposed to practice those teachings through the performance of ritual, meditation and study until 'signs' of readiness for the next stage of practice are evident. Such signs may range from evidence of intense emotion (such as the repetition of a refuge prayer) 'until one is trembling with devotion and tears are falling' to the production of dramatic transformations in the initiate's phenomenology such as the experience of oneself as a multiheaded, multilimbed deity complete with architectural and geographic surround. Further transformations of that experience will be discussed later.

Once an initiation ceremony or Wang Kur has been performed and the relevant instructions for the practice of the ritual-drama or Sadhana have been imparted, the initiate might appear to have received all that he or she needs to know and the ethnographer might be tempted to pack up his or her notebooks. Yet it is explicitly taught that this knowledge cannot be apprehended without major changes in the phenomenology of the practitioner which must be produced by repeated practice of the teachings themselves over a long period of time. The need for exegesis is implicit in the Lamas' instructions. However, the Lamas are explicit in warning the initiates that such an exegesis constitutes a transformation in the phenomenology of the practitioner, not an intellectual abstraction. Their pedagogy appears to consist of a cycle of exploration that involves the receipt of instructions and an initial hermeneutic context within which they may be understood, followed by 'practice' and resultant experience. Based upon the initiate's experience, the Guru provides additional or more subtle hermeneutics coupled with modified or new instructions for practice.

Turner (1974) suggested, with regard to puberty rites, that initiation rituals may serve to promote cognitive development to the level of abstract adult thought that which Piaget called 'formal operations'. The Tibetan Tantric Lamas who taught us see the Tantric teachings as multivocal metaphors addressing levels of world-view beyond Piaget's formal operations. Just as a child's cognitive development to formal operational thought will, after age 12 or so, permit him or her to understand an allegory like *Alice in Wonderland* on a new level—that of metaphor—so Tantric teachers[5] believe that a process of post-adult cognitive development must take place in order for the Lam Dre' teachings to be understood. 'Enlightenment', then, is conceived as a developmental process, rather than a state.

It is made clear at the beginning that if the initiate is to derive the 'fruits' of the Lam Dre' practices he or she is going to have to live the ritual-drama or Sadhana and must incorporate it into his or her experience completely. This is accomplished through the protracted practice of meditation in conjunction with prescribed practices of thought and behaviour in non-meditative states.[6]

Description of the Initiation Cycle

The Lam Dre' initiation cycle is divided into two major parts, the Nang Sum or Triple Teaching and the Gyud Sum or Triple Tantra. The Nang Sum is the more accessible part of the teachings while the Gyud Sum is the more esoteric part. We might expect that the Nang Sum part of the initiation would be amenable to treatment with reference primarily to the cultural categories of mundane experience. It should be noted, however, that one high Lama who came to the initiation at Puruwala had already completed a 12-year cave-retreat meditating the relatively exoteric Nang Sum teachings. Such preparation was considered impressive but not inappropriate. My teachers explicitly base their instructions upon several major premises as follows:

- Knowledge changes the mind of the knower, and conversely knowledge is changed (or is structured) by the mind of the knower. Hence, learning a system of thought and practice changes the mind of the learner such that subsequent explorations of that same system are predicated upon new experiential and intellectual premises which, in turn, change the meaning of that system. Those changes in understanding both require and make comprehensible further instruction.
- For this reason higher truths cannot be presented directly to the initiate. At best they would be incapable of comprehending them, at worst they would be distorted and misunderstood, perhaps in ways that would be harmful to the student or to the teachings. This is a major reason for the secrecy that surrounds these instructions. Many of the most secret instructions are 'orally' transmitted across generations of teachers and students, while access to high Tantric texts is generally restricted to initiates.
- Rather than serving as the explicit presentation of objective information, the teachings are presented explicitly as psychotropic devices designed to facilitate the generation of a mind that is capable of knowing those higher truths. In other words my

teachers consider that teaching, or at least Dharma teaching, consists in the students' manipulation of their subjective reality through the psychotropic use of ritual control strategies and supporting hermeneutics.

- Consequently the teachings consist in a hierarchy of what Tantric teachers call (in English gloss) 'views'. Each level of view is sought through the manipulation of experience (by means of ritual and meditation) conjunctive with supporting hermeneutics (cosmology). It is understood that these are 'partial views' which are presented for heuristic reasons. The truth value of a view is its transcendent quality. Each successive view is intended to be transcended by the progressive changes in consciousness that it facilitates. This succession of views continues until the final transcendence that is enlightenment.

The next level of view then is not seen as being inherently true. Rather, if the initiate acts as if it is true it will shape her or his mind such that a higher level view may generate. Thus, it is an extreme example of what Regna Darnell (1979) called 'deferred communication' with reference to discourse by Cree elders. Tantric teachers explicitly understand the instruction and initiations to consist in multilevelled metaphors that will be differently understood contingent upon the initiate's ability to use meditation practice to 'unfold' the experiences that our teachers say are an important stage of the realization of the ritual symbology to which they have been initiated. The act of initiation, then, operates on two levels. The student receives initiation to a new social role (i.e., 'Tantric person') and, at the same time, is authorized and instructed in the use of powerful ritual tools designed to facilitate the production of non-ordinary states of mind.

As already mentioned, the Lam Dre' teachings, and indeed Tantric teachings in general, are self-consciously predicated upon the assumption that knowledge changes the knower. As a corollary, in order to gain 'higher' knowledge one must change the mental conditions that create the projections which constitute our experience, our reality. At each stage in the Lam Dre' teachings the same set of postulates are presented to the students, but each time within a different, and from the teachers' perspective, a 'higher' interpretive phenomenological framework, an understanding upon which a still higher understanding may be predicated.

By way of example, the beginner sees a meditation deity as a being external to himself or herself. An intermediate practitioner might realize that the deity does not inherently exist but is a set of multivocal symbols which integrates meaning across multiple domains of experience and which may also be 'unfolded' through meditation to reveal deeper meanings that are antecedent to conscious experience but which are the stuff of which that experience is constructed. The deity, then, for that practitioner, is the map for a mind-state which is the goal of a particular meditation practice. A more advanced practitioner might recognize that the deity is closer to being inherently real than they are themselves because the archetypal experiences that comprise the deity reflect, and so constitute portals to awareness of, the underlying processes that create their ordinary reality experience. These prototypical experiences are lower order projections of those processes and hence are proximate to the experience of the universal 'mind stuff' (to use Heisenberg's term) that comprises our experience of the world. Such a view is also called Mahamudra or the 'Great Symbol'.

The Initiation Process

I shall bypass the first two months of the teachings—the Nang Sum here, and will limit myself to the more esoteric Gyud Sum part.[7]

The Gyud Sum teachings involve sets of Wang Kur or ritual initiations that empower the initiate to practise particular meditations. In addition, there is the reading of texts relevant to the practice of the meditations. There is Ti or the offering of traditional secret instructions by the highest Lamas on the practice of the meditation and finally there is 'Lama teaching' that is developed within the relationship between initiates and individual adepts. The Lam Dre' initiation cycle involves a great many Wang Kur, relevant instructions and subsequent practice of meditation and ritual. The Wangs are presented in a fixed sequence, each contingent upon receiving the previous one.[8] The initiate is expected to 'realize the fruits' of the practices in the order in which they are taught. By way of illustration I will present a short description of one of the preliminary practices, called the Mandala offering. There are two kinds of Mandalas, the 'offering Mandala' (or offering of the universe) and the 'visualized Mandala' (or universe of the deity). The offering Mandala may be understood as the initial ritual renunciation of the phenomenal world and the visualized Mandala may be understood initially as the substitution of what my teachers called a 'celestial' or higher phenomenal world. The offering Mandala consists in the creation of a symbolic representation of the universe as the practitioner ordinarily experiences it.

As part of the exercise the initiate uses various colours of dyed rice[9] to create a symbolic world upon a convex silver plate. The offering Mandala is a multivocal symbol wherein the piles of rice represent the 'five continents' arising from a 'vast ocean' represented by the silver plate; at another level they represent the myriad objects of consciousness constructed through the five 'Skandas' or sensory domains, arising from the 'stainless ocean' of pure consciousness (i.e., consciousness without an object or 'Sunyata'). Having created this 'offering Mandala' representing the phenomenal world, she or he intones a Mantra and sweeps the piles of rice from the plate with her or his arm. Thus, the practitioner symbolizes the sweeping away of the phenomenal world, leaving only consciousness itself. Most initiates complete 100,000 offering Mandalas as a preliminary or 'foundation' practice, although some Lamas require 300,000 repetitions or more from their students.

The Lamas who taught us about the Mandala offering were adamant that while even the most deluded of initiates can comprehend the Mandala offering as a symbolic giving up of the 'ordinary' world or 'the world of appearances', the initiate must repeat the Sadhana until it becomes an 'experiential' reality. It is repeatedly stated that it is the generation of the experience rather than the number of repetitions of the ritual which is important. That is to say, the Mandala offering must become a personal and very real experience which constitutes a transform of the Sadhana itself. Various signs, relating to the intensity and completeness of the generated experience, are mentioned as indicators of successful transcoding.

The Mandala of the Deity

After the Mandala offering, the wiping away of 'ordinary reality', the initiate proceeds to construct the extraordinary reality of the deity. This constitutes the vehicle whereby his or her phenomenal world will be re-created. Step by step a complex visual image of the deity and the universe of the deity are constructed in the initiate's imagination. Each aspect of the visualization is described in painstaking detail. The importance of clearly experiencing the visualizations is frequently emphasized. Over and over again the initiates are told that they must 'really know' that they are the deity and the deity's Mandala. In all, the basic instructions for the complete imagery require about fifty pages of text. Such an initial description is further elaborated in much greater detail by the teachers. That is, we are told exactly how a specific symbol should be imaged whereas the initial instructions merely told us which symbol to visualize. The Sadhana presents many sets of symbols that are transformed into other sets of symbols only to be transformed again. If one permits even the slightest distraction one is likely to lose track altogether. Once the initiates have entered this path they are expected to live it twenty-four hours a day. The initiate does not dissolve the deity visualization, but rather arises from the session as the deity. We are encouraged to maintain the image of ourselves and all other appearances as being the Mandala or universe of the deity. Our teachers acknowledge that such imagery is very difficult for most students to create or maintain but they repeatedly emphasize the importance of doing so, providing us with a number of exercises designed to help us to sustain the appropriate imagery. For example, the initiate mentally transmutes their food into nectar and offers it to a sacred syllable which they visualize in their heart-centre.[10] All appearances are to be seen as the deity, and all sounds are to be heard as the Mantra of the deity.

At night the initiate dissolves all of the deities into an empty symbolic field called Sunyata or (in English gloss) 'the plenum void' or 'emptiness'. When the initiate awakens, they arise as the deity, thereby reiterating the theme of the Sadhana. It is made clear that a student who wants 'the fruits' of this practice must do it fully. She or he must be the deity and the Mandala of the deity full time for years. Only with such effort can he or she realize the full meaning encoded by the practice. In order to achieve this end it is common for the initiate to do a series of meditation retreats after receiving the teachings to intersperse various stages of initiation with retreats.[11] It is recognized that the task of creating oneself as the deity is one which is difficult to accomplish while interacting with people who are enmeshed in ordinary or 'consensus' reality.

Clearly, the process of deliberately creating oneself as the deity and the universe of the deity consists in a personal experience of a carefully articulated non-ordinary reality which, at one level, symbolically mirrors the universe of external appearances, the 'world of the senses' in what our teachers called a 'purified', and what I would gloss as an 'archetypical' form. Each symbolic element of that 'universe of the deity' has, associated with it, multiple meanings which integrate various domains of experience. In that sense this symbology is multivocal (Turner, 1969, 1970, 1974). These multiple meanings are explicitly discussed by the Tantric teachers who add to them the concept of meditative 'unfoldment' which extends the concept of symbol multivocality to mean symbolic synthesis across modes of consciousness.

Now, the final stage of symbol visualization will be discussed.

The Process of Completion

The final stage requires that the initiate, while imagining himself or herself as the deity, visualize, 'inside the body of the deity', a corresponding 'body Mandala' consisting of the structure of 'veins' or energy channels and the 'airs' or movement of energy within them. Predicated upon those he/she visualizes a set of inner Chakras ('energy centres'[12]) such as the 64 vein Nirmanichakra at the navel, the eight vein Dharmachakra at the heart centre and so on. Cross points in the five Chakras are visualized as deities. In all, the practitioner must learn to visualize 157 deities, each with its colours, ornaments, 116 physical marks and specific location. The practitioner also mentally transforms the sense organs (the physical organs themselves) into the forms of deities, adding another five to the total 'inner creation' Mandala. One of our teachers mentions that these 162 are only the main ones. As was noted previously, the above described 'Inner Creation' Mandala is visualized at the same time as the 'Outer Creation' Mandala including oneself as the deity and all of the surrounding deities and symbols.

Most of the practices at this stage consist in breathing exercises. These are strategies for manipulating the airs and elements, moving them around in the veins. The initiates are taught that it is these processes which produce conscious experience. Clearly the initiate will require a high level of meditative skill in order to create and maintain the visualization, to complete the process of creation of the Mandala of the central deity and all of the surrounding deities. The Mandala of the deity is designed to collapse in upon itself in the same sequence of practised structural transformations through which it is created. These transformations are spatially organized in developmental sequences, from the periphery to the centre of the Mandala, culminating in the goal symbolic field called Sunyata or emptiness, better translated as the 'plenum void' or consciousness without an object. By producing, manipulating and dissolving the Mandala of the deity the initiate will learn that ordinary reality is also a Mandala. In this process the practitioner's experience of self and other is distilled to elemental form in a set of multivocal symbols which correspond initially to a relatively anthropomorphic body with pseudo-geographic and pseudo-architectural surrounds. Later on he/she will experience himself/herself as both the deity and as the Mandala of the deity. Finally, through the medium of the inner Mandala, described above, he/she will experience himself/herself as being, in his or her nature, the process that underlies the creation of the outer form of the deity and the universe of the deity.

Thus, the entirety of phenomenal experience is mapped onto the psycho-physical body of the practitioner. Each of the primal elements of experience corresponds to a primal body structure and process. More complex and composite experiences are attributed to more complex and composite structures of veins which represent transformations upon these lower order symbols. The transformations from primal structure to primal experience (i.e., of the effect of moving the 'airs' in the 'veins'), from primal to archetypal experience and finally to mundane experience are articulated in the morphological pattern whereby the veins and airs elaborate to form the outer world or the 'world of the senses'. Again, while this is a cosmological map of the forces which are believed to underlay experience, its major function is as a map for experience.

The Vajra Body as Symbolic Control System

It appears that the deity map of the body is intended as a symbolic control system. My teachers do not pretend to their Tantric students that the deities to be visualized have inherent existence. The practitioner is expected to be able to come to experience the veins and elements as the Guna or essence, the qualities of the deity, without having to have recourse to a pseudo-physical form. At this point in the initiation cycle the Lamas make it apparent to the students that the deities are symbolic strategies for manipulating psychological processes. The first, albeit long and arduous, step is to establish this symbolic paradigm in the experience of the practitioner. The second part of this ritual process is to link, through intellectual discourse as well as through sets of transformations of symbols in the initiate's visualization practices, the paradigm to all facets of the practitioners' experience (both 'ordinary' and 'extraordinary') of the world. If the initiate can accomplish this practice he/she is now in a position to fold the projection back in upon itself. In so doing he/she aims to transform and disengage from awareness the composite elements which constitute the lower order objects of consciousness upon which ordinary experience is predicated. The goal of such global disentrainment of the cognitive models or experiences antecedent to ordinary experience is to generate the symbolic field upon which they, in turn, are predicated. According to my teachers, diligent practice may enable the initiate to further penetrate to the experience of consciousness itself or consciousness without an object, Sunyata. The bench mark of Sunyata or 'the plenum void' is the criterion for epistemological objectivity—the 'only' basis for knowing.

Understanding Inner Signs

It can be suggested here following Laughlin et al., (1984), that the deity and associated mental techniques ('Yogas'[13]) have been developed over time because these particular signs have proven to be efficacious codes for the keying and activation (i.e., activation in consciousness) of deep, genetically and neuro-physiologically based elements of experience. These non-ordinary experiences constitute lower order components of ordinary experience and, as such, are experiential precursors to Sunyata, the target symbolic field.

This hypothesis implies that the 'outer sign' as presented to the practitioner must be keyed in some way to 'universal' or genetically based signs. Webber (1979) postulated that outer signs represent the cultural, sub-cultural, and perhaps idiosyncratic transforms of genetically based universal signs. For example, focusing one's attention on the experience of the breath at one's nostrils, which Tibetan Tantrists would call an 'outer sign', does, for many individuals, yield spontaneously the arising of an internally generated experience, which Tantrists call the 'arising sign' and which a number of initiates have described variously as resembling 'a crystalline structure', 'fish eggs', or 'a crystal network'. While interviewees have usually made reference to such visual descriptors, most also mention kinaesthetic, auditory (e.g., the 'music of the spheres' was mentioned by several interviewees) and other sensory experiences, described as allegorical to the visual experience. I have interviewed several meditation teachers with extensive cross-cultural experience and all claim that the only culture-specific variation in students' reports of the results of extensive work with this practice is that of the choice of descriptive metaphor. It seems possible that all are having essentially[14] the same experience.

With regard to deity visualizations, Webber (ibid.) posited two stages of internalization of the object of meditation. In the first stage, the practitioner creates a stable mental replica of the outer sign. He notes that practitioners report that this 'inner sign' tends to elaborate itself, with the apparently spontaneous appearance of additional detail as well as changes in appearance. The inner sign may also become animate, again without the conscious intervention of the practitioner. Hence the inner sign represents a transcoding of the outer sign which produces a personal object of meditation. With extensive meditation upon this inner sign, a further transcoding is possible, producing the universal or 'arising' sign. The assertion here is that culture-specific symbology may be used to generate experiences for which the potential exists in all human beings. The teachers assured us that such an arising sign constitutes a universal transcoding of the object of meditation or 'outer sign' which will occur with sufficient practice regardless of the cultural background of the practitioner. Where they would agree that the outer form of a deity, for example, is mediated by cultural background, the 'essence' or final inner transcoding of the deity is posited as inherent in the human mind (see also Webber, 1979). This experience of the outer sign being displaced in awareness by the arising sign is called 'Jhana', a Pali[15] term which translates as 'absorption'. Such an experience may involve visual, olfactory, kinaesthetic or auditory modalities and is remarkable for its affective intensity (Laughlin et al., 1984; Shearer et al., 1977; Webber, 1979). The universal sign that arises in response to meditation upon the object is called an 'arising sign'—hence, this is the practice of 'arising Yoga'.

Understandably, no specific teachings are offered regarding the attributes of the arising sign, nor is the initiate necessarily informed that such an experience may occur. It is considered necessary that the practitioner should produce it through his/her own efforts. My teachers emphasize that this stage, although it may take years of diligent practice to reach and may not be reached by all practitioners, is only the beginning. One continues to meditate upon the arising sign as a vehicle for further transformation. For some practitioners, classified as of 'superior ability', absorption into the universal or arising sign may lead to the experience of Sunyata, a clear awareness that Tantrics believe is 'pure consciousness', or consciousness without an object. This final transformation in consciousness is the target symbolic field, the 'ground of being', and the experiential bench mark from which perspective conventional concepts of 'illusion' and 'reality' are seen as semantically equivalent fallacies. While such an experience constitutes 'enlightenment', the Lamas are quick to point out that this event marks only the first stage of enlightenment or first 'Bhumi'. There are 13 Bhumis.

Final Comments

I return to my earlier points: (1) the ethnographic truncation of our representation of our informants' range of conscious experience, (2) asking questions about non-ordinary states of consciousness, and (3) the ethnographic telescoping of time-frame with regard to ritual initiation. These three issues are central to a study of religion which respects the knowledge and experience of our cross-cultural teachers.

Whether or not my teachers' hermeneutic system is valid within other cultures' frames of reference is a matter for a separate discussion. For an ethnographer it is sufficient that this hermeneutic system is antecedent to the world-view of its adherents. I suggest that, as researchers, working with people whose world-views are based upon experience that is systematically transformed through the use of techniques such as ritual practice and meditation, it is inappropriate to base our research upon assumptions, experience and questions that ignore that experience. We are obliged to consider the intentionality of ritual from our informant's/teacher's perspectives and experiences. It is the experience of transformation with which both the teachers and initiates at Lam Dre' were concerned. For them, the ritual's purpose is to yield experiences that render new levels of hermeneutics understandable and, more importantly, make further symbolic penetration possible. Invariably the Lamas' answers to questions about the meanings of practices take the form of instructions for mental-exercises designed to enhance the initiate's personal transcoding of those practices. Furthermore, successful transcoding (i.e., the generation of the inner sign followed by the arising sign) is only an interim goal of the practice. When the initiate achieves a new level of transcoding of the meditation object, the Lamas provide him or her with new instructions for seeking the next level.

Models for the analysis of rituals that are unable to incorporate successive transformations of key symbols across shifts in modes of consciousness must invariably ignore those transformative qualities of ritual which are definitive for many of our informants. So, too, must they fail to recognize the difference in experience and therefore in meaning between the practice of ritual adepts and that of non-adepts. Perhaps, too, such models preclude our teachers teaching us their culture's discoveries about human nature. Analyses of ritual through conventional intellectual symbolic exegesis provide valuable insight into the ways in which rituals do, to paraphrase Wallace (1972), 'the work of religion'. Tibetan Tantric teachers provide such scholarly exegesis as a part of their epistemological programme and some Lamas recognize that exegesis within a Western cultural idiom is useful for Western initiates. The Lamas who taught the Lam Dre' clearly believe that deeper understanding, the understanding which constitutes the value of this ritual cycle, may only be apprehended through meditative exegesis. They also believe that analyses of their ritual epistemologies which omit this essential pedagogical component can only 'devalue' their culture's contributions to human understanding.

It can be noted, after Turner (1974), that because their semiotic operating ranges transcend the boundaries of ordinary time and space, the elements and processes of ritual integrate broad ranges of cognitive and social phenomena within a phenomenal matrix that is beyond the bounds of ordinary experience. Such a semiotic matrix necessarily cuts across that range of cognitive elements and processes which produce our ordinary experience, but is not limited to that sub-matrix. Ritual then is a vehicle with which we activate in our awareness cognitive matrices which may subsume all or part of, but are not limited to, those which produce the reality we ordinarily experience. Ritual then, frees us of the reality of ordinary or 'normal waking state' time and space to experience and formulate alternate realities which cut across or render meaningless the categories and constraints of 'ordinary' reality.

Our informants have been telling us all along that their ritual systems constitute epistemological pedagogies through which the practitioner's cognized model of reality is transformed in the direction of greater isomorphism with that set of principles and processes which comprise natural law (Chagnon, 1977; Evans-Wentz, 1958; Firth, 1967; Laughlin et al., 1984). We have not heard them, in part, because our colonial and post-colonial ethnographic discourse has tended to minimize the inclusion of references to non-Western pedagogies as a basis for acquiring knowledge and tends to use Western cultural models as the baseline for the evaluation of such epistemological claims. Initiation as a subset of ritual may be understood as the introduction of a system of semiotic operators that function as cognitive/ phenomenological devices to integrate, as a symbolic control system, various symbolic elements and transformational processes which underlie human experience in a matrix that is free of normal spatial and temporal determinants. In this non-ordinary reality,[16] the symbolizing process is freed from the matrix within which cultural or personal conditioning has bound it. Its elements exist in limenality or lessened coalescence and are ultimately re-combined to form a new matrix, a new social and cognitive reality. To paraphrase Anthony Wallace (1972), ritual is where the work of religion is done. There is ample support in the literature for the contention that ritual-practitioners usually regard their practice as making possible more ontologically valid reality-experience. Further, it would appear that the initiates' progress through the series of initiations and practices that constitutes an initiation cycle often may involve multiple levels of ritually introduced experience which are thought by the teachers and initiates to constitute a hierarchy of states of consciousness. Tibetan teachers have developed a vast and complex lateral and hierarchical taxonomy of mind-states to be attained through application of ritual as the technology of their epistemological system (Beyer, 1978; Evans-Wentz, 1958) but are not unique in this regard. For example Reichel-Dolmatoff's (1971) Amazonian teachers refer to 'seven levels of knowing' that may be sequentially attained through appropriate initiation and ritual practice, Rinzai Zen recognizes three 'Kenshos' or levels of enlightenment[17] while Jainism recognizes 'Twelve Facets of Reality' (Chitrabhanu, 1980). Similarly, Marcel Griaule (1965) reports that Dogon secret society initiates seek to attain successive levels of knowing through their ritual-initiation cycle.

Questions regarding the purpose of initiation are often answered by anthropologists' informants with reference to shifts in consciousness such that the 'reality' experienced by the initiate during the liminal and post-initiation phases differs dramatically from their former experience. Such an insider's view implies a developmental perspective that accounts for the greater truth-value that is attributed to the experience of adepts within such ritual-epistemologies. If ritual and ritual initiation can function to precipitate experience that is not a part of the 'normal waking state' of consciousness, as the ethnographic record seems to indicate that it can (e.g., Cove, 1987; d'Aquilly et al., 1979; Katz, 1982, 1984; Webber, 1979), then any theoretical formulations dealing with these phenomena must take into account data relevant to the production, experience, and ontological consequences of such shifts in consciousness.

The field worker faces a quite practical problem when confronted with informants who claim that their world-views and decision-making processes are mediated by experience derived from one or more transformations of consciousness. He or she is likely to ask questions that, at best, reveal a lack of relevant experience. Further, it is likely that the sorts of explanation that are offered to a naive questioner are very different than those likely to be offered to a fellow practitioner. For the informant, the researcher may appear to be stubbornly denying very real experience that is the essence of ritual pedagogy.[18] Tibetan Tantric teachers are quite willing to discuss Dharma[19] with Western scientists. As a group, however, they see us as rather obstinate primitives who must be talked down to. With great courtesy they make it clear that unless we are willing to make the effort to generate the experience upon which understanding must be based, there is little that they can do except humour us.

Most tragically, often the field worker never finds out that he or she has been dealt with according to perceived limitations in his or her experience. If we are genuinely interested in our informants' unique experience, it may be necessary for some researchers to undertake the training necessary to convince our informants that we are capable of inter-subjectivity (see Katz, 1982; Tart, 1975).

A further common deficit in anthropological treatments of ritual initiation results from a tendency to treat the ceremony as an isolated event apart from the extremely lengthy period of preparation leading up to it. Some authors (Jorgensen, 1972; Jung, 1944, 1952, 1956; Katz, 1982; Whiting et al., 1958) have taken this preparation into account though none have considered preparation and ceremony as a single phenomenon.[20] My teachers tell me that the preparation is essential because (to use a Tibetan metaphor) it produces 'fertile soil' in which the initiation ceremony 'plants a seed'. In addition, after initiation, only the individual's regular, (usually daily) recapitulation of the initiation process through personal practice can produce 'the fruit' which is the goal of a ritual cycle (see also Katz, 1982; Laughlin et al., 1984; Reichel-Dolmatoff, 1971). The ethnographic record, then, requires a theoretical treatment of initiation ritual.

Respecting the Cross-cultural Practitioners' Experience

The theoretical concerns discussed above are particularly relevant to the analysis of Tibetan Tantric initiation and ritual practice. The Lam Dre' initiation cycle which is my ethnographic focus here was, according to Tibetan historical sources, developed by the Indian sage Virupa at the ancient Nalanda University. Tibetan Buddhists have preserved a ritual system which was developed by Indian Buddhists who brought these traditions to Tibet around 600 AD. Tibetan monastic institutions have done an excellent job, for over thirteen centuries, of preserving written and oral teachings which were originally adopted from India. Through a carefully controlled programme of oral transmission they have maintained lineages of adept practitioners passing the oral instructions and discipline from master to student.[21]

The entire purpose of that ancient school's teachings was its intent to evoke in the individual Yogis who applied its techniques a 'direct' experience of Buddhist tenets. Given that this avowedly epistemological enterprise is predicated upon the ritual control of experience, an adequate theoretical formulation must model the relationship between a system of ritual-initiation and the practitioners' phenomenology. Further, such a model must account for short- and long-term changes in the ritual practitioner's world-view as a consequence of initiation and ritual activity. Anthropologists have long studied ritual and ritualinitiation. Unfortunately existing conceptual and methodological tools seem to cause more problems than they solve when applied to a ritual system as complex as that employed by Tibetan Tantrists. The Tibetan system, while extremely sophisticated, is not unique in its use of ritual based pedagogical strategies. Theoretical and methodological biases have resulted in the failure of field workers to ask the sort of questions which would allow them to elicit and model technologies for the realization of cosmologies in the cultures they study. Griaule (1965), for example, worked for 12 years with the Dogon before his teachers felt he was ready to be taught cosmology. Even so, this instruction was given as if to a child. Similar experiences are reported by other authors (Chagnon, 1977; Given, 1990; Reichel-Dolmatoff, 1971). I suggest that, where our informants base their teaching upon ritually derived experience, the logical prerequisite for producing what Geertz (1973) calls 'thick description' is 'thick participation' on the part of the researcher. This approach requires that one meet one's cross-cultural teacher on 'their' terms as far as possible, including sincere participation in culture-specific pedagogy. Even with my efforts in this regard, my own work reflects the information available to a very junior practitioner. That information is, of course, further distorted because I must examine it and discuss it within conceptual frameworks provided by my own, not the Tibetan teachers' culture. My ethnographic example demonstrates that it is necessary for Western scientists to examine ritual pedagogy both with, and without, reference to the host culture's hermeneutics. It is necessary to study the phenomenological as well as the social-structural concomitants of ritual practice.

Perhaps more importantly, this example demonstrates that we, as anthropologists, must be willing to undergo change, to place our concepts and ourselves at risk. Such an enterprise, according to my Tibetan teachers, will inevitably require a careful re-examination of our personal as well as our professional a priori assumptions regarding the nature of mind, the process of knowing and our concepts of research and pedagogy. For some social scientists the laudable questioning of Eurocentric teaching, research and theory construction involves primarily applications of European conflict theory by Asians, Latin Americans, Arabs, Africans and other non-Europeans. Such a focus constricts theoretical scope while remaining essentially European in its concerns and conceptual formulations. A more powerful challenge to Eurocentric epistemological and pedagogical models is offered by that majority of other cultures who predicate the transmission of knowledge upon the ritual-transformation of the knower. Research and teaching consist in the transmission of culture. If we are serious about opening that process to include the cultural other, the form of such inclusion must take into account other cultures' strategies of education for experience.

Notes

1. The term Tantra has come to refer to the practice of esoteric ritual techniques in order to attain rapid enlightenment. Tantrayana (yana=way) is also referred to as the Vajrayana or 'thunderbolt path'. A discussion of the three levels of practice—Hinayana, Mahayana and Tantrayana is provided in Given (1990).
2. I refer the reader to the works of Bourgignon (1973), Harner (1973, 1980), Katz (1982, 1984), Laughlin et al. (1979), Lex (1979), McManus (1979), Shearer (1977, 1979) and Webber (1979) for discussions of relevant issues.
3. His Holiness is also referred to as the Sakyapa or head of the Sakya lineage. As such, his religious status is comparable, within the Sakya lineage to that of His Holiness, Tenzin Gyatso, the head of the Gelug lineage who is also the legitimate ruler of Tibet and is best known as the Dalai Lama.
4. One's Root Guru is the Lama from whom one has received the highest teachings. The relationship can be one of considerable personal intimacy although many students will rarely see their Root Guru, receiving most of their guidance from other teachers. The essential dimension of the relationship with the Root Guru is that of the 'direct-transmission' of the meditation experience or 'empowerment' which takes place during the Wang Kur or ritual of initiation and through contact with the Lama. The Lam Dre' is an initiation to one form of 'Guru Yoga'. It was taught that the Root Guru 'takes on the Karma' of the student and that thenceforth the students and teacher's Karma were 'yoked' (the root of the term Yoga means 'to yoke').
5. Throughout this article I avoid the ethnographic convention which would have me refer to the Tibetans who were so kind as to teach me about the Tibetan form of the Buddha Dharma as 'informants'. The label 'teachers' better reflects the nature of our relationship and, I would argue, of the appropriate relationship between a culture member and a cross-cultural researcher. Where I am less certain about the roles of interviewer and interviewee I use the more conventional term.
6. I have described the sequence and the teachings in detail elsewhere (Given, 1990). The information runs to hundreds of pages of precise instructions regarding techniques to be used by the initiates to manipulate their consciousness such as to be able to generate the experiences upon which particular doctrines are based. My purpose here is to elucidate several principles upon which such practices appear to be based, on the evidence of my own experience as an initiate as well as that of extensive interviews with initiates, and to provide a brief example of such a practice.

7. For ethical reasons I will not reveal specific meditation or ritual instructions with sufficient detail to permit unauthorized practice or teaching. In the Tibetan Tantric tradition, only a practitioner who has been authorized to do so may transmit a particular practice.
8. So important are the appropriate initiations that the practitioners were issued with a document upon which each initiation was listed; a stamp was to be placed beside it upon completion of the Wang Kur. This 'Dharma passport' was required in order to gain access to the next initiation. One Lama pointed out to me that the document would be very useful to the initiates because we would undoubtedly require further instruction as our practice progressed after the initiation cycle was over. Most Lamas would be reluctant to discuss Tantric practices unless we could demonstrate that we had received the appropriate authorization for practice.
9. Other symbolic media, including hand Mudras or gestures, may also be used to construct the Mandala.
10. The heart Chakra or energy centre is visualized in the centre of one's chest.
11. The Lam Dre' is more commonly offered as a three-year retreat. Several Lamas explained to me, during instruction sessions, that a number of meditation retreats would normally be interspersed with the initiations and instructions. One Lama pointed out that this allowed monks and nuns from various parts of Tibet to receive all of the initiations and essential transmissions during one extended trip and they could then receive personal guidance nearer their home monasteries. The initiates were repeatedly told that, while they were receiving all of the essential instructions, they would have to do years of practice and seek additional personal instruction in order to realize their meaning.
12. The Chakras are usually visualized as multi-spoked wheels. The locations of the main Chakras correspond roughly with those of neural plexus.
13. Yoga is usually glossed as 'way' in the sense of 'Bhakti Yoga' as the way of Bhakti or devotion. Yoga can also refer to a specific technique or set of techniques such that a given practice may embody a variety of Yogas. In the case of the Hevajra Tantra which is the focus of Lam Dre', there are 10 main Yogas associated with more advanced practice.
14. I imply essentialism quite deliberately here.
15. Pali is the language in which the historical Buddha's teachings are recorded (i.e., the Pali Canon). The historical Buddha likely taught in both Kosalese and Maghadese.
16. That is in an Alternate State of Consciousness or A.S.C.
17. I depend on a Japanese Zen Roshi and thorough discussions with several Japanese Zen monks.

18. In Levi-Strauss's words, 'rituals think through man'. To paraphrase Cezanne, the initiate comes to understand the ritual by 'becoming its consciousness' (Merleau-Ponty, 1977).
19. The Sanskrit term Dharma and Pali word Dhamma are usually translated as 'religious teachings'. For my Lama teachers Dharma is the study of the process of coming to know and as such encompasses the Western categories of science and religion. I suggest that a better English gloss might be 'epistemology'.
20. Extensive periods of preparation often constitute a major part of the mythology of initiation (see Evans-Wentz, 1928).
21. It is reasonable to argue that relatively few changes have taken place in the basic form of the Lam Dre' initiation cycle. The 26 written texts of the Lam Dre' date from specific times, places and authors while the transmission of the oral tradition has passed through a relatively small number of high Lamas. The lineage is taught to initiates and does not appear to be telescoped. I suggest too, that the practice of integrating oral and textual transmission with the meditation exercises which are considered necessary for what my teachers call the 'unfoldment' of these practices has a stabilizing affect. Finally, as mentioned earlier, Tibetan Tantric teachers make clear distinctions among textual transmission, the oral transmission of lineage teaching, and the more idiosyncratic form of Lama teaching, which places considerable emphasis upon the need to perfectly replicate the former two categories.

14 Globalization and Religion

Beyond the Primacy of the Political

Ananta Kumar Giri

Globalization has become the sign of our times but like most other contemporary signs it has become a contested one as its complex unfoldment in the world and discourses about it have led to radically divergent debates, positions and perceptions. Not long ago, the discourse of globalization was mainly confined to the domains of economy and politics. But of late there has been a broadening of focus to attend to the cultural and 'subjective' dimensions of globalization as global processes now touch upon the thresholds of self and culture, breaking down insularities, and creating new trajectories of flow and interpenetration, which deeply affect the everyday life of individuals (Hannerz, 1992; Robertson, 1992). Scholars of globalization are now concerned with 'sociocultural processes and forms of life which are emerging as the global begins to replace the nation-state as the decisive framework for social life' (Featherstone and Lash, 1995). They provide us a multidimensional view and a 'perspectival' construction of the contemporary global-human condition. While for Robertson (1992), the constitutive variables in the global human-condition today are self, national society, world system of societies, and the humankind, for Appadurai (1990) these are the global flows in mediascapes, ethnoscapes, technoscapes, and ideascapes, and Hannerz (1992) looks at this cultural complexity today as a configuration of four non-reducible variables—state, market, movements and forms of life.

Globalization of religion, spirituality and religious movements is an important aspect of this broader process of globalization which takes us beyond the primacy of the political and the economic and urges us to understand the dynamics of religion as it undergoes transformation within itself and diffuses across the global terrain. Our contemporary moment is characterized by a global resurgence of religion which is taking place in all varieties of social systems (from the technologically most complex to the technologically simple societies) and is manifesting itself in many forms—from religious fundamentalism to a spiritual renewal of self and society. The resurgence is, in a manner of speaking, contrary to the prediction of the prophets of modernity that with the march of time, religion will lose its public significance and, if at all, will persist only as a residue in individual lives, as an aspect of personal faith. As one perceptive student (Sacks, 1991) of contemporary religious resurgence tells us:

> Faith persists and in persisting allows us to build a world more human than one in which men, nations or economic systems have become gods. Twenty years ago it seemed as if religion had run its course in the modern world. Today a more considered view would be that its story has hardly yet begun.

As we begin to understand this unfolding story of the persistence of faith in our contemporary globalized world, we witness within each of the world religion a double transformation—a progressive, practical and dialogical transformation on the one hand and a conservative fundamentalism on the other. In order to understand the link between religion and globalization, it is helpful to understand this double transformation going on within each of the world religions rather than to focus only on global diffusion since what is being diffused under the condition of globalization is not unchanged religion per se but either progressive, practical, spiritual and dialogical religion or fundamentalism or both. Mobilization of religion is not confined to either fundamentalist or political mobilization. Religious mobilization at the contemporary juncture also refers to ethical and aesthetic mobilization and the mobilization of a practical spirituality. While ethical mobilization makes religions responsible for ameliorating the condition of suffering in the lives of others, aesthetic mobilization focuses on appropriate self-cultivation and spiritual transformation in the life of the actors. In the mobilization of a practical spirituality, the followers of religious movements realize that spiritual realization is possible only through addressing the concrete problems of men and women who live in their midst. As E.H. Cousins (1985) tells us in his *Global Spirituality*: 'People of faith now rediscover the material dimensions of existence and their spiritual significance.'

True, major world religions have always had a concern throughout history to extend themselves globally but in the contemporary period of globalization there is an intensification of global relationships within religions and some shift in the method and object of their diffusion across the world. While earlier, globalization of religion was primarily accompanied by conquest, now the will to conquer and convert is slowly giving way to acknowledge members of other religions as fellow pilgrims in the global heritage of a spiritual humanity and be engaged in dialogue with them—a dialogue which is not confined only to verbal communication and rational exchange of faiths and argumentation but includes varieties of practices of love and programmes of concrete and embodied togetherness. But by globalization of religion, both in the common parlance as well as in scholarly discourse, what we predominantly have in mind is the globalization of politically motivated fundamentalism and militant religious movements. Surely when we look at the religious scenario of the world, we find instances of such religious globalization. While here it is easy to pick on the globalization of Islamic fundamentalism—from Afghanistan to Chechnya, but there are instances of globalization of fundamentalism from Christianity and Hindus as well. The conservative New Christian Right in the United States which altered the terms of discourse in American society under the leadership of evangelists such as Jerry Fallwell has been globalized (Beyer, 1990) and any visitor to the US and UK can easily notice the intense mobilization of Hindu fundamentalist movements such as Visva Hindu Parishad (VHP) and Rastriya Swayam Sevak Sangha (RSS).

But globalization of fundamentalist and militant religious movements does not exhaust the religious scenario of the contemporary globalized world. If VHP has been globalized so has been Swadhyaya—a socio-spiritual movement in contemporary India which works on self-development and social transformation. Swadhyaya works in UK, US, Caribbean and Africa. Unlike VHP and RSS, Swadhyaya in a country like England is not mobilizing the Hindus against either the Muslims or Christians but encouraging them to be engaged in varieties of constructive activities and to be open towards other religious faiths. In Swadhyaya we witness an ethical and spiritual mobilization of religion in the direction of a more inclusive ethical awareness, struggle for a practical spirituality—a mobilization which transcends the familiar boundaries of the outsider and the insider, good and evil. But ethical mobilization here is not just doing well for the other but also developing oneself, making oneself a servant of God and a work of art for creating beautiful and just relationships in society (Giri and Philip, 2000). Ethical mobilization includes an aesthetic mobilization of self for appropriate self-development, self-fashioning and self-cultivation.

Globalization of Devotional Hinduism

Globalization of Hinduism at the contemporary juncture while involving the globalization of a much more militant Hinduism such as Visva Hindu Parishad (VHP) and Rastriya Swayam Sevak Sangha (RSS) whose activities are widespread in a country like England also includes spread of initiatives such as Swadhyaya which embodies an ethical, aesthetic and spiritual mobilization. The same is also true of the Sai Baba movement in Bali which owes its inspiration to the life, mission and work of Satya Sai Baba and the movement which follows him in India. In Bali, while providing a constructive critique of and alternative to the highly ritualized Adat religion which is the customary religion of the land, the Sai Baba movement also provides an alternative to the state sponsored Agama Hinduism which has become part of a bureaucratic state and whose ethical agenda lacks a dimension of depth and self-development. As Leo Howe (1999) tells us: '... devotees of Sai Baba, while valuing their Balinese identity in some contexts' are also striving for a more global and deeper identity:

> This new identity is about the individual in the world or more precisely the individual in his or her specific relationship to the universal God. It is an identity based on the essential self deep within one. Experienced and dedicated devotees frequently speak about improving and developing themselves. Overtime their nascent identity progressively takes on a specific shape. It is molded by the change in life-style that members undergo. (ibid.)

The Swadhyaya initiative in England and the Sai Baba movement in Bali both have a history of around 20 years in their respective countries. Swadhyaya came to England in 1978 and Sai Baba to Bali in 1981. Let us begin with the vision and dynamics of Swadhyaya. Swadhyaya is a socio-spiritual initiative in self-development and social transformation in India. It started with the spiritual discourses of its main source of inspiration, Pandurang Shastri Athavale who is called Dadajee (elder brother). After silent work in villages in Gujarat for 30 years, it took a socially active turn in the building of many Prayogas for self-development such as the community worship centre and community farming. Bhaktipheri is the foundational Prayoga or experiment of Swadhyaya where the participants go to meet interested people near and far without any expectation. Swadhyaya in England emerged from the pioneering Bhaktipheri that Swadhyayees from Bombay (now Mumbai), the coordinating headquarters of Swadhyaya, had undertaken in London and Leicester. The Gujarati Hindus of England—Swadhyaya has it most active base in Gujarat in India—many of whom had earlier come from East Africa started taking part in this unfolding movement. They also started doing intense Bhaktipheri and this made Swadhyaya spread. In this initial phase, Swadhyayees were listening to the audio cassettes of Dadajee in the Swadhyaya Kendra. But then came the phase of video cassettes and on Sundays, the day of the Swadhyaya Kendra, Swadhyayees attend Dadajee's video Prabachana as an act of worship. This is similar to the way the followers of Sai Baba participate in the Bhajan meetings in India which is for them an act of worship (Babb, 1987).

Some of the participants of Swadhyaya in England had also participated in the Bhajan Mandalis of Satya Sai Baba in East Africa, but they found just attending Bhajans is inadequate to fulfil their desire for more concrete social action. Swadhyaya's practice of devotional labour or Shramabhakti where participants join and share their labour and time together with a spirit of devotion provided them an alternative. There are different projects for the offer of Shramabhakti in India as it is in England. But three unique projects of Swadhyaya in England are—Sneha Care (a care of affection), Eikya Utpadan (production of unity) and Poonam Milan (meeting on the fool moon day).

Sneha Care is a day care centre which is a Prayoga of Swadhyaya for the Swadhyayees of London to offer their efficiency of taking care of the elderly at the feet of God. They take part in this activity for their own self-development. The whole day care centre is run on the basis of the Shramabhakti of the participants. For instance, the care workers are devotional volunteers. The same is true of those who drive the van to pick up and to drop the users. The Swadhyaya Sneha Care centre runs in East London and is catering to five local authorities. Those who work in the kitchen are also Swadhyaya volunteers. The volunteers are called Pujaris or worshippers. The day care centre needs 10 Pujaris every day but there are 60 to 70 people in London ready to render their Shramabhakti. Some of them have to drive for hours to join the day care centre. The centre is managed by Hemanta Bhai and Bhiru Behen who are professional care workers working with the social welfare system of UK. Since other care workers are not professionally trained, they are given training in hygiene and in the maintenance of client-confidentiality.

The day care centre was earlier running three days a week but now it is running two days a week as it has moved to a new community centre. There is a growing demand for this service of Sneha Care from the people of Asian community as the mainstream social service system of UK is not sensitive to the cultural world of the Asians. According to Hemanta Bhai:

> The centre charges a fee of 35 pounds per person per day to the local authorities which are much less compared to other private contractors. The objective here is not to make money but to provide a model to the local society and provide a platform to the Swadhyayees where they practise to give their prime time.

Eikya Utpadan or production of unity is another Prayoga of Swadhyaya. In this the women participants of Swadhyaya meet around an activity such as preparing food together. In the Hindu families in England even if it is not an extended family if there are more than one woman in the house it becomes difficult for them to agree on the food items to prepare. The Swadhyaya Prayoga of Eikya Utpadan helps them to produce unity among women in the household as well as in the larger society. Another Prayoga or experiment is the Poonam Milan or meeting on the full moon day. In this, women meet on the full moon day just to be with themselves.

Peter Beyer (1994) argues that in the globalized world pure religion is at a discount and religion in order to be able to influence the believers as well as to have wider public influence has to be applied. In

Swadhyaya we see many applied activities of religion though unlike Beyer's presupposition, these activities are not only immanent, they also embody a vibrant link with the transcendent in the form of practical spirituality. Yogeswara Krishi is another applied or practical project of Swadhyaya in which Swadhyayees come and offer their devotional labour in the field of agriculture. Whatever is produced from this becomes the impersonal wealth which is shared with the needy members of the community as a gift from God.

When Swadhyaya began in England there was a feeling of uncertainty on the part of the participants whether they would be able to go to another person's house without prior appointment as part of Bhaktipheri. But encouraged by Dadajee, Swadhyayees started doing it. Now, they also undertake Bhaktipheri in distant towns. For example, Swadhyayees of East London go in Bhaktipheri to Nottingham, and of Leicester, to Cambridge. They go in Bhaktipheri once a month for one weekend. For them to leave their work and to join in Bhaktipheri requires a great deal of preparation but through this they learn to develop themselves and live for others and for God.

Swadhyaya provides the participants frames for creative identity formation. This is especially true of the younger generation. Living in the English society both in the school and in the wider society they are asked questions about their religion. Children are subjected to such derisive comments in the school: 'Oh! your religion has monkey God (referring to Hanuman) and Elephant God (referring to Ganesh).' Swadhyaya teaches the participants about the symbolic meaning of such Gods as well as about the scientific basis of the religious rituals. In the context of a coming of a post-traditionalist rationality and globalization, the challenge of justification of religious belief is an important one but Swadhyaya's response to it is not confined only to a rational reconstruction of religious rituals but includes experiments in practical spirituality and Prayogas of self-development and holding the hands of the other. Justification here is much more than Habermasian (Habermas, 1993) rational argumentation and application which is divorced from a transcendental inspiration of love, and practice in these experiments while embodying a critique of scholastic reason is much more than rational strategies of Bourdieu (2000).

In London and Leicester RSS and VHP also work. While the participants of Sakhas of RSS appreciate the role of Swadhyaya they complain that Swadhyaya does not fight with those who attack Hindus and does not do enough to save the culture. In a discussion on this held in Nottingham during my visit, one Swadhyayee activist told the Sakha activist: 'While by culture Sakha means the culture of the land and has a territorial notion of culture, Swadhyaya has a much wider notion of culture which is Vedic. Protection and nurturance of this culture requires silent cultural work.' Swadhyaya further argues that Hindu culture cannot be saved by building temples. Hindus in England seem to be taking satisfaction in the fact that they are buying churches to build temples as many of the churches are suffering from the problem of low attendance. Swadhyayees warn the builders of temples that if they do not make religion a practical and spiritual quest in the life of the participants then temples would have the same fate as the mainline churches in the West. Swadhyaya is engaged in a constructive critique and reconstruction of Hinduism. Bhaktipheri is a social force in Swadhyaya. The Sai Baba movement in Bali is also engaged in a critique and reconstruction of both the ritualistic Hinduism of Bali—the Adat religion—and its more formalized Agama religion. This movement is working in Bali since 1981 and it has centres in many towns. Though it does not have any formal membership, approximately 5,000 to 6,000 people regularly attend the meeting. While in Adat religion, being a member of the temple congregation one has to pay membership fee, in the devotional Hinduism of the Sai Baba movement there is no such requirement for payment of fees. The centres on the other hand have both educational programmes in which religious education is imparted as well as community development programmes for the spiritual development of the participants. As Howe (1999) tells us: 'Members make charitable donations (money, materials, labour) to help others whether these are followers or not. They also help to clean and renovate hospitals, schools, Balinese temples, and commercial facilities.'

Followers of Sai Baba in Bali also 'condemn competitive ritual display, gambling, cock-fighting and the slaughtering and eating of animals, all of which are central to local Adat religion' (ibid.). They also provide an alternative to orthodoxy and hierarchy in both the Adat and the Agama religions. Though the Sai Baba movement in India bears the mark of class and caste distinction, in Bali it is relatively egalitarian. It 'provides the unique combination of personal and loving relationship with a loving God together with a relatively egalitarian theology and social organization which help maintain the struggle against the inequalities embedded in Balinese institutions' (ibid.).

There seems to have taken place some shift in the globalization of the Sai Baba movement. The Sai Baba movement in India is much more controlled by hierarchies of caste and class than it is in Bali (Babb, 1987). Probably the Balinese under the weight of hierarchical social and religious institutions have interpreted the universal message of love of Sai Baba in a much more radical manner than probably what was intended. Though Bhajan is a key activity in both the Sai Baba movement in India and Bali, in Bali social outreach programmes in which there is voluntary sharing of not only resources but also time and labour seems to be more. But this voluntary sharing of time and labour seems minuscule compared to its intensity, scale and primacy in Swadhyaya. In Swadhyaya, devotional travel and sharing of devotional labour are foundational activities. The Sai Baba initiative in Bali can reflect on the need to create more platforms of sharing of devotional labour and through this generate resources for community development. Though the community development activities in the Sai Baba movement are supported by the donation of participants, it still carries the egoistic traces of the giver but for the spiritual development of the participants and for the realization of a more dignified equality, it is important that the activities do not run on the patronage of the rich clients. In the Swadhyaya movement in both England and India the rich participants do not have a determinant voice. This is possible because the primary source of wealth in Swadhyaya is not money (either the state grant or donation from private philanthropists) but time and labour which are deployed with a spirit of Bhakti in several initiatives in generating well-being such as Sneha Care and Yogeswara Krishi. The deployment of devotional labour and sharing of time in these initiatives create wealth which in turn is spent for the amelioration of suffering in the community and for undertaking new community development programmes. The Sai Baba initiative can consider to make devotional labour a key ingredient in its devotional engagement. It can also rethink the primacy it accords to miracles by having a dialogue with Swadhyaya which does not have any faith in miracles and has an intellectual and rational approach to religious practices and rituals. At the same time, the Swadhyaya movement in India and England can learn from the Sai Baba initiative in Bali the way and the extent to which it has been able to overcome the hierarchy of caste. Though in its rhetoric and certain domain of its practice, Swadhyaya has been able to overcome the distinction of caste, caste hierarchy is still a major challenge in the socio-spiritual movement of Swadhyaya.

Other Examples of Practical Spirituality

The works of Swadhyaya in England and Sai Baba in Bali provide us a different picture of globalization of religion. And this picture can be enlarged with the example of Christian socio-religious movements like 'Habitat for Humanity' which, operational since 1976, builds houses for low income families in 1,500 US communities and around 60 countries in the world for people of all religious faiths without any effort to convert the beneficiaries to Christianity (Giri, forthcoming). Globalization of Habitat has a more esteemed and radical predecessor in liberation theology. Liberation theology has been a major radical movement within Latin American Catholic religion for fighting for the rights of the poor and the oppressed. Its globalization continues to stir the imagination of many seeking souls and social movements across the world including India.

There are many instances of movements of practical and critical spirituality in contemporary Buddhism and Islam too. We get an invitational intimation of these in a recent essay by Fred Dallmayr, the pre-eminent scholar of cross-cultural understanding of our times, where critical spiritual movements are 'dedicated to the goal of social change and the removal of oppressive inequities' (Dallmayr, 1996). In contemporary Buddhist liberation movements, there is a 'redefinition of the traditional Buddhist notion of suffering *(Dukha)* and its overcoming: a redefinition which shifts attention to social and political causes of human suffering and the possibility of their correction or removal' (ibid.). In such movements, there is a 'profound change in Buddhist soteriology', namely, a change from 'highly personal and other-worldly notion of liberation to a social, economic and this-worldly liberation' (ibid.). But the issue of transcendence-immanence confronts us here as well: should the this-worldly orientation of Buddhist liberation movements be cut off from transcendental engagement? If movements of practical spirituality become 'completely embroiled in this-worldly struggles and activities, what happens to the liberating transcendence of such embroilment?' (ibid.). Political mobilization is not the only exhaustive vehicle of expression of practical spirituality as Dallmayr urges us to realize:

> ... care must be taken to differentiate or distance religion (and philosophy) from totalizing political ideologies .... In the case of Buddhism, this involves a careful reassessment of the notion of non-attachment or non-attached action, that is, of an agency which, wedded to social service, remains yet unattached to selfish gain or the lure of power and domination. With specific regard to liberation, this reassessment brings back into the view the idea of a double 'gesture' of affirmation and transcendence (of constitutive agency)—or in traditional Mahayana terminology, the project of a 'self-emptying' of emptiness itself. (ibid.: 18)

Dallmayr presents us the work and thought of Japanese Zen master Masao Abe who develops the notion of an 'affirmative and dynamic Sunyata, that is, of an emptiness that transcends or transmutes itself in the direction of a compassionate social engagement' (ibid.: 19). Before the movements of practical spirituality Abe boldly proposes a '"kenotic" (meaning self-emptying) rendering of human willing and acting—a reformulation which both preserves and transcends human initiative, namely, by embedding the latter in the framework of emptiness' (ibid.: 20).

In order to provide us a glimpse of critical spiritual voices in contemporary Islam, Dallmayr first presents us the work of Mohammad Arkoun, Professor of Islamic history and philosophy at the Sorbornne and author of numerous books and essays on the contemporary significance of Islam. Arkoun charts a path of critical and creative Islam, different from both clerical dogmatism and elitism and urges Muslim intellectuals to 'become active participants in debates concerning the present condition and prospects of the evolving global village' (ibid.: 25). 'At the same time, while adopting a "liberal" stance of open-mindedness', Arkoun is critical of some liberal predilections, especially 'the predilections for an agnostic secularism and a market-centred politics' (ibid.). Arkoun's life work 'has always addressed a question crucial to both Muslims and non-Muslims in the contemporary world: the question of the proper relation between self and other' (ibid.) and in this process of exploration Arkoun presents us the calling of a liberating faith, a socially and politically engaged faith, which is different from fundamentalism, 'marked by the indiscriminate fusion of religion and politics and the ultimate surrender of faith to power objectives' (ibid.: 27). For Arkoun, instead of ideological fundamentalist mobilization, practical spirituality must tap 'deeper religious resources located beyond, and even repressed by sheer power politics' (ibid.).

The other voice of critical spirituality that Dallmayr presents us from contemporary Islam is that of Maulana Wahiduddin Khan, from the Centre for Islamic Studies in Delhi. The Maulana's Centre has been spreading the message of a gentle, non-militant religious piety in the midst of violent turns in religion and politics in both India and Pakistan. Khan considers the religious mobilization in the name of Hindutva and Islamization as misguided in the 'world-wide context of progressive democratization' (ibid.: 30). The Maulana distinguishes between two methods to bring about change: one by revolutionary violence, the other by persuasion or exhortation. For Dallmayr, 'the basic difference of methods is ultimately between a willful striving for power and a 'self-emptying' liberation from injustice' (ibid.: 30).

Beyond the Primacy of the Political

These examples of religious globalization can help us rethink some of the contemporary theories of religion and globalization. One of the major interlocutors here is Canadian scholar of religion, Peter Beyer who argues that in a globalized society religion can have public influence only through sub-societal political mobilization since in a supposedly de-mystified, post-traditional and post-metaphysical world, it is difficult to have the public influence of religion at the level of entire society, not to speak of the entire world (Beyer, 1990). For Beyer and his kind, politics is the only route between religion and globalization. But sub-societal political mobilization is not the only response of religion to the processes of globalization. There is also a trans-social and transnational mobilization in religions now in the direction of a more inclusive ethical awareness, struggle for a dignified society, and practical spirituality, a mobilization which transcends the familiar boundaries of the outsider and the insider, good and evil. In such works of religion of, as exemplified in the works of Swadhyaya, Habitat and Sai Baba, public influence works through voluntary action, ethical and spiritual mobilization for the common good rather than through the logic of power, control and political mobilization.

Beyer further argues that 'pure religion' is at a disadvantage in the global society and the solution to its increasing and inevitable privatization lies in finding 'effective religious applications' (ibid.). Thus in order to be of interest to both believers and non-believers, religions have to undertake activities which ameliorate the conditions of poverty and suffering, and build the foundations of common good. And through this act of building it should encourage the participants to develop themselves ethically, morally and spiritually. But the practical activities of religion are not just 'applied' where application is dissociated from what is called a 'transcendental inspiration of love'. The applied activities of religion manifest themselves though various projects—both the life projects where the actors are committed to a cause and live in accordance with such a commitment and social projects where religious movements are engaged in a concrete activity as building houses as in the case of Habitat—but these projects are not merely instances of 'application'; they are manifestations of an integral mode of engagement where applied activities are nourished by a spiritual relationship with the 'transcendent'. Thus, the applied projects of such movements of practical spirituality are different from the projects of mere application which is the case with many development projects of our times.

Beyer (1990) also tells us that globalization of religion does not lead to the 'death of God'; 'God can still be loved but it is more difficult to fear him.' Instead of lamenting this shift, this shift from fear to love can be looked at as a new source of inspiration in the field of religious action. Love of God, in place of fear of God, becomes a source of creative social action which embodies a concern both for the development of the other and the spiritual development of self. Such a love of God is a source of inspiration behind 'Habitat for Humanity' and Swadhyaya. In fact, Swadhyaya strives to deepen Gandhi's Satyagraha with the experiment of what it calls Premagraha—striving for love.

Under conditions of globalization, conventional issues of religious morality such as sin get a new meaning. In the past, moral considerations meant 'sin, ignorance, etc.,' but now there is a transformation in the ethico-moral horizons of religions where the condition of our life and society—the nature of poverty, social justice etc.,—is the subject of ethico-moral engagement. In fact, there is an ethical transformation at work in world religions where ethics is much more concerned with quality of our conduct in this world, with self-development and responsibility to the other. In such a mode of engagement, ethics is not just for the other; it is also for self-cultivation and spiritual realization. Here what is done to the other is not done for the sake of other per se but for God, where God stands at the mid-point of relationship between self and other. Such an orientation to God is an important source of ethical mobilization in the socio-spiritual movements around the world.

Another important issue in the field of religion and globalization is the issue of justification of religious belief. In a globalized world there is limit to self-justificatory claims of religion, as for that matter, limit to any self-justificatory claims which does not want to participate in a process of mutual validation. Anthony Giddens (1999) makes this clear in his recent work *Runaway World: How Globalization Is Reshaping Our Lives*:

> Religion is normally associated with the idea of faith, a sort of emotional leap into belief. Yet in a cosmopolitan world, more people than ever before are regularly in contact with others who think differently from them. They are required to justify their beliefs, in an implicit way, at least, both to themselves and others.

But Giddens does not inquire further into different ways of justification and like Jurgen Habermas seems to be confined to rationality and argumentation as the only mode of justification (Habermas, 1993). But the examples of Swadhyaya and Habitat show that justification of one's faith is not through rational argumentation alone but also through one's participation in concrete projects of practical spirituality which are embodiments of aesthetic and ethical projects of love. But though Beyer emphasizes sub-societal political mobilization as the route through which religions become globalized, what he (Beyer, 1994) writes in his subsequent book, *Religion and Globalization*, deserves our careful consideration:

> Does the globalized context mean the gradual erosion of the religious system as system, to be replaced by a highly diverse ecology of religious culture? And are we heading toward the development of a broadly cultural 'religion of humanity' as the typical religion of the future?

Final Comments

When we look around we find an affirmative response to the above questions of the present and future. Religion of the future has to be a religion of humanity and both ethical and aesthetic mobilizations have to be our activities as participants in religious activities and spiritual seeking. While ethical mobilization makes religions much more concerned with the quality of our conduct in this world and the quality of life and social relationships, aesthetic mobilization urges religions to create appropriate climate for the self-development and spiritual realization of not only believers but also all interested people so that all of us concerned can make our lives a work of art and a lamp of God. But realization of this future, from the womb of multiple strivings within the present, has inevitably to face the conflict and inadequate understanding of the present, not to mention the politically entrenched interest groups who would like to use religion to kill others (Felix, 2000).

References

Achcar, Gilbert, 2004. 'Marxists and Religion: Yesterday and Today', *International Viewpoint*. http://www.internationalviewpoint.org/spip.php?article622.

——, 2007. 'Religion and Politics Today from a Marxian Perspective', *Socialist Register 2008*.

Ackerman, Robert, 1991. 'Preface', in F.M. Cornford, *From Religion to Philosophy*. New Jersey: Princeton University Press.

Afary, J. and Kevin, B. Anderson, 2005. *Foucault and the Iranian Revolution*. Chicago: The University of Chicago Press.

Agrawala, V.S., 1981. *Ancient Indian Folk Cults*. Varanasi: Prithivi Prakashan.

Ahmad, Aijaz, 1994. *In Theory*. London: Verso.

Althusser, L. and Balibar, É., 1997. *Reading Capital*. London: Verso.

Ambedkar, B.R., 1950. 'Buddha and the Future of His Religion', *Mahabodhi Society Journal,* May.

Appadurai, Arjun, 1990. 'Disjuncture and Difference in the Global Culture Economy', in Mike Featherstone (ed.), *Global Culture: Nationalism, Globalization and Modernity*. London: Sage Publications.

Babb, Lawrence A., 1987. *Redemptive Encounters: Three Modern Styles in the Hindu Tradition*. Delhi: Oxford University Press.

Bales, Kevin, 2004. (1999). *Disposable People: New Slavery in the Global Economy*. Berkeley: University of California Press.

Barnhardt, J.E., 1977. *The Study of Religion and Its Meaning: New Explorations in Light of Karl Popper and Emile Durkheim*. The Hague: Mouton.

Beck, R., 2006. 'Spiritual Pollution: The Dilemma of Sociomoral Disgust and the Ethic of Love', *Journal of Psychology and Theology*, 34(1): 53–65.

Bedi, Vanjara, 1994. *Punjabi Lokdhara Vishvakosh* (Vol. 7). New Delhi: National Book Shop.

Bendix, Reinhard, 1977. *Max Weber: An Intellectual Portrait*. Berkeley: University of California Press.

Benjamin, W., 1996. *Selected Writings*. Cambridge: Harvard University Press.

Benoit, Hubert, 1990 (1955). *Zen and the Psychology of Transformation*. Rochester VT: Inner Traditions International.

Berkouwer, G.C., 1958. *Dogmatische Studiën. De zonde: Oorsprong en kennis der zonde* (Vol. 1). Kampen: Kok.

——, 1960. *Dogmatische Studiën. De zonde: Wezen en verbreiding der zonde* (Vol. 2). Kampen: Kok.

Bertrand, Michèle, 1979. *Le statut de la religion chez Marx et Engels*. Paris: Éditions Sociales.

Beteille, A., 2000. *Antinomies of Society: Essays on Ideologies and Institutions*. New Delhi: Oxford University Press.

——, 2001. 'Civil Society and Good Society', *Sociological Bulletin*, 50(2): 286–307.

Beyer, Peter F., 1990. 'Globalization and the Public Influence of Religion', in Mike Featherstone (ed.), *Global Cultures*. London: Sage Publications.

——, 1994. *Religion and Globalization*. London: Sage Publications.

Beyer, Stephen, 1978. *The Cult of Tara*. Berkeley: University of California Press.

Bhatt, Chetan, 2007. 'Frontlines and Interstices in the War on Terror', *Development and Change Forum*, 38(6): 1073–93.

Bhatti, H.S., 2000. *Folk Religion: Change and Continuity*. Jaipur: Rawat Publications.

Bianchi, Ugo, 1994. *The Notion of Religion in Comparative Research* (ed.). Roma: L'erma.

Blumenberg, Hans, 1983. *The Legitimacy of Modern Age*. Cambridge: MIT Press.

Bourdieu, Pierre, 2000. *Pascalian Meditations*. Cambridge: Polity Press.

Bourgignon, Erika. 1973. *Religion, Altered States of Consciousness and Social Change*. Columbus: Ohio State University Press.

Bousquet, G.H., 1969. 'Marx et Engels se sont-ils interéssés aux questions islamiques?', *Studia Islamica*, 30: 119–30.

Bowker, John, 2002. *God: A Brief History*. London: Dorling Kindersley.

Breckman, Warren. 1999. *Marx, the Young Hegelians, and the Origins of Radical Social Theory*. Cambridge: Cambridge University Press.

Bredemeier, H.C. and Stephenson, R.M., 1970. *The Analysis of Social Systems*. New York: Holt Rinehart and Winston.

Brow, Robert, 1982. 'Origins of Religion', in R.P. Beaver et al. (eds.), *The World Religions*. England: Lion Publishing.

Brubaker, Rogers, 1984. *The Limits of Rationality: An Essay on the Social and Moral Thought of Max Weber*. London: George Allen and Unwin.

Burling, Robbins, 1963. *Rengsanggri: Family and Kinship in a Garo Village*. Philadelphia: University of Pennsylvania Press.

Cascardi, J.A., 1992. *The Subject of Modernity*. Cambridge: Cambridge University Press.

Cassinelli, C.W., 1964. 'Introduction to the Principality of Sakya', *American Anthropologist*, 66(5): 1105–09.

Chagnon, Napoleon, 1977. *Yanomamo: The Fierce People*. New York: Holt, Rinehart and Winston.

Cherbonnier, E. La B., 1956. *Hardness of Heart: A Contemporary Interpretation of Sin*. London: Victor Gollancz.

Chisholm, Roderick, 1989. *On Metaphysics*. Minneapolis: University of Minnesota Press.

Chitrabhanu, Gurudev, 1980. *Twelve Facets of Reality: The Jain Path to Freedom*. New York: Dodd and Mead.

Clive, Geoffrey, 1965. *The Philosophy of Nietzsche*. USA: Meridian.

Coomaraswamy, A.K., 1971. *Yaksas*. New Delhi: Munshiram Manoharlal.

Cornford, F.M., 1991. *From Religion to Philosophy*. New Jersey: Princeton University Press.

Cousins, E.F., 1985. *Global Spirituality*. Madras: University of Madras Press.

Cove, John J., 1987. 'Reflections in a Shaman's Mirror', in John Cove (ed.), *Shattered Images: Dialogues and Meditations on Tsimshian Narratives*. Ottawa: Carleton University Press.

Crooke, William, 1968. *The Popular Religion and Folklore of Northern India*. New Delhi: Munshiram Manoharlal.

Dallmayr, F., 1981. *Twilight of Subjectivity*. Amherst: UMP.

——, 1996. 'Liberation Perspectives: East and West', Paper presented at the Silver Jubilee Workshop on Social Criticism, Cultural Creativity and the Contemporary Dialectics of Transformations. Madras: Madras Institute of Development Studies.

Dalton, E.T., 1847. *Some Accounts of the Garrow Tribes of the Valley of Assam.* New Delhi: Cosmo Publishers.

d'Aquilly, Eugene et al., 1979. *The Spectrum of Ritual: A Biogenetic Structural Analysis.* New York: Columbia University Press.

Darnell, Regna, 1979. *Personal communication.*

Davis, Mike, 2004. 'Planet of Slums', *New Left Review II,* 26: 5–34.

——, 2006. *Planet of Slums*. London: Verso.

De Martino, Ernesto, 1977. *La fine del mondo. Contributo all'analisi delle apocalissi culturali.* Torino: Einaudi.

Derrida, Jacques, 1994. *Specters of Marx, the State of the Debt, the Work of Mourning and the New International.* London: Routledge.

Divedi, H.P., 1961. *Cultural Significance of the Fairs of Punjab*: *Census of India* (Vol. 15). Part vii-B.

Dreyfus, George B.J., 1997. *Recognizing Reality: Dharmakîrti's Philosophy and its Tibetan Interpretations.* Albany: State University of New York Press.

Durkheim, E., 1912. 'The Elementary Forms of Religious Life', http://www.mdx.ac.uk/WWW/STUDY/xdur.htm# Durkheim1912.

——, 1926. *The Elementary Forms of Religious Life.* London: Allen and Unwin.

——, 1982. *The Rules of Sociological Method.* New York: Free Press.

Eliade, Mircea, 1964. *Shamanism*. Princeton: Princeton University Press.

Ellin, Joseph, 1995. *Morality and the Meaning of Life: An Introduction to Ethical Theory.* New York: Harcourt Brace.

Ellul, J., 1985. *The Humiliation of the Word*. Grand Rapids: Eerdmans.

Engels, Friedrich, 1987. *The Condition of the Working Class in England.* London: Penguin.

Evans-Wentz, W.Y., 1928. *Tibet's Great Yogi Milarepa.* Oxford: Oxford University Press.

——, 1958. *Tibetan Yoga and Secret Doctrines.* New York: Oxford University Press.

——, 1960. *The Tibetan Book of the Dead.* Oxford: Oxford University Press.

Featherstone, M. and Scott, Lash, 1995. 'Globalization, Modernity and the Spatialization of Social Theory: An Introduction', in M. Featherstone (ed.), *Global Modernities*. London: Sage Publications.

Feil, Ernest, 1992. 'From the Classic Religio to Modern Religion', in Michel Despland and Gerard Vallee (eds.), *Religion in History: the Word, the Idea, the Reality.* Waterloo: WLUP.

Feuerbach, L., 1957. *The Essence of Christianity.* New York: Harper and Row.

Finelli, Roberto, 1987. *Astrazione e dialettica dal romanticismo al capitalismo (saggio su Marx)*. Roma: Bulzoni Editore.

Finsterbusch, K. and Mckenna, G., 1986. *Taking Sides.* Connecticut: Dushkin.

Firth, Raymond, 1936. *We the Tikopia: A Sociological Study of Kinship in Primitive Polynesia.* London: George Allen and Unwin Ltd.

——, 1967. *Tikopia Ritual and Belief.* Boston: Beacon Press.

Fraser, Giles, 2002. *Redeeming Nietzsche: On the Piety of Unbelief.* London: Routledge.

Frazer, J.G., 1926. *The Worship of Nature* (Vol. 1). London: Macmillan and Company.

Gandhi, L., 1998. *Post Colonial Theory.* New Delhi: Oxford University Press.

Geertz, Clifford, 1973. 'Thick Description: Toward an Interpretive Theory of Culture' in Clifford Geertz (ed.), *The Interpretation of Cultures: Selected Essays by Clifford Geertz*. New York: Basic Books.

Gendlin, Eugene, 1997 (1962). *Experiencing and the Creation of Meaning: A Philosophical Approach to the Subjective.* Evanston: Northwestern University Press.

Gerth, H.H. and Mills, C.W., 2000. *From Max Weber: Essays in Sociology.* London: Routledge.

Giddens, Anthony. 1972. *Emile Durkheim: Selected Writings* (ed.). Cambridge: Cambridge University Press.

——, 1984. *The Constitution of Society.* UK: Polity Press.

——, 1993. *Sociology.* UK: Polity Press.

——, 1999. *Runaway World: How Globalization is Reshaping Our Lives.* London: Profile Books.

Gill, H.S., 1975. *Folk Art of the Punjab.* Patiala: Punjabi University.

Giri, Ananta K. (Forthcoming). *Building in the Margins of Shacks: The Vision and Projects of Habitat for Humanity.* New Delhi: Orient Longmans.

Giri, Ananta K. and Philip, Q.V.U., 2000. 'Reconstituting Development as a Shared Responsibility: Ethics and a Creative Shaping of Human Possibilities', *Working Paper*. Madras: Madras Institute of Development Studies.

Given, B.J., 1990. *Tibetan Tantra—One View: An Asian Model for the Ritual Control of Experience* (Unpublished manuscript). Ottawa: Carleton University.

Gohain, C.B., 1977. *Human Sacrifice and Head Hunting in North-East India.* Assam: Lawyer's Book Stall.

Goody, Jack, 2007. *The Theft of History.* Cambridge: Cambridge University Press.

Gray, John, 2007. *Black Mass: Apocalyptic Religion and the Death of Utopia.* London: Allen Lane.

Griaule, Marcel, 1965. *Conversations with Ogotemmeli.* London: Oxford University Press.

Grupp, Jeffrey, 2005. 'The R-Theory of Time, or Replacement Presentism: The Buddhist Philosophy of Time', *Indian International Journal of Buddhist Studies*, 6: 51–122.

——, 2006a. 'Blob Theory: N-adic Properties Do Not Exist', *Sorites*, 17: 104–131.

——, 2006b. 'Mereological Nihilism: Quantum Atomism and the Impossibility of Material Constitution', *Axiomathes*, 16(3): 245–386.

Habermas, Jurgen, 1993. *Justification and Application.* Cambridge: Polity Press.

Hamilton, F.B., 1820. *An Account of Assam.* London: Macmillan and Company.

Hannerz, Ulf, 1992. *Transnational Connections.* London: Routledge.

Harman, G. and Thomson, J.J., 2000. *Moral Relativism Moral Objectivity.* Malden: Blackwell Publishers.

Harner, Michael, 1973. 'Common Themes in South American Yage Experiences', in M. Harner (ed.), *Hallucinogens and Shamanism.* New York: Oxford University Press.

——, 1980. *The Way of the Shaman.* New York: Bantam.

Harrison, P., 1990. *Religion and the Religions in the English Enlightenment.* Cambridge: Cambridge University Press.

Harvey, David, 2003. *The New Imperialism.* Oxford: Oxford University Press.

Harvey, Peter, 2000. *An Introduction to Buddhist Ethics.* New York: Cambridge University Press.

Hasnain, Nadeem, 1983. *Tribal India Today*. New Delhi: Harnam Publication.

Hegel, G.W.F., 1967. *The Phenomenology of Mind*. New York: Harper Colophon.

Heidegger, M., 1977. *The Question Concerning Technology and Other Essays*. New York: Harper and Row.

Hick, J., 1989. *An Interpretation of Religion*. London: McMillan.

Hiriyanna, M., 1975. *Indian Conception of Values*. Mysore: Kavyalay Publishers.

Hopkins, N.S., 1990. 'Engels and Ibn Khaldun', *Alif: Journal of Comparative Poetics*, 10.

Howe, Leo, 1999. 'Sai Baba in Bali: Identity, Social Conflict and the Politics of Religious Truth', *Working Paper, Department of Social Anthropology*. Cambridge: University of Cambridge.

Jorgensen, J.G., 1972. *The Sun Dance Religion: Power for the Powerless*. Chicago: The University of Chicago Press.

Jung, C.G., 1944. *Psychology and Alchemy*. Princeton: Princeton University Press.

——, 1952. *Symbols of Transformation*. Princeton: Princeton University Press.

——, 1956. *Mysterium Conjunctionis*. Princeton: Princeton University Press.

Kalberg, Stephen, 1999. 'Max Weber's Critique of Recent Comparative-Historical Sociology and a Reconstruction of His Analysis of the Rise of Confucianism in China', in Jennifer Lehmann (ed.), *Current Perspectives in Social Theory*. Stamford: JAI Press.

Kar, B., 2006–2007. 'Secularism and Spiritualism: An Appraisal', *Philosophy and the Life World. Vidyasagar University Journal of Philosophy*, 9: 70–79.

Kar, P.C., 1967. 'A Point of View on the Garo in Transition', in Ralhin Mitra and Barun Das Gupta (eds.), *A Common Perspective for North-East India*. Calcutta: Pannalal Das Gupta Publishers.

Katz, Richard, 1982. *Boiling Energy: Community Healing Among the Kalahari/Kung*. Cambridge: Harvard University Press.

——, 1984. 'Accepting Boiling Energy: The Experience of !Kia-Healing Among The !Kung', *Ethos*, 10: 344–368.

Koshul, Basit, 2005. *The Postmodern Significance of Max Weber's Legacy: Disenchanting Disenchantment*. New York: Palgrave MacMillan.

Kouvelakis, Stathis, 2003. *Philosophy and Revolution: From Kant to Marx*. London: Verso.

Lafargue, Paul, 2006. *La religion du Capital.* Paris: l'Aube.

Laughlin, C.D. et al., 1979. 'The Spectrum of Ritual', in d'Aquilly Eugene et al. (eds.), *The Spectrum of Ritual: A Biogenetic Structural Analysis.* New York: Columbia University Press.

——, 1984. 'Neurognosis, Individuation and Tibetan Arising Yoga Practice', *Phoenix: The Journal of Transpersonal Anthropology,* 8(1/2): 91–106.

Lex, Barbara, 1979. 'The Neurobiology of Ritual Trance', in d'Aquilly Eugene et al., (eds.), *The Spectrum of Ritual: A Biogenetic Structural Analysis.* New York: Columbia University Press.

Löwy, Michael, 1996. *The War of the Gods: Religion and Politics in Latin America.* London: Verso.

——, 2005. 'Marxism and Religion: Opiate of the People', http://newsocialist.org/newsite/index.php?id=243.

——, 2006. 'Le capitalisme comme religion: Walter Benjamin et Max Weber', *Raisons politiques*, 23(3): 203–19.

Lyman, S.M., 1978. *The Seven Deadly Sins: Society and Evil.* New York: St. Martin's Press.

Lyon, D., 1999. *Postmodernity.* Buckingham: Open University Press.

MacIntyre, Alasdair, 1971. *Marxism and Christianity.* Harmondsworth: Pelican.

Majumdar, Kadernath, 1906. *Mymensingh-Ar-Itihas.* Calcutta: Sanal and Company.

Maloney, C. et al., 1981. *Beliefs and Fertility in Bangladesh* (Unpublished manuscript). Dhaka: International Centre for Diarrhoeal Disease Research Bangladesh.

Mann, Heinrich, 1939. *The Living Thoughts of Nietzsche, The Living Thoughts Library.* London: Cassell.

Marx, Karl, 1841. '*The Difference between the Democritean and Epicurean Philosophy of Nature*', http://www.marxists.org/archive/marx/works/1841/dr-theses.

——, 1847. '*The Communism of the Rheinischer Beobachter*', http://marxists.org/archive/marx/works/1847/09/12.htm.

——, 1863. '*Theories of Surplus Value*', http://www.marxists.org/archive/marx/works/1863/theories-surplus value.

——, 1875. '*Critique of the Gotha Programme*', http://www.marxists.org/archive/marx/works/1875/gotha/index.htm.

——, 1970. *A Contribution to the Critique of Political Economy.*

——, 1973. *Grundrisse*. London: Penguin.

——, 1974. *The First International and After: Political Writings* (Vol. 3) London: Penguin.

——, 1990. *Capital* (Vol. 1). London: Penguin.

——, 2007. *Dispatches for the New York Tribune: Selected Journalism of Karl Marx*. London: Penguin.

Marx, K. and Engels, F., 1850. *'Review of Daumer'*, http://marxists.org/archive/marx/works/1850/02/daumer.htm.

——, 1975. *The Holy Family*. Moscow: Progress Publishers.

——, 1998. *The German Ideology*. New York: Prometheus.

McCutcehon, R., 1997. *Manufacturing Religion*. Oxford: Oxford University Press.

McLellan, David, 1987. *Marxism and Religion*. London: Macmillan.

McManus, John, 1979. 'Ritual and Human Social Cognition', in d'Aquilly Eugene et al., (eds.), *The Spectrum of Ritual: A Biogenetic Structural Analysis*. New York: Columbia University Press.

Merleau-Ponty, M., 1977. 'Cezanne's Doubt', in J. Dolgin et al. (eds.), *Symbolic Anthropology*. New York: Columbia University Press.

Mette, H.J., 1934. *Historische-Kritische Gesamtausgabe*. Munich: Beck.

Mitchell, D.W., 2002. *Buddhism*. New York: Oxford University Press.

Mohanty, A.K., 2004. *Karma*. Utkal University: Department of Special Assistance in Philosophy.

Mohapatra, P.K., 2000. *Personal Identity*. New Delhi: Decent Books.

Mol, Hans, 1979. 'The Origin and Function of Religion: A Critique of, and Alternative to, Durkheim's Interpretation of the Religion of Australian Aborigines', *Journal for the Scientific Study of Religion*, 18: 379–89.

Möller, F.P., 1997. *Words of Light and Life: From Sin to Salvation* (Vol. 3). Pretoria: Van Schaik.

Moreland, J.P., 2001. *Universals*. Montreal and Kingston: McGill-Queen's University Press.

Neil, G. and Robert, A. Jones, 2004. *Durkheim's Philosophy Lectures: Notes from the Lycée de Sens Course*, 1883–1884 (eds.). New York: Cambridge University Press.

Nietzsche, Friedrich, 1967. *On the Genealogy of Morals and Ecce Homo*. New York: Vintage Books.

——, 1968. *The Portable Nietzsche*. New York: The Viking Press.

——, 1974. *The Gay Science*. New York: Vintage Books.

——, 1978. *Thus Spoke Zarathustra*. New York: Penguin Books.

——, 1986. *Human, All Too Human: A Book for Free Sprits*. Great Britain: Cambridge University Press.

——, 1989. *Beyond Good and Evil: Prelude to a Philosophy of the Future*. New York: Vintage Books.

——, 2000. *The Birth of Tragedy*. Oxford: Oxford University Press.

Oberoi, Harjot, 1994. *The Construction of Religious Boundaries*. London: Oxford University Press.

Osipova, Elina, 1989. 'Emile Durkheim's Sociology', in F.M. Volkov (ed.), *A History of Classical Sociology*. USSR: Progress Publishers.

Playfair, Major, 1909. *The Garo*. Gauhati: United Publishers.

Prasad, R., 1989. *Causation and Retributive Morality*. New Delhi: ICPR.

Pye, Michael, 1994. 'The Notion of Religion in Comparative Research', *Selected Proceedings of the XVI IAHR Congress*.

Radhakrishnan, S., 1971. *The Hindu View of Life*. London: Unwin Books.

Raines, John, 2002. *Marx on Religion* (ed.). Philadelphia: Temple University Press.

Raju, P.T., 1998. (1992). *The Philosophical Traditions of India*. Delhi: Motilal Banarsidass.

Rancière, Jacques, 1989. 'The Concept of "Critique" and the "Critique of Political Economy"', in A. Rattansi (ed.), *Ideology, Method and Marx*. London: Routledge.

Reichel-Dolmatoff, Gerardo, 1971. *Amazonian Cosmos*. Chicago: The University of Chicago Press.

Rheinstein, Max, 1954. *Max Weber on Law in Economy and Society*. Cambridge: Harvard University Press.

Ricard, M. and Thuan, T.X., 2001. *The Quantum and the Lotus*. New York: Three Rivers Press.

Robertson, Ronald, 1992. *Globalization: Social Theory and the Global Culture*. London: Sage Publications.

Rodinson, Maxime, 1977. *Islam and Capitalism*. London: Penguin.

Rose, H.A., 1970. *A Glossary of the Tribes and Castes of the Punjab and Northwest Frontier Province*. Patiala: Languages Department.

Ross, E.A., 1973. (1907). *Sin and Society: An Analysis of Latter Day Iniquity*. New York: Harper Torch books.

Roth, Robyn Alice, 2002. 'Nietzsche's Use of Atheism', in R. White (ed.), *Nietzsche*. Aldershot: Ashgate Dartmouth.

Saberwal, S., 2001. 'Democracy and Civil Society in India, Integral or Accidental', *Sociological Bulletin*, 50(2): 192–205.

Sacks, Jonathan, 1991. *The Persistence of Faith: Religion, Morality, and Society in a Secular Age*. London: Weidenfield and Nicholson.

Said, Edward, 1994. *Orientalism*. Toronto: Random House.

Saler, Michael, 2004. 'Modernity, Disenchantment and the Ironic Imagination', *Philosophy and Literature*, 28(1): 137–49.

Sangma, S.M., 1981. *History and Culture of the Garos*. New Delhi: Books Today.

Sattar, A., 1975. *Tribal Culture in Bangladesh*. Dhaka: Muktadhara.

Scaff, Leonard, 1989. *Fleeing the Iron Cage: Culture, Politics, and Modernity in the Thought of Max Weber*. Berkeley: University of California Press.

Schluchter, Wolfgang, 1981. *The Rise of Western Rationalization: Max Weber's Developmental History*. Berkeley: University of California Press.

Schutz, Alfred, 1967. *The Phenomenology of the Social World*. Evanston IL: Northwestern University Press.

Schuurman, E., 1993. 'Problemen en Crisis Van de Opgezweepte Westerse Technologische Cultuur', *Koers*, 58(3): 353–68.

Sharpe, Eric, 1983. *Understanding Religion*. London: Duckworth.

Shearer, J. et al., 1977. *A Biogenetic Structural Model of Phenomenological Phases* (Unpublished manuscript). Ottawa: Carleton University.

——, 1979. 'Waking, Sleeping and Cross-Phase Transference', Paper presented at the Canadian Ethnological Society Annual Meetings. Canada: Banff, Alberta.

Siegel, P.N., 2005. *The Meek and the Militant*. Chicago: Haymarket.

Singh, Surjeet, 1981. 'Semiotic Structure of Sanjhi', *Pakha Sanjam*, XIV: 197–252.

Sinha, T.C., 1966. *The Psyche of the Garos*. Calcutta: Anthropological Survey of India.

Small, Robin, 2001. *Nietzsche in Context*. Aldershot: Ashgate.

Smith, Douglas, 2000. 'Introduction', in F. Nietzsche, *The Birth of Tragedy*. Oxford: Oxford University Press.

Sprinker, Michael, 1999. *Ghostly Demarcations* (ed.). London: Verso.

Statistical Abstract of Punjab 2001. Chandigarh, 2002, Punjab Government Publication.

Staal, F., 1989. *Rules Without Meaning*. New York: Peter Lang.

Stcherbatsky, F.T., 1962 (1930). *Buddhist Logic* (Vol. 1). New York: Dover.

Stevens, Jacob, 2004. 'Exorcizing the Manifesto', *New Left Review*, 28: 151–60.

Swedberg, Richard, 2005. *The Max Weber Dictionary: Key Words and Central Concepts*. Stanford: Stanford University Press.

Tabatabaii, M.H., 1984. *Al-Mizan fi Tafsir al-Quran* (Vol. 1). Tehran: Ismaeylian Publication.

Tart, Charles, 1969. *Altered States of Consciousness*. New York: Wiley.

——, 1975. *States of Consciousness*. New York: Dutton.

Temple, Richard, 1969. *Legends of Punjab*. Patiala: Languages Department.

The Encyclopedia Britannica, 1984, 'Religion, A Study of', in *The Encyclopedia Britannica* (Vol. 15). Chicago: Encyclopedia Britannica Inc.

Thio, A., 1995. *Deviant Behaviour*. New York: Harper Collins.

Tocqueville, A.De., 1954. *Democracy in America.* New York: Vintage Books.

Toscano, Alberto, 2008a. 'Marxism Expatriated: Alain Badiou's Turn', in Jacques Bidet and Stathis Kouvelakis (eds.), *Critical Companion to Contemporary Marxism*. Leiden: Brill.

——, 2008b. 'The Open Secret of Real Abstraction', *Rethinking Marxism,* 20(2): 273–87.

Troeltsch, Ernst, 1971. *Social Teachings of the Christain Churchs*. New York: MacMillan.

Troisi, J., 1978. *Tribal Religion.* New Delhi: Manohar.

Turner, Stephen, 2000. *The Cambridge Companion to Weber.* Cambridge: Cambridge University Press.

Turner, V.W., 1969. *The Ritual Process*. Chicago: Aldine.

——, 1970. *The Forest of Symbols*. Ithaca: Cornell University Press.

——, 1974. *Dramas, Fields and Metaphors*. Ithaca: Cornell University Press.

Tylor, E.B., 1958. *The Origins of Culture*. New York: Harper and Row.

Virno, Paolo, 2003. *Scienze sociali e 'natura umana'*. Soveria Mannelli: Rubbettino.

Wallace, A.F.C., 1972. 'Paradigmatic Processes in Culture Change', *American Anthropologist,* 74: 467–78.

Weaver, D.F., 2003. 'Taking sin seriously', *Journal of Religious Ethics*, 31(1): 45–74.

Webber, Mark, 1979. 'The Mechanism of Symbolic Penetration', *Departmental Working Paper V, Department of Sociology and Anthropology.* Ottawa: Carleton University.

Weber, Max, 1958. *The Religion of India: The Sociology of Hinduism and Buddhism.* New York: Free Press.

——, 1967. *Ancient Judaism.* New York: Free Press.

——, 1968. *The Religion of China: Confucianism and Taoism.* New York: Free Press.

——, 1978. *Economy and Society: An Outline of Interpretive Sociology.* Berkeley: University of California Press.

——, 1993. *Collected Essays in the Sociology of Religion.* Boston: Beacon Press.

——, 1999. *Essays in Economic Sociology.* Princeton: Princeton University Press.

——, 2004. *The Vocation Lectures: Science as a Vocation, Politics as a Vocation.* Indianapolis: Hackett Publishing Company.

——, 2006. *The Protestant Ethic and the Spirit of Capitalism.* New York: Routledge.

Werner, Max, 1975. *Hegel's Phenomenology of Mind.* New York: Harper and Row.

Whiting, J.W.M. et al., 1958. 'The Function of Male Initiation Ceremonies at Puberty', in Eleanor E. Maccoby et al. (eds.), *Readings in Social Psychology.* New York: Holt, Rinehart and Winston.

Wicks, Robert, 2007. *Friedrich Nietzsche.* Stanford University: Online Database.

Wilfred, Felix, 2000. *Asian Dreams and Christian Hopes.* Delhi: ISPCK Publications.

Zangcham, S., (n.d.) *Garo Sanskritir-Ka-Yekti Dik.* Bangladesh: Jalchatra Dharma Palli Adivasi Parishad.

Zizek, Slavoj, 2006. *How to Read Lacan.* London: Granta Books.

Notes on Contributors

Harvinder Singh Bhatti is a Professor in the Department of Sociology and Social Anthropology at Punjabi University (India). His research area includes folk religion of Punjab (India). Harvinder Singh Bhatti has also written a book on the folk religion of Punjab.

Ananta Kumar Giri is currently on the faculty of Madras Institute of Development Studies, Chennai (India) and has worked and taught in many universities in India and abroad including University of Kentucky (USA), Aalborg University (Denmark) and University of Freiburg (Germany). Ananta Kumar Giri has written a number of books including *Global Transformations: Postmodernity and Beyond (1998)*, *Conversations and Transformations: Toward a New Ethics of Self and Society (2002)*, *Reflections and Mobilizations: Dialogues with Movements and Voluntary Organizations (2004)*, *Self-Development and Social Transformations? The Vision and Practice of Self-Study Mobilization of Swadhyaya (2007)* and *The Modern Prince and Modern Sage: Transforming Power and Freedom (2008)*.

Brian J. Given is an Associate Professor in the Department of Sociology and Anthropology at Carleton University (Canada). The area of his interest includes immigrant and refugee settlement and adaptation, cultural survival, belief systems, ritual and meditation systems, Tibetan culture and religion, Buddhism, ethnohistory, culture and technology. His book about trade in weapons with aboriginal populations in North America during the early contact period in the 17th century *A Most Pernicious Thing* was published in 1994. He is currently completing a book about the Tibetan-Canadian communities.

Jeffrey Grupp is an Adjunct Professor of Purdue University (USA). His research emphasis is Indian Buddhism, philosophy of quantum physics and economic issues in philosophy.

Zahidul Islam is a Professor of the Department of Anthropology at the University of Dhaka (Bangladesh). His research interests include ethnography and urban issues. Zahidul Islam also acts as a Consultant of Food Planning and Monitoring Unit (FPMU), Government of Bangladesh.

Mahmoud Khatami is a Professor of Philosophy at the University of Tehran (Iran). He has written a number of books including *Phenomenology of Religion (2003)* and *Modernity and Religion (2005)*.

S.M. Arif Mahmud is a lecturer in the Department of Anthropology at the University of Dhaka (Bangladesh). His research area includes ethnic studies and ethnography, rural development, urban issues and migration.

P.K. Mohapatra is a Professor of Philosophy at Utkal University (India). He also acted as a Senior Fellow of the Indian Council of Philosophical Research. P.K. Mohapatra obtained the degree of Doctor of Philosophy as a Commonwealth Scholar at the University of Keele (England). He was a Fulbright Visiting Fellow in the United States in 1989 and served as an adjunct faculty at the Temple University (Philadelphia). P.K. Mohapatra has written many books including *Personal Identity (1983)*, *Concepts and Problems (1988)* and *Ethics and Society* (Forthcoming).

Soumyajit Patra is a lecturer in the Department of Sociology at Vidyasagar University (India). He has obtained his Ph.D. from the University of Kalyani (India). Soumyajit Patra was awarded Research Fellowship from the Ministry of Welfare (Government of India). His research area includes tribal culture, gender issues and sociology of religion. Recently, Soumyajit Patra was invited to present a paper in an international seminar on 'Alternative Expressions of the Numinous' held at the University of Queensland (Australia).

Swapan Kumar Pramanick served for a long time as Professor of Sociology in the Department of Sociology at the University of Calcutta (India). He is now the Vice-Chancellor of Vidyasagar University (India). His area of interest includes Indian social structure and rural sociology. Swapan Kumar Pramanick has written a number of books including *The Sociology of G.S. Ghurye (1994)* and *Panchayats and People: The West Bengal Experience (1994)*.

Kathleen A. Riddell is associated with the Department of Religious Studies at McMaster University (Canada). Her work is interdisciplinary, but concentrates on the anthropology of religion that involves the secularization-privatization thesis. The primary exemplar of her research is American Civil Religion and American Icons and Mythos. Kathleen A. Riddell is also interested in the works of Friedrich Nietzsche, Max Weber and Arjun Appadurai.

Håkan Sandgren is on the faculty of the University of Queensland (Australia). His research interests include philosophy of religion, religious festivals and the influence of modern technology on religious practices.

Anton Senekal is an Associate Professor of sociology and is Chair of the Department of Sociology at the University of Johannesburg (South Africa). Anton Senekal has obtained D. Litt. in sociology. His research interests include family sociology, military sociology, methodology and social problems.

Pramod Kumar Singh is currently on the faculty of the Department of Philosophy and Religion at Banaras Hindu University (India). He completed doctoral studies from the same university. Pramod Kumar Singh has been awarded many scholarships and fellowships including a Post-Doctoral Fellowship (ICHR) in 2003. He is interested in Indian Philosophy, particularly in Kashmir Vaibhasika and Kashmir Saivism. He is the editor of the journal *Anusilana*.

Alberto Toscano is a lecturer in sociology at Goldsmiths, University of London (UK) and the editor of the journal *Historical Materialism*. He has written a number of books including *The Theatre of Production: Philosophy and Individuation Between Kant and Deleuze (2006)*. Alberto Toscano is the translator of Alain Badiou's *The Century (2007)* and *Handbook of Inaesthetics (2005)*. He is currently writing a book on the politics of fanaticism.

Index